BEING & BECOMING

The memoir of a former Catholic priest

by

Walter Keady

CASTLETREE
BOOKS

CASTLETREE
BOOKS

To

former friends and confreres,

and the women I loved

CHAPTERS

Preface

This is the story of my engagement with religion – mental, emotional, physical, and relational – from conservative Catholic to freewheeling agnostic. The memoir covers about twenty-five years of my life and for the most part does not include events that are not relevant to the religious narrative.

I was born into a milieu in which Catholicism was not only a religion but also a culture and a defense against all mores that threatened the Irish Catholic way of life. Ireland had freed itself from English domination a mere twelve years before I was born – my father fought in the war of independence – having endured hundreds of years of alien governance. During those centuries of subjugation the country had retained its Catholic religion in spite of – or perhaps because of – the ruling power's attempt to subvert it to the established religion of its empire.

So Ireland free was going to be Ireland Catholic, and the educating of its youth would be under the control of the Church. I was subjected to that education, where we were not merely taught Catholic doctrine but were also trained to live as Catholics. Other religions were mentioned only to say that they were false and that their adherents were doomed to hell.

According to the standards of the time, education was 'beaten in' to the young. We learned through fear: corporal punishment was the norm, and it was applied by teachers to enforce scholarship and adherence to the Catholic Church as well as to impose discipline.

I accepted all that I was taught: the closed and coherent system of Catholic beliefs appealed to my tidy mind. So I grew up, not only intent on living my faith, but anxious also that others would gain the promised kingdom of heaven. From those sentiments it was a relatively easy step – apart from assuming the obligation of celibacy, which did cause me considerable anguish – to decide on becoming a Catholic priest.

It was only after I went to Brazil as a missionary and

became exposed to the wider world outside of Irish Catholicism that I critically examined the theology I had been taught, and discovered its flaws. From there it was a logical step to losing faith in the religion I was brought up to revere and practice. Rejection of celibacy might be the immediate motive, but loss of belief in the Church's teaching was the defining cause of my transition from believer to agnostic.

I have tried to be honest in my tale and to avoid self-serving excuses. If there be a Higher Power I trust It will forgive my lapses.

Acknowledgments

I thank my wife, Jennifer, for her encouragement and support in my undertaking this daunting task, and for her very helpful comments on the manuscript.

I also thank the members of Taconic Writers and my friend Eamon Grennan for reading the entire manuscript and for their many insightful comments.

I am most grateful to Josephine Hausam for undertaking the task of line editing the manuscript.

And I thank David Cole Wheeler for his wonderful cover design.

Growing Up Catholic in Ireland

Religion Is Beaten In

Baldy stood up from his desk, reached into the drawer, and pulled out the black leather strap. *"Lamh amach –* hand out," he told the lad at the end of the class that was standing around his desk.

The little fellow with the torn gansy stretched out his left hand. Baldy drew the strap back over his shoulder and brought it down with a heavy thwack on the outstretched palm. Two more thwacks followed on the now reddened hand.

"An lamh eile anois – the other hand now." Baldy, his face contorted with passion, meted out the same treatment to the lad's right palm. "That'll teach you not to miss mass on Sunday."

He returned the strap to the drawer and sat again. The punished lad buried his hands in his oxters to dull the pain and scrunched his eyes so as not to cry. I and the rest of the newly-promoted class looked on. Lesson learned: missing Sunday mass was not only a mortal sin, as our previous teacher, Mrs. Kelly, had taught us, but was now punishable with six hard slaps from

1

Baldy's strap. Mrs. Kelly lived in Cong and attended church there, so she didn't know if any of her pupils missed Sunday mass. Baldy lived in The Neale and went to mass here, and he had warned us on our first day in his classroom that if anyone missed Sunday mass he'd "come down on him like a ton of bricks."

Baldy was known in the parish as a cross teacher. Which meant he used his black strap a lot to beat learning and manners and responsibility into his pupils. In his classroom he had six classes, from third to eighth, about twenty-five boys in all. He made us work hard and he was said by parents and other parishioners to be "a great teacher entirely." Class was supposed to end at three o'clock but Baldy never let his pupils go before four. And he gave us a lot of homework: sums and spellings and compositions, and poems we had to learn by heart.

He made us work even harder and gave even more beatings with his leather strap when he was preparing us for the annual diocesan catechism exam. For that event he stopped teaching everything else a month beforehand, and for homework he had us learn by heart a hundred or more catechism questions and lots of prayers and long lists of other things like the seven deadly sins, the cardinal virtues, the litany of the Blessed Virgin, the twelve spiritual and the twelve corporal works of mercy. And we better know the answers, with every word just right; it didn't matter that we didn't understand what the words meant as long as we could recite them without a mistake.

"What is the Immaculate Conception?" One morning, a week before the exam, Baldy looked enquiringly at the pupils standing in an arc around his desk. No one dared put up a hand for fear of getting it wrong. I was quite confident that I knew the answer but I wasn't about to take the risk.

2

"Walsh," Baldy barked, pointing to a victim.

Walsh looked blankly at him.

"Come on, boy; I wrote it on the board yesterday."

"Sir, Jesus was born with an immaculate constipation."

Several lads grinned: we all knew Walsh was an eejit. But Baldy spotted one of the grins. "Since you're smiling, Donovan, I suppose you know the answer."

"I wasn't smiling, sir."

"Well, give me the answer anyway."

Donovan had a good shot at it but he wasn't able to articulate it exactly as the catechism put it; neither were the next eight lads that Baldy put on the spot. Eventually he pointed to me. "Keady!"

"The Blessed Virgin Mary by a singular privilege of grace was preserved free from the stain of original sin and this privilege is called her Immaculate Conception." I had learned it by heart and got it all out in one breath lest I forgot it if I paused.

"*Togha fir* – best man," said Baldy. He got up from his chair and reached for the strap. "All those who failed to answer correctly step forward. I'll warm your palms for you; you should have learned this by heart last night." Ten lads got their hands stung with four thwacks apiece.

Baldy never seemed to tire wielding the strap; from the look on his face it appeared he might even be enjoying it. He used that strap all day every day for the entire month we spent preparing for the catechism exam. I studied hard and learned all the material by heart; I was fortunate in having a good memory, which kept me safe from beatings.

On the day of the exam I was bursting to show off what I knew, but was deprived of the opportunity. The priest sent by the archbishop to test us, a jolly-looking man with a great shock of red hair, put a few easy questions to boys he picked at random; he

3

never called on me and spent the rest of the time chatting with Baldy while we pupils, relieved that it was over, looked on in silence.

Michael

I was awakened one morning by the sound of a crying baby. When I went downstairs to the kitchen – I was always the first child up in the morning – Daddy was holding the tiny creature in his arms. "A new baby brother arrived last night," he said.

"Where's Mammy?" I didn't think to ask where the baby brother came from and Daddy didn't explain..

"Mammy isn't well. She's staying in bed today."

Mammy stayed in bed for a couple of days, and the baby stayed with her; Daddy said we weren't to go into her room. We heard our baby brother crying now and again. When, finally, Mammy came downstairs she looked tired. On Saturday Daddy brought the baby back to the church to be baptized. We knew what that meant, having learnt about it in catechism class: we were all born with a stain on our souls and baptism took it away. When Daddy came home he said the baby's name was Michael.

The Stations

The parish of The Neale comprised the village itself and clusters of houses, called townlands, located within an approximate three-mile radius. The village consisted of seventeen houses, the church, the school, the post office, two pubs which were also grocery shops, a carpenter shop, and a smithy. The townlands were of varying sizes, ranging from two to ten houses. Our townland was called Castletree; it had only one other house. One of the village pub-grocery shops sent around a lorry as a shop-on-wheels every week to sell household goods to the people of the townlands, and to buy eggs and wool from the farmers.

Twice each year an event called The Stations – mass and confessions in a chosen house – took place in each townland. The privileged families – selected by rotation – prepared for the great event by painting and cleaning house and yard. Since our townland had only two houses it was included in an adjoining townland for the Stations. The priest arrived at about half past seven in the morning, and all the residents of the townland gathered. He heard confessions in the kitchen; then, using the kitchen table for altar, said mass. The congregation crowded round as best it could.

Mass was followed by breakfast for the priest, who was joined at table by the man of the house and a few privileged guests. Much preparation went into making the meal a special one. We children liked to visit the Station house after school that day since there was sure to be some cake left over from the breakfast.

We learned about the origin of the Stations in Baldy's class. "Irish history," he told us, "is largely the seven-hundred-year story of the English trying to crush the spirit of the Irish people." I was enthralled with the stories of such Irish heroes as the O'Neills and O'Donnells and Patrick Sarsfield, who almost rid the country of the foreign invader. And I felt crushed when Baldy told of their ultimate failure and of the flight of the Wild Geese and the dark days of the Penal Laws that followed. England was Protestant and Ireland was Catholic and the wicked English tried to make the holy Irish abandon the faith of our fathers and convert to their own false religion. But they didn't succeed, Baldy told us triumphantly. Though priests were proscribed by English law and a price was put on their heads, young Irish lads still escaped to European Catholic countries to train and be ordained and return as priests to Ireland. And, though declared outlaws, they kept the faith alive in our people by saying mass in houses and out of the way places where the English couldn't find them. That was the origin of the Stations: the custom of saying mass in people's houses was preserved as a reminder of our precious Catholic heritage.

The story of our religious persecution by the foreign enemy did much to strengthen my adherence to the Catholic faith of my forefathers. I was especially stirred by the hymn which began "*Faith of our fathers living still, in spite of dungeon, fire, and sword.....* The seeds of militant Catholicism were being sown within me.

Serving mass

"Going to Sunday mass is an obligation imposed on us all by Almighty God Himself," Baldy told us one Friday. "But serving the priest at mass is a privilege to be enjoyed by only a few." And he selected the boys who would receive that privilege. He chose only those, he said, who had demonstrated an ability to learn quickly and memorize accurately. He had a roster of such boys from fourth to eighth class. He added me from the new third class, and then kept me after school for the next several Fridays to teach me the mass responses. "They're in Latin," he said, "and you'll have to memorize them." When he decided that I was proficient he included me among the six servers for second mass the following Sunday. I felt terribly important when I put on the red soutane and white surplice in the sacristy – my mother had to make the surplice – and marched out onto the altar in full view of the congregation.

I soon noticed that some boys garbled the Latin responses so as not to keep the priest waiting. And sometimes they even put non-Latin words into their responses, either for fun or through ignorance. When we said the Latin prayer *Confiteor* at the beginning of mass we had to bow from the waist and thump our craws while we said *mea culpa, mea culpa, mea maxima culpa* – through my fault, through my fault, through my most grievous fault. One boy learned from his older brother that a funny way to say this was *me a cowboy, me a cowboy, me a Mexican cowboy.* We all thought that was hilarious and some boys – but not I, fearing it would be a sin – said it at mass. Fortunately for the culprits, neither Baldy nor the priest ever heard them.

Death

My years in Baldy's class went by, and I grew in knowledge and fear of God and religion, the Catholic religion of course, which Baldy taught was the only true religion. I never heard of any other creed, except Protestantism, which, he told us, was false and un-Irish, and whose members were doomed to hell. Protestants weren't really Irish anyway, Baldy said; their ancestors stole the land from the Irish Catholics and, as landlords, imposed their rule on the country for hundreds of years, until we Irish defeated them and gained our independence.

As I learned about the Catholic faith and the laws that God imposed on us I feared for the salvation of my parents. Neither my father nor my mother showed any signs of being seriously religious: they went to mass on Sundays all right, but they went to Confession and Communion only at Easter – after the priest

7

had thundered from the altar that all were bound to fulfil their Easter duty under pain of mortal sin. And though they took part in the nightly rosary when Grandpa made us all kneel in the kitchen before we went to bed, they never seemed terribly interested in praying. So I prayed for them that they'd avoid the flames of hell. My fears for them were exacerbated by what Baldy taught in catechism class. "When a person dies," he wrote on the board, "his soul goes immediately before the throne of God to be judged." We obediently transcribed the sentence into our copybooks. Then he added, "if he dies in the state of mortal sin he is cast into hell for all eternity." He continued writing: "on the Last Day at the General Judgment our souls and bodies will be re-united; the just will go up to Heaven for all eternity, the evil will burn eternally down in hell." So what if my parents died in the state of mortal sin?

That fear was heightened when Pat, our next-door neighbor, was suddenly, violently, killed. The poor old man – he was fifty-nine – was coming home in his cart when the horse ran out of control and threw him onto the road. All through that night we heard the anguished screams of his youngest daughter, Tess. Next day after school Mammy told us to go visit the deceased man's house and pray for his soul. It was my first sight of a dead person. Pat, with bruises on his pale face, and looking smaller than the man I remembered, was laid out in his own bed, dressed in a Franciscan habit. My worried thoughts, as I knelt to pray for the repose of his soul, were on the poor man's eternal dwelling. He died suddenly; what if he hadn't time to repent of his sins?

"Where did his soul go?" I asked Tess who was in the kitchen and had stopped crying for the moment. Tess and I were great friends, though I was only eight and she was eighteen; she had even asked me to marry her and promised she'd wait for me to grow up.

Tess started crying again. "Oh God!" She blubbered some more, then said, "he was at confession for his sodality last Saturday, so I know he's in heaven now." She rolled her eyes upward and cried again. "But I want him here, God," she wailed. "I miss my Daddy."

When I was nine, tragedy struck my own family. Michael, just a year and a half, died one night while I and my other siblings slept. I came downstairs in the morning to find Mammy crying and Daddy standing by the fire and baby Michael lying dead on the couch.

"He got convulsions," Mammy said between bouts of sobbing. "He developed a high fever during the night and went into ..." She broke down again.

"I cycled to Ballinrobe to fetch the doctor," Daddy added. "But by the time he got here poor Michael was dead."

My siblings, on hearing Mammy's wailing, came downstairs in a rush. "He's a little angel in heaven now," Mammy consoled Mary and Kitty, who were crying, too; they used to play little mothers to their baby brother. I and my brothers didn't cry: boys were not supposed to show that womanly sign of weakness.

All day Mammy wailed, while we boys stayed outside in the sheds and the girls stayed in the house. The neighboring women came and sat in the kitchen to console Mammy, while the men stood outside the back door sharing Daddy's un-demonstrated grief. In the afternoon the undertaker arrived in his motor hearse and carried a little white coffin into the kitchen. Michael's body was placed in it and my brothers and I were called in to kiss him goodbye on his cold forehead. Then we children and Daddy and the neighbors walked behind the hearse to The Neale parish graveyard. Mammy stayed home because,

Daddy said, "that's the custom when a child dies". Some neighbors had dug a grave, the priest came and blessed it, the little coffin was lowered into it and covered over with clay, and we all went home.

About six months later another baby boy arrived, in the same way that Michael came. Mammy was unwell again for several days but neither she nor Daddy gave us any explanation as to where the baby came from and we asked no questions. After a few days the baby was baptized in The Neale church and given the name John. He looked so like Michael that it almost seemed as if Michael had came back to life. When John was exactly the same age as Michael had been, just over a year and a half, he, too, died one night of convulsions. The same sad procession of events took place, and, for a long time after, Mammy cried whenever the names of Michael or John were mentioned.

Grandpa

We lived in my grandfather's house. Grandpa was a farmer and living on his farm meant there were many chores for us children to do. When we got home from school and had dinner – which was always fat bacon, cabbage, and potatoes, kept warm by the fire after the grown-ups' dinner at one – we were assigned work duties for the rest of the day. Depending on the season, those could be anything from cleaning out the cowshed to weeding or thinning turnips and mangolds to sowing potatoes to helping feed cattle and sheep. During the summer holidays we helped to save the hay and wheat and oats. In October the school closed for two weeks so we children could help harvest the potatoes. All year round the cows had to be milked morning and

Grandpa

evening. I liked milking: loved the warm smell of the animals and the plash of the milk on the side of the bucket as I squeezed it from the cow's teats. But, like my siblings, I hated thinning turnips: that chore had to be done always in wet, still-chilly, April or May, kneeling in the muddy troughs between drills; the worst part was when, after spending an eternity crawling ever so slowly along, plucking out the unwanted seedlings and leaving one to grow every eight inches or so, I'd look back to find I had completed only about ten yards, and there were still another fifty to go.

"Who took my cap?" Grandpa shouted, coming down to the kitchen one Saturday when we were finishing dinner – Grandpa was a contrary man and lately had taken to eating his meals in an upstairs room he called the parlor. We all denied having touched or even seen his headgear.

"Everyone go search for it," Daddy said, to placate the old man who seemed to be always angry at us.

We scattered and searched the house, the yard, the sheds, without success. Eventually, during a break, with Grandpa standing at the back door glaring suspiciously at his grandchildren, Kitty pointed at the old man's head. "Grandpa," she shouted, "you're wearing it."

Grandpa grunted, felt with his hand to ensure the missing

lid was there, then turned and limped inside without a word. His behavior – he had never been friendly to his grandchildren, or to his daughter-in-law – had recently become unbearable: he shouted at Mammy a lot and made it clear that he didn't want us living in his house. The year was 1946, John had just died, the war had ended, Tom was away at boarding school – he won a County Scholarship to Mount St. Joseph's College in Roscrea – and house construction was underway again in the country. So Mammy and Daddy decided to leave Grandpa's house. They packed our belongings, put them into the horse cart, and we went to live in a rented house in The Neale village. It was a miserable house, dark and dingy, and infested with rats that lived in the walls and gnawed through the floorboards at night while Seamus and I tried to sleep in our bedroom in the upstairs loft. We kept a flashlamp and our shoes at the ready by the bed we shared, and threw the shoes at the rats when they appeared through new-gnawed holes in the floor.

When we left his house neither I nor my siblings questioned why Grandpa was so unfriendly that we had to leave. Many years later Seamus discovered why: researching the family genealogy, he talked with some of the old people who knew Grandpa and uncovered the probable cause of the old man's anger. He had been reared on a small farm and as a young man went to Australia, where he made a fortune farming sheep. He returned home a wealthy man and bought a house – the one we lived in at Castletree – and large farm. In due course he married into an affluent family, and fathered five children. Then his wife – our grandmother – died from a miscarriage. Seamus was told the story of her death by an old cousin: Grandpa was playing cards downstairs in the kitchen with some neighbors and ignored the screams of his wife who was hemorrhaging to death upstairs.

He married again shortly after, into more money, and had another son. But because he had been a difficult man to get along with, his five older children left home as soon as they were able. Tommy, his second son – my father – emigrated to America after taking part in the Irish War of Independence and being shot at during the ensuing Civil War. In New York he met and married Margaret Murray – my mother – who had also emigrated from Mayo about the same time. Three children were born to them, Tom, Mary, and Kitty. They were living in the Bronx when Grandpa wrote in the summer of 1933 and asked my father to come home and take over his farm. He was getting too old to manage it by himself, he wrote, and his youngest son who had been living with him had bought a shop in Ballinrobe and had gone to live there.

My father was a plasterer – and had worked on the Empire State Building – but now because of the Great Depression he was out of work. So he and his young family set sail for Ireland and arrived in Castletree in due course. Grandpa, now a man of some wealth and a bit of a snob, had selected a woman from a moneyed family to marry his son. My father, for some unknown reason, had never told his father he had married, so when he arrived with my mother and the children Grandpa was furious at the let-down to his plans and his pride. He was even more angry when he heard that my mother was the daughter of a mere small farmer. So he refused to hand over the farm and my parents went to live in Castlebar, near where my mother had grown up. I was born there in November of 1934 and when Seamus was born just a year later my parents had five children under the age of five to care for. In 1937 the family moved to Dublin where my father could find more reliable work. When, after the outbreak of World War II the building industry came to a halt, my parents, now with six

13

children – <u>Bridie was born after we moved to Dublin</u> – were in dire straits. My father   persuaded Grandpa to let us live in Castletree, which we did till the war ended.

Left front, with siblings, 1944

Discovering Sex

Initial Shock

I was eleven when we moved to The Neale, had been a mass server for two years, and was becoming quite pious. One Sunday morning, after serving second mass, as I and my fellow servers were disrobing in the sacristy, Father Jimmy tapped me on the shoulder.

"I understand you're living in the village now?"

"I am, Father."

"I have a favor to ask of you."

My eyes widened: to be even spoken to by the priest was a privilege; to be asked to do him a favor ...! "Yes, Father."

"I'd like you to serve my mass on weekday mornings at nine o'clock."

"Of course, Father." Then I remembered school. The priest noticed my worried look.

"What's the matter?"

"School starts at half nine, Father, and Mr. Baldy is very strict about us being on time.

Father Jimmy smiled, " I'll talk to your teacher and I'm sure he'll allow you to arrive a few minutes late."

The Neale School

The priest talked to Baldy. And Baldy allowed. So I served Father Jimmy's mass every morning for the next two years, and became more and more attached to my faith. I believed everything I was taught in matters of religion. How could I not? Baldy and Father Jimmy believed those things. Anyway Catholic teaching was compelling, however difficult its content might be. So my faith never wavered, even when its content became more difficult, which it did when knowledge of sex was thrust into my life.

Until I was about twelve years old I had no idea how human life was propagated and didn't have any curiosity about it. This despite living on a farm and seeing roosters mate with hens on a daily basis, knowing all about rams being let in among the ewes at a certain time of year so the ewes would give birth to lambs in the spring, driving cows in heat – *bulling*, we called that condition – to the bull and watching the bull mount the cow. Not even when my mother gave birth to the two boys in Grandpa's house did I make the connection between animal and human propagation. Until one particular day ....

16

Baldy was a man of regular habits, one of which was to bring the *Irish Independent* newspaper to school every day. Another was to visit the outhouse – the school had no indoor toilets – before dismissing us for lunch . His son, Des, who was in my class and who hated his father because Baldy beat him, too, always grabbed the newspaper during his father's absence to look at the headlines. I shared in this viewing because he and I were good friends. One day, Des pointed to the Births column on the front page.

"Let's see who got foaled today," he chortled.

A light turned on in my brain: I had seen foals being born. Was this how children were born as well? My first reaction was disgust: my parents couldn't possibly ...?

Sex then entered my life by degrees. The first degree occurred when I became better acquainted with girls. Which happened when school classes were amalgamated. Up to the time I was in fifth class we had four teachers, two for the boys and two for the girls. When the total enrollment of school pupils fell to seventy Baldy told us that henceforth there would be only three teachers in the school. Boys' and girls' classes would be merged; he himself would teach fifth through eighth.

The entry of girls brought significant changes to Baldy's treatment of his pupils. He never used his leather strap on the girls, and lessened greatly his abuse of the boys. He separated boys from girls in the classroom, having girls occupy the right side and boys the left. We boys were fascinated to have girls in close proximity, and we discussed among ourselves which girl each boy liked best. Though we never informed the girls of our choices, or even talked to them, we decided that certain girls belonged to particular boys. I liked looking at Bridgie more than any other girl, gazing at her often when we were standing around Baldy's desk during reading and spelling sessions. She had a

17

dreamy look when she returned my gaze and I felt sure she liked me.

Although, due to the foal incident with Des and the newspaper, I became aware of the general nature of sex, I didn't learn that there was any kind of pleasure or sin connected with it. The only time Baldy ever touched on the subject was when he made us learn the Ten Commandments by heart, including *thou shalt not commit adultery* and *thou shalt not covet thy neighbor's wife*. Although he explained in some detail what was forbidden by the other Commandments – for instance that *thou shalt not kill* included anger and backside kicking – he dismissed the sixth and ninth with the comment that they involved undue intimacy between members of the opposite sex and that we needn't worry about those commandments for now. My parents never mentioned sex or the facts of life.

So when puberty struck after we moved to The Neale, and I found myself enjoying the new pleasure of an engorged penis, I had no inkling of the disapproval with which God's Holy Church frowned on such rapture. I discovered that penis swelling and its concomitant physical pleasure occurred whenever I looked at pictures of ladies in their underwear in the magazines that my mother was now able to buy, or when I looked at ladies' bare legs as they cycled by with their skirts blown back by the wind. Almost every day was windy.

The Sinfulness of Sex

Enlightenment – the proper word for what proved to be a darkening experience – regarding the evil of sexual pleasure came only after I went to secondary school. Baldy prepared me– I was the brightest pupil in the school, he told my parents, though he

18

rarely praised me – for the County Council scholarship, as he had prepared my older brother Tom four years earlier. I won the scholarship, and at the age of thirteen was sent as a boarder to Mount St. Joseph's College, Roscrea, where Tom was already a student; my wishes in the matter weren't consulted by parents or teacher. The College, a secondary school for boys run by Cistercian monks, was eighty miles from The Neale. It was there, in first year Christian Doctrine class, that I learned about Holy Purity, the sinfulness of sexual enjoyment, and the dangers sex held for my eternal salvation.

I was horrified to hear that those delightful sensations of pleasure I got from my swollen penis were sinful. Mortally sinful. The only good news was that since I hadn't known of their heinousness when I was enjoying them I didn't actually commit mortal sin.

Mt St. Joseph's College, Roscrea

"They're called material sins," Father Kevin told us in Christian Doctrine class, meaning, he explained, that although they constituted what the Church called grave matter, a person couldn't be held responsible if he didn't know they were sins when he was committing them. However, that only absolved me from the past. From now on I couldn't partake of those pleasures without committing mortal sin and placing my soul on the precipice of hell. I further learned that there was a plethora of sins associated with sex, under the headings of thoughts, words, and deeds. All of them were mortal – there were no venial sex sins, Father Kevin said. Even thoughts, which by now were constantly bombarding my imagination in the form of women's bodily parts, were mortally sinful. A single impure thought – thoughts about sex were called impure thoughts – could send me tumbling down to hell if I deliberately took pleasure in it. I decided I didn't have to worry about impure words or deeds since I never talked about sex or performed sexual acts. At least I thought I didn't until I went to confession to a devout monk.

"I had bad thoughts eleven times, Father." Sexual thoughts were also referred to as bad thoughts; they came unbidden and it was impossible to tell if I took pleasure in them, so I confessed them to be safe.

The white-cowled figure across the grill showed no reaction. Relieved, I was about to continue my litany of other sins when he asked, "did you touch yourself?"

Oh God! Couldn't I even touch my own body without committing sin? Was that what the monk meant? "I don't understand, Father." Kicking for touch to find out more.

"Did you touch your private parts while you were thinking those thoughts?"

"No, Father." I hadn't, but neither had I known that such

an action would be sinful.

"Very well. Continue."

Dear God! I was walking through a minefield of sexual sins during every waking minute. And I wasn't even safe during sleep since I was more than once awakened at night by feelings of intense pleasure in my nether regions, and found a sticky substance in my pajama pants next morning. "Sexual pleasure is sinful if you enjoy it," Father Kevin had said in class. So, did I enjoy what happened in my sleep? I was asleep, so I could hardly be held responsible for what my body did in that state. But after I was awakened by the pleasure, did I enjoy it? Maybe inadvertently? But was my inadvertent enjoyment sinful? Mortally sinful? Did I have to confess it? What misery! I hated having to confess sins of sex; the embarrassment of acknowledging them was almost as painful as my fear of hell.

A problem I had – and apparently other College boys had it, too – was shyness in asking questions about sex. I feared that by asking such questions in Christian Doctrine class I'd be implying that I performed those acts. A solution to the dilemma presented itself in the Gift Shop attached to the monastery Guest House where the monks sold visitors pious objects, including books dealing with Holy Purity – the virtue opposed to sexual sin. When we went to the monastery chapel for weekly confession we were allowed to visit the Gift Shop. The books on Holy Purity were popular reading, and from them I learned in awful detail the myriad pathways to hell that sexual pleasure provided. I stored those pathways in my memory, and recalled them to torture myself when preparing for confession.

Return to Dublin

I made it onto the College junior rugby team in my second

year. One afternoon in January after practice I showered and was hurrying to the five-to-seven study period when I was stopped by the new College President. Tommy the Tiger was a much-feared monk who had been so nicknamed on his first day in office.

"Please come with me." The Tiger's tone was gentle but I expected I was in for it: he only hauled boys into his office because they had committed serious offenses. Though I couldn't remember anything terrible I had done. The Tiger remained standing while I shut the door, then he said without preamble, "I'm very sorry to tell you that your sister Kitty has died."

I felt as if I'd been struck in the gut by a rugby ball. True, Kitty had been ill for over a year, diagnosed with bone cancer at the age of fifteen, but no one had told me it was a fatal disease. And when I said goodbye to her before returning to school after the Christmas holidays she seemed all right. I couldn't restrain the tears: Kitty and I had been very close. My Uncle Walter came in his car to fetch me and I got home in time for the funeral mass and burial. Mammy told me that the priest gave her Extreme

On Roscrea Junior Rugby team, 1950; front, second from right.

Unction the day she died so she was sure the poor girl was in heaven now.

A month later Mammy wrote to say the family had moved back to Dublin. So for Easter and summer holidays I went to our new home, a newly-built rented house that was equipped with electricity and a bathroom, luxuries we didn't have in either Grandpa's or the house in The Neale. My parents informed me shortly after I came home for the summer that from now on I was to attend the local Christian Brothers School in Fairview, because it was less expensive, and because my scholarship money would pay for Seamus as well. Seamus was already at school there since they moved to Dublin.

I was now fifteen, and my father got me a trade union card so I could earn some money working as an apprentice plasterer over the summer. I worked on a building site for two months, from eight to six Monday to Friday and from eight to one on Saturday, and earned thirty shillings a week. From this I was able to give some money to my mother. The raunchy stories my much older fellow workmen told each other during those work-days taught me many more details about sex and sexual behavior, details that both disgusted and titillated me.

In September I started school at the Christian Brothers, a very unpleasant experience after two years with the mellow monks of Roscrea. The Brothers were exam-oriented and they beat their students unmercifully to make them pass the Intermediate and Leaving Certificate exams. One Brother in particular, whom we called Gunner, was outrageously violent, and his face betrayed orgasmic excitement when he used his leather strap – which he did constantly. Another teacher, a layman nicknamed Nailer because he was forever either biting or filing his nails during class, seemed terribly unhappy except when he was using his strap on some unfortunate student. I managed to escape the beatings of both sadists by memorizing vast quantities of school subject matter.

Dublin proved to be a source of much temptation in my battle with sexual sin. Impure thoughts and looks attacked without letup. Pretty girls and women were everywhere, cycling by with flying skirts – Dublin was a city of bicycles – or sitting next to me on buses, when their slightest touch inflamed my libido. Even the bus itself by the very vibration of its engine swelled the joint and threatened pleasure. The cinema, to which I soon became addicted, was a pleasure palace of Satan himself; many films showed saucy women displaying their wares on massive screens to tempt the fragile flesh of my lusty youth.

I went to confession on Saturday nights to unload my mountain of weekly wickedness: impure thoughts fifteen times, unchaste looks nineteen times, unchaste acts with myself three times but I don't know if I enjoyed them. Then Communion on Sunday morning made my soul as pure as an angel's. After mass I'd cycle home for breakfast feeling light as air, my soul once again the temple of God. An hour later Tom would return from a later mass with the Sunday newspapers, mostly English. Ah, the English Sunday papers! They usually had pictures of almost naked ladies, the sight of which immediately caused me to sully my just-purified soul. And I had to wait till Saturday to be cleansed again. What if I died in the meantime?

Soon I was old enough to go to dances, where I found new sources of sin. The slow foxtrot brought contact with girls' soft breasts; which, combined with the dimming of the lights and the girls' hair tickling my face, made avoidance of sin well-nigh impossible. The tango, Gunner warned, was an immoral dance, which we must not engage in. I danced it anyway, my body tingling to the soft touch of my partner's thighs.

24

Walter Keady

Leaving School

When I was sixteen, the year I took the Intermediate Certificate, my parents had me sit for the Civil Service Clerical Officers exam. I scored a high place and was offered a job the following year. My parents decided I should leave school to take the job, despite the advice of a teacher who said I would do much better later on if I stayed in school to take the Leaving Certificate. However, since my family needed the money I'd earn as a Clerical Officer, I became a working adult at the age of seventeen. So I began a new life. Even after giving my mother half my pay I had money in my pocket, and I was old enough now to enjoy the company of girls.

A challenge I had to contend with on leaving school was one that most lads of my age had to face in the Ireland of the 1950s. It was called *Vocation*, by which was meant a 'calling' to the priestly or Religious life. For two years I had gone to a secondary school run by Cistercian monks and for another two years to a school run by Christian Brothers. In both, the idea of a Religious Vocation was subtly insinuated, was always present, and was sometimes overtly promoted. So I couldn't leave school without asking myself the question that had been put more than once by teachers and preachers: is God calling me to the Higher Life? And those teachers and preachers had always made clear that a Religious Vocation was the highest life to which anyone could aspire. I almost succumbed to the urge to give up all for Christ, but decided in the end that the celibate life was not for me: the lure of the female was too strong for my young body to reject. So I turned my back on the notion of a priestly vocation, thinking I had made a final decision in the matter. Ha!

Left, on holidays with the grown-ups, Salthill, Galway, 1952

A Very Catholic Organization

Joining Maria Duce

"They're very Catholic," Brennan said, "and they have a six-point program to reform society."

I wasn't aware that society needed reforming; in fact, I wasn't even sure what Brennan meant by society. But I said nothing, not wanting to display my ignorance. We were on top of a double-decker bus, riding home after playing a football match in the Phoenix Park on a Sunday morning in November. I was feeling happy: we'd won the match and I had played awfully well. Gaelic football was my life these days and I had a promising future in the game.

"And they're very sociable," Brennan pursued, responding to my silence. "There are plenty of girls in the organization, and they have lots of parties."

"Indeed!" Now he was getting my attention. My social life had been negligible since I left school; the people I worked with in the Civil Service were all much older and they were a pretty dull lot, and my football team-mates left in a hurry after games so that I never really got to know them. I was friends with Brennan because we were at the Christian Brothers school together.

"I met a very nice girl there,"he went on, then paused, before adding shyly, "I'm doing a line with her."

"That's wonderful." Meeting girls was something I would like very much. Right now I had no social entrée into the world of women.

"Would you like to came to a meeting of the organization?"

I would since there were girls in it. So that evening I went with Brennan to what he described as a social event. It was held in an upstairs room in a rundown-looking Georgian building, number 5 Cavendish Row, across the street from the Gate Theatre. The people were mostly young, friendly, enthusiastic, and they projected happiness. The happiness bit struck me particularly: they seemed terribly cheerful and they laughed a lot. When I discovered that they were pious as well I was ready to join them. Since leaving school my conscience had been nagging me for slacking off in my religious duties: mass on Sunday, confession and communion just once a month, and overall carelessness in the matter of chastity.

The social began with a prayer, for which all knelt; it was led by an older man whom people addressed as Mr. Agar. After the prayer all sat on not-very-comfortable cane chairs while a serious-looking young man with horn-rimmed glasses introduced and played on a gramophone a program of classical music. Which thrilled me: I had recently discovered the joys of serious music. Afterwards, a few of the women served tea and biscuits and Brennan introduced me to various people, including several young ladies. The latter, however, showed no particular interest in me, and I was too shy to engage them in conversation.

"Would you like to know more abut the organization?" a

sparrow-fart of a fellow, who introduced himself as Austin, asked me. I noticed that they all referred to the group as the organization.

"Yes, I would."

"Great!" the sparrow-fart chirped. "Come on over here and I'll tell you a bit about it." He led the way to a corner and found two unoccupied chairs. "The Catholic Church" he intoned, like a priest orating from the pulpit, "is the one true Church and ought to be acknowledged as such by States and Nations." He paused, then wagged an admonitory finger. "That's the principal on which our organization was founded."

"I see." Though I didn't at all. I had been taught that the Catholic Church was the one true church of course, but never heard that States were obliged to bow before it. In fact I had never heard anything about the obligation of the State to do anything other than to collect taxes and to fight wars when it felt threatened by other States. However, I supposed that recognizing the Catholic Church as the one true Church was a reasonable demand to make of the State: it would be simply acknowledging a fact.

"Jesus Christ is King of the Universe and must be recognized as such." Austin was working up a head of sermonical steam.

"So how do you go about ... I mean what do you do about it?" I interjected in a hurry to keep the subject at a conversational level; I didn't feel like being preached to by this pipsqueak: the fellow couldn't be more than about five feet small.

Austin wagged a triumphant finger. "This is what Maria Duce is all about," he crowed. "We –"

"Maria Duce?" I raised an eyebrow.

"Oh! Didn't anyone tell you?" His wide eyes suggested that my ignorance was culpable and beyond his comprehension.

29

"That's the name of our organization. Maria Duce is the Latin for Mary Leading. As in leading an army." He stared enquiringly to ensure I understood. "We, the members of Maria Duce, are the army of the Blessed Virgin Mary. We dedicate ourselves to fighting for the recognition of Her Son's Kingship in the world."

"I see." But again I didn't have a clue as to what the fellow was talking about. However, this organization might provide the support I needed to renew my spiritual fervor. "What do the members do?"

Austin paused to strike a match and light a cigarette. He took a long puff, then issued a dragon-like exhalation of smoke through his his nostrils. "We do a lot of things to spread the word about the Social Rights of Christ the King: for example, we give public lectures, we publish a newspaper that we distribute widely, we write letters to the newspapers, we sell the papal encyclicals and the works of Father Fahey, we recruit new members for the organization. And, most importantly, we train our members to play their part in the fight for the Social Rights of Christ the King." He paused to pick a strand from the unfiltered cigarette off the tip of his tongue.

"What would I do if I became a member?"

He tapped ash from his cigarette onto the floor and coughed – I recognized a smoker's cough: Mammy was making the same disgusting sounds since she started smoking a few years before. After he recovered his voice Austin said, "when you become a member we'll assign you to a Branch; we're organized into Branches, you see. At the meeting – each Branch has a weekly meeting – you'll learn about the Divine Plan for Social Order." He intoned this last phrase in a distinctly reverential mode, as if it was a prayer. "Between meetings you'll be working with the rest of us to bring about the reign of Christ the King in

Irish society by distributing our newspaper and selling books."

Books! I loved books. "What books do you sell?"

"Mostly papal encyclicals, and the works of Father Fahey."

"Who's Father Fahey?"

Austin pulled on his cigarette. "If you become a member you'll learn all about him in due course." He looked at me, challenge in his eyes. "Do you want to join?"

"Sure." The sparrow-fart had an enthusiasm and an air of authority that I was beginning to find irresistible.

"Good!" He dropped the remains of his cigarette on the floor and stamped on it. "I'll assign you to the St Catherine of Sienna Branch, which meets here every Tuesday at seven. Claire!" He called to a young woman who was chatting with others nearby. She came over. "Walter – it is Walter, isn't it?" He pulled out another cigarette.

"Yes."

"I'd like you to meet Claire; she's the First Officer of St Catherine's. Claire, Walter would like to join your Branch."

Claire smiled at me. "We'll be very pleased to welcome you." Willowy, with a beautiful face. "We already have six members, including myself. Five are women so we'll be delighted to have another man in our midst."

I went home tickled: I had found new friends and an organization to keep me on the straight and narrow. And lots of pretty girls.

The Branch Meeting

The Branch meeting on Tuesday evening was intense, warm, and sociable. Four women and I were present when Claire began to recite the rosary, for which we all knelt around the table. Two more members, a man introduced as Christy and a very attractive young woman called Marjorie, arrived after the rosary. The minutes of the previous meeting were read, as was the treasurer's report. Then Claire read a few pages of a book by Father Fahey that dealt with the Divine Plan for Social Order, and the members discussed it at length.

When Brennan told me on the bus about the six-point program to reform society he was simply repeating the official objective of the organization. The statement meant nothing to me at the time since it gave no inkling of the radical reform that Maria Duce intended for Irish society. The study portion of the Branch meeting introduced me now to some of those revolutionary ideas. It would take the better part of a year of such study groups, as well as lectures, readings, and informal discussions, for me to fully understand the proposed reform.

At the end of the study period Claire announced the churches at which, she said, *Fiat* would be distributed next Sunday. She called for volunteers.

"What is *Fiat*?" I asked.

"It's the Maria Duce newspaper." She reached into her bag, pulled out a copy, and handed it to me. "It contains articles that explain the Divine Plan for Social Order. We distribute it outside churches on Sundays."

I looked over the eight-page slightly less than newspaper-size publication, printed on glossy paper with large headlines condemning Communism, Freemasonry, and Zionism – enemies of the Church, it said – and calling on all Catholics to support the Divine Plan for Social Order. "What do you charge for it?"

Everyone smiled. "We don't exactly charge," Claire said. "We sort of give it away. But we do invite people to leave a donation."

"Sometimes they take it and give you sweet feck all,"

Christy grumbled.

Christy and I volunteered for St Peter's Church in Phibsboro: it was about a fifteen minute bike ride from my home, and I didn't have a football match till the afternoon. Claire assured us that we'd be helped by members from other Branches.

Sunday morning I went to seven o'clock mass at my parish church, then dashed home and made my breakfast – the rest of the family were still in bed – and hurried to St. Peter's. Christy was already there with several hundred copies of *Fiat*. People were beginning to stream out of the eight o'clock mass.

Christy handed me a bundle of papers, then waved a copy at the exiting congregation, shouting, "Read *Fiat*, the Catholic newspaper. Fight Communism and Freemasonry, the enemies of the Church. Learn all about the Catholic Plan for Social Order."

There were several gates leading out of the church grounds. Christy stood at one, I at another. Jimmy, from another Branch, raced up on his bike, grabbed copies of the paper and went to a third gate. Five or six minutes later the eight o'clock congregation had dissipated.

"How many did you sell?" Christy asked me when we huddled.

"Only five," I confessed. "But one man gave me a ten shilling note."

"Jaysus!" Christy stared at me. "I sold eleven and only got four and ninepence."

"I sold seven," Jimmy said. He took coins from his pocket and counted. "Six and thruppence."

We stayed at our posts through the nine, ten, eleven, half-eleven, and twelve, masses and distributed a total of a hundred and forty six copies, for which we got four pounds thirteen and eightpence. I found that most people ignored me; only the occasional one took a paper and gave a donation. One man took a copy and, while searching his pockets for change, said, "good lad yourself; them Jews is the ruination of the country."

Afterwards, I hurried home for dinner, which my parents prepared together, the one meal of the week at which all members of the family were present. Then I grabbed my togs and boots and cycled to Clontarf to play a football match. That evening I met Jimmy and Christy and we went to a dance at the Crystal Ballroom. I was happy: my social life had taken off.

Austin

I soon fell under the spell of Austin, a miniature fanatic with a brilliant mind, whose reasoning was flawless in teasing out the logical conclusions of Papal teaching.

"Listen," he said, lighting another cigarette. "The Pope's infallible, right?"

"Right." Six of us sat around a table in Forte's café on O'Connell Street, all drinking coffee and most puffing cigarettes. No one disagreed with Austin's statement: the Pope had himself declared infallible by the Vatican Council.

"So what he teaches about faith and morals is infallibly true." Austin stabbed the air with his cigarette to drive home the point.

"Right," we chorused again.

"And he teaches that the Catholic Church is the one true Church."

He sipped coffee; we all nodded assent.

"And he teaches that error has no rights; only truth has rights."

"Right," we chorused.

"So the Catholic Church, and it alone, has a right to be

acknowledged as the One True Church."

"Absolutely," we chanted in unison.

"And," Austin waved his ash-laden cigarette, "it must be acknowledged as such by States and Nations." He tapped the ash into his saucer. "Which," he said, "the Irish Constitution doesn't do."

"I've a question." Mick pointed a nicotine-stained finger at Austin. "I read somewhere that when de Valera was drafting the Constitution in 1937 he asked the advice of bishops and theologians to make sure the document paid due deference to the teaching of the Church. So how come he didn't do it right if he got all that advice?"

Austin smirked. "Good question, Mick." He sipped coffee and dragged on his cigarette. "Dev maintains that he did the right thing. However, there's a very strong suspicion that he was under the thumb of certain Masonic and Jewish organizations when he submitted the draft Constitution to be ratified by the people of Ireland." Austin's expressionless eyes suggested that he knew more than he was willing to say.

"Excuse my ignorance," I said. "What does the Constitution say that we don't agree with?"

"I can answer that." Mick tapped my shoulder. "Article 44 says that the State recognizes the special position of the Holy Catholic Apostolic and Roman Church as the guardian of the Faith professed by the great majority of the citizens."

"Good man," Austin said, emitting a cloud of smoke through his nose.

"Well, what's wrong with that?" It seemed pretty strong stuff to me.

"What's wrong with it?" Austin's stern expression reminded me of Baldy reacting to a pupil who gave an incorrect answer. "All it does is recognize the mathematical fact that the vast majority of Irish people are Catholics."

"More coffee anyone?" The waitress looked accusingly at us; we had been here for more than an hour and had ordered only one round of coffee.

"No thanks," we all said. She stared at us some more, then went away.

"So what should it say?" I was still struggling to understand the Divine Plan.

Mick sniggered. "You have a lot to learn, Walter."

"What it should say, " Austin said evenly, "is that the State acknowledges that the Catholic Church is the one true religion established by Jesus Christ."

"Protestants and Jews won't like that too much." Mick grinned.

"Feck Protestants and Jews," Christy said. Even among Maria Duce fanatics, I had learned, he was regarded as extremely intolerant of all who weren't true believers.

"All other religions should be *tolerated* by the State." Austin emphasized the word. "They should be allowed to practice their beliefs as long as they don't interfere with the true religion."

Indoctrination

Father Fahey

At a Tuesday Branch meeting Claire announced that Father Fahey would be giving his monthly lecture on Sunday at noon and that we should all try to attend.   I had been to several of his lectures already and was anxious for more.   Father Fahey, a member of the Holy Ghost Congregation and the spiritual leader of Maria Duce, fascinated me. A small man about seventy with rosy cheeks and incongruously sensual-looking lips, he had

dedicated his life to writing and preaching about the Divine Plan, and he founded Maria Duce to propagate it. He was a mediocre speaker, but he expounded the Divine Plan with a captivating sincerity. His books, though difficult, were de rigeur study material for Maria Duce members, who worshiped the Founder. A saintly man, they proclaimed, a man ahead of his time, whose wisdom would one day be acknowledged by

Father Fahey

37

all the world when the reign of Christ the King was established. Outside of the organization, however, Father Fahey was regarded as a fanatic and an anti-Semite, even by most Irish bishops. As indeed were we members of Maria Duce. *They're out to establish a confessional State,* one detractor wrote in a letter to a national newspaper. *If they have their way they'll allow only the Catholic faith to be practiced in Ireland and they'll burn at the stake all those they regard as heretics.*

The room in Cavendish Row could accommodate about fifty people and it was filled on Sunday at noon when the great little man arrived. We all stood; he knelt at a priedieu placed for him at the head of the room and pulled a beads from the pocket of his shabby raincoat. Everyone knelt as he began the rosary. The members responded with enthusiasm. When it was finished he rose and faced his audience from behind a lectern.

"I'd like to talk to you this morning about the second of the six-point plan: The State must recognize the Catholic Church as divinely appointed to teach man what favors or hinders his supernatural destiny."

I could feel the audience settling into their chairs: this was the kind of stuff we wanted to hear.

"Since the Catholic Church is the Body of Christ," the little priest pronounced in his reedy, barely audible, voice, "through which He rules and is the Sovereign Ruler of all rulers, it must be acknowledged as the one true church by States and Nations...."

Then, for more than an hour he hammered home the logical consequences of his opening statements. The enthusiasm of the audience was reflected in their hearty clapping when he ended his lecture. I myself was mightily stirred, though my mind felt exhausted by the effort to follow his train of thought. I resolved to spend my scanty savings on his books and to read a portion of them every day.

In January, 1954 we were informed that Father Fahey was gravely ill and not expected to live. Two days later we got the news that he had died. The members were in shock. Someone got hold of a photo of Father Fahey's corpse, laid out in mass vestments, and presented a copy to each member. It was rather macabre, but members saw it as a souvenir of our saint-in-the-making. Many of us attended the funeral at the Holy Ghost College in Kimmage where Father Fahey had lived and worked; I was thrilled to find myself standing close to Eamon de Valera, at the back of the church as the priest's body was carried in and placed on a catafalque in front of the high altar. Dev had been a friend of Father Fahey who was one of the theologians from whom he sought advice when drafting the religion article of the Irish Constitution.

Shortly after, Austin told us in Forte's café that the Maria Duce Executive now feared the Archbishop might suppress the organization since our founder was no longer here to protect us.

Archbishop McQuaid and Eamon de Valera

John Charles McQuaid, the Archbishop of Dublin, was a former member of the Holy Ghost Order and a one-time student of Father Fahey. A dour unfriendly prelate, his scowl was known to evoke terror in any priest in his diocese who committed even the slightest infraction of the many rules he laid down for his clergy. He, too, had given theological advice to de Valera when the latter was writing the Article on religion in the Constitution. And he was a strict enforcer of Catholic doctrine in public life. Among other prohibitions, he forbade Catholics to attend Trinity College because he regarded its Protestant ethos as inimical to the faith of young Catholics.

Yet even this hardline stickler for doctrinal purity found Maria Duce's commitment to Catholic hegemony extreme. Or perhaps, as Austin suspected, he resented the fact that the organization, run by mere 'lay people,' was not sufficiently under his thumb. Whatever the reason, he had tolerated Maria Duce because of his reverence for Father Fahey, his one-time professor and mentor. But it came as no surprise to the Executive when, less than a year after Father Fahey's death, they were summoned to the archiepiscopal palace, where the prelate informed them that they could no longer use the name of Mary in the title of the organization. Relieved that they had not been suppressed entirely, the Executive chose *Firinne*, the Irish word for *truth*, as the new name of the organization. With his acceptance of that title and having made clear his authority, his Grace allowed the Organization to continue.

The Organization

The Executive of Maria Duce, now Firinne, was made up of president, vice-president, secretary, treasurer, and several other

40

members. Lower down in the hierarchy, each Branch was ruled by a First Officer who also attended meetings of the Executive. As I got to know the members of the Executive, I found them to be kind and thoughtful people who were horrified at accusations that implementing the Divine Plan would lead to a government in which heretics would be persecuted. Nevertheless, they were the leaders of an organization that upheld and promoted the Vatican-approved doctrine that the Catholic Church alone was the true Church of Christ and that all other religions were false.

The Firinne leadership did not consider itself extreme, it was simply following Catholic doctrine to its logical conclusion with its six-point plan. In keeping with the teachings of papal encyclicals, it expected the State to tolerate other religions, but only after it recognized the Catholic Church as the one true religion. It also believed that the Church's foes were involved in a Satanic conspiracy to deny the Rights of Christ the King and impose a godless world government to replace the Divinely instituted Holy Catholic Church. The Executive, and the members they indoctrinated, lived in the happy world of the unencumbered-by-doubt. We were certain that our Cause was Right and we pursued it with a faith and zeal that we believed would ultimately lead to success and vindication. We believed our viewpoint was that of visionaries who saw the world *sub specie aeternitatis* – from the aspect of eternity.

Some members, however, reveled in being considered fanatics, devotees of The Cause. They had no time for intellectual tolerance of error, believing that extremism in the cause of truth was no vice and moderation in its pursuit no virtue. Though I personally did not believe in persecuting the invincibly ignorant, still, as I listened to members' conversations in Forte's café, I had to acknowledge that occasional statements of some could easily lead an outsider to believe we would not be averse to burning heretics at the stake.

Shortly after Father Fahey's death I was appointed First Officer of the St. Catherine of Sienna Branch, and given responsibility for the distribution of Fiat. I was thrilled that the Executive had recognized my talent and leadership. As a First Officer I was invited to their meetings, where I embraced the Firinne Weltanschauung and became even more dedicated to the Cause.

Danny Kaye

"Guess who's coming to Dublin?" Tony asked one night in Forte's, as a half dozen of us sat drinking coffee and smoking and discussing the ills of the world and our solutions for those ills.

"Are you talking about Danny Kaye?" Mick blew sly smoke in Tony's face.

Tony ignored him. "Danny Kaye, the Communist, is coming here next week to perform at the Theatre Royal."

"Are we going to shoot him?" Christy asked. "Fecking Communists should be shot, you know. They have a helluva nerve coming here."

"Unfortunately, killing Communists is still against the fifth commandment," Tony said. "But we are going to picket him."

"Count me in," Colman said. "Though I do like him."

"I saw The Inspector General, last year," Mick said. "It was hilarious."

"An Inspector general is generally expected to inspect generally," Colman mimicked.

"Why are we picketing him?" I asked, a bit timidly; I was still learning who was acceptable and who was not and why.

"Walter!" Tony glared at me. "You're an officer in this organization, for God's sake. You have to be on top of those things."

I was crushed. Tony was a figure of awe to us: the smartest man in the organization, it was agreed whenever we discussed the membership among our coterie of Forte coffee drinkers. He was also acknowledged to be the most fanatical. But he rarely came to our café sessions, so we felt privileged to have him join us.

"Danny Kaye is what Joe McCarthy calls a crypto-Communist," Colman gently explained to me. He himself had felt the lash of Tony's scolding at another time.

"Ah! If Joe McCarthy be against him who shall be for him?" I sang. At that time McCarthy was conducting his witch hunt for American Communists, fellow-travelers, crypto-Communists. Firinne was on his side of course, for he was a Catholic and a crusading champion against godless Communism. Most American Catholics supported him, too, especially the American Catholic Press – except for a couple of so-called liberal Catholic papers. Firinne followed his hearings in the American Senate, and vilified in lectures and in Fiat those public figures whom McCarthy fingered as tarnished by any shade of pink.

"Kaye supports known Communists in Hollywood," Mick added. "He says they have a right to say whatever they like!"

We all laughed at that. Error had no rights, according to Catholic theology. And certainly Communists had no right to preach their pernicious doctrines. In Firinne we always associated the word *pernicious* with false doctrines.

"I need volunteers to picket him on Saturday."

"I'll do it," all but I volunteered.

"Sorry, Tony," I said. "I've a football match that I can't afford to miss."

Tony gave me a disdainful look. "Go play your football

match if you must."

I might have backed down except that I didn't like Tony's arrogance.

It was not the first time that Firinne had picketed celebrities: just before I joined they had picketed Orson Welles when he appeared at the Gate Theatre, and for the same reason that they were now about to picket Danny Kaye. There were stories, always insinuated but never fully told, of Firinne members who attended a Communist rally in Dublin a few years back in order to heckle the speakers, and who were said to have thrown a Communist supporter into the Liffey. I hoped they wouldn't do that on Saturday: I liked Danny Kaye.

Defending The Cause

The Barrow

An organization devoted to a Cause could find no better place to promote that Cause than a busy street corner of a city at night. That at least was the thinking of the Firinne Executive when it established *The Barrow*. Physically, the barrow was a pushcart fitted with sloping sides to hold a medley of religious literature for sale, including pamphlets, papal encyclicals, and various books. Strategically, it was a magnet that caused friends and enemies to stop and discuss the Divine Plan. Almost every night of the week the barrow was stationed at the intersection of O'Connell and Abbey streets, across from Mooney's pub. Sales, though mostly desultory, were occasionally brisk, and discussions of their contents were sometimes acrimonious. We Firinne members liked those discussions because it allowed us to engage with, and try to convert, those who didn't believe in our Cause.

In addition to distributing Fiat on Sunday mornings I volunteered to man the barrow on Monday nights with my fellow member and friend, Jimmy. I found the experience both rewarding and frustrating. The reward came whenever a stranger approached, browsed the literature for a few minutes, then smiled, asked some friendly questions, and made a purchase. The frustration arose whenever – and this happened fairly often – I stared into a hostile face and listened to contradictory statements. It wasn't the disagreement that frustrated me, but what I felt was the closed mind that the discordant tone betrayed. I was shocked to find that not even those I'd call otherwise good Catholics were convinced of the rightness of our Cause: Jimmy and I had many arguments with fervent Catholics who thought we were fanatics who wanted to return the Church to the bad old days of the Spanish Inquisition.

"Why can't you leave the Protestants alone? Live and let live, I say." The woman was old and poorly-dressed, but well-spoken.

I responded respectfully – she was probably as old as my mother, who was a little over fifty. "The Protestant religion is false," I told her. "It's an offence to Almighty God. The Catholic Church is the only true Church and it must be acknowledged as such by the State."

The woman smiled. "How do you know the Catholic Church is the true Church anyway?"

The nerve of her! "The Pope says –"

" – Never mind what the Pope says. Look at all the bad popes we've had. Haven't you ever heard of Alexander VI?"

I had learned how to reply to such specious arguments. "Bad popes only prove that the Church is indestructible and founded by God Himself. It has survived even the wickedness of its leaders."

"You'd like to burn all the Protestants at the stake, wouldn't you?" The woman fired back. "Like they did in the old days?"

"No. They –"

" – You've a lot to learn, lad." She turned her back and wandered off.

A prim-looking middle-age well-dressed man approached one night and browsed with obvious disdain the Papal Encyclicals laid out on the barrow. "You fellows ought to be locked up for proselytizing like this in public," he barked.

It was a cold night. I was tired after a long day and wasn't in the mood for an argument. "It's a free country," I said.

"You fellows don't want a free country; you'd like it to be a fecking dictatorship lorded over by your bloody Pope."

One of those anti-Catholic zealots! His tone roused my ire and despite my weariness I prepared to take him on. But Jimmy stepped in.

"Are you a Catholic?" he asked politely, staring at the man. When Jimmy was polite I knew he was about to wade in with verbal fists flailing. He was the nicest fellow, with a wonderful sense of the absurd, and we had become pals, but he attacked with terrier tenacity anyone who challenged the Cause.

"I was. Until I got wise to the pack of lies the priests were telling us."

"What particular lies?" Jimmy was still polite, though now there was an edge in his tone.

"What I want to know is why I had to have religion and all the lies that go with it beaten into me at school." The man scowled. "Bloody beaten into me! Jesus! Why is the Catholic Church in charge of education anyway?"

Point four of the Divine Plan! I jumped in with a direct quote. *"The Education of Youth ought always to envisage youth as members of the Mystical Body of Christ.* So the Catholic Church has the right to control education. "

"Christ!" The fellow laughed. "That's terrible *raiméis* altogether. Do you fellows ever really listen to yourselves when

47

you spout that kind of drivel?"

"You're the one that's full of *raiméis*," Politeness gone, Jimmy was shouting now. "In answer to your question, the Catholic Church is preparing people for the next life as well as this, so it has the right and duty to control the education of the young."

"It has no such goddam right," the man scoffed. "What your organization is looking for is a fecking country ruled by the bloody Pope, in which all members march in lock step to orthodox Catholic doctrine."

"We want Catholic education for Catholics." Jimmy was breathing heavily. "Those who aren't Catholic can wallow in their ignorance for all I care. Like those fellows." He pointed to a group of Protestant clergymen who had just passed and were recognizable by their mode of dress.

"What about people like me who don't believe in any religion?" The man was annoyed now. "All the National Schools are run by priests, but I don't want my kids to have their minds poisoned by the stuff they preach. So what am I to do?"

"Go back to being a practicing Catholic," Jimmy said. The man looked angrily at him and walked off.

Shortly after, Marjorie and Tina, attractive young Firinne members, stopped by. They'd been to the cinema and were on their way to Forte's for coffee. It was almost ten o'clock, our closing time, so Jimmy and I pushed the barrow to its lodging in Lower Gardiner Street and returned to the café to join them. We had a delightful time. While Tina was very pretty, Marjorie was stunning; I had been eyeing her with more than a casual interest for some time. However, she was several years older than I and anyway she was so elegant in dress and manner that she seemed unattainable. But a fellow could dream. We stayed so long in the café that I barely caught the last bus home.

A fellow in workman's clothes and seeming somewhat jarred came by one night. He picked up a pamphlet, browsed for a few moments, then walked around the Barrow reading the pamphlet cover and pointing a finger at Jimmy.

"I see yez have here an encyclical by Pope Leo called *The Workers' Charter.*"

"A great encyclical," Jimmy enthused. "It's considered to be –"

" – So what I want to know is this." The jarred one prodded Jimmy on the shoulder with a finger. "What are youz guys doin' for the workin' man?"

"A good question." Jimmy stepped back. "We – and the Pope of course – believe in social justice for the working man."

"Me, too." The man burped. "Sorry!" He put his hand to his mouth. "I believe in any kind of justice for the workin' man."

"Good man yourself," Jimmy said.

"The workin' man," the inebriated one stepped closer and prodded Jimmy's shoulder again, "is at the bottom of the totem pole in this country of ours. He does the most of the work and gets the littlest of the money."

"You're absolutely right," Jimmy agreed. "I'm a working man myself."

"Good on ye." The fellow extended his hand. "Let's shake on that."

Jimmy shook his hand, then hurried into a recitation of the Fifth Point. "Now, what *the Divine Plan for Social Order* demands is that the doctrine contained in the Papal Encyclicals – like *The Workers' Charter* of Pope Leo XIII that you have in your hand – *ought to be reduced to practice in such wise as to promote the virtuous life of individual members of the Mystical Body of Christ organized in families, Vocational Associations, and*

States."

"Jaysus!" The joxer shook his head as if to clear the cobwebs from his brain. "Words like them would banjax the brains of a saint, so they would. Not to mind a poor workin' man like meself. Listen!" Hands on hips, he faced us, swaying slightly. "I might not be as well educated as youz guys, and I may have a few jars in me tonight, which I'll admit I have, but I know what the workin' man needs." He wagged an admonitory finger at Jimmy. "He needs work, that's what he needs. And he needs a fair day's wages for a fair day's work." He glared at me. "Now tell me that yez are all for that and yez 'll have my support."

"Oh yes! We believe in a living wage," I said. "A man should be able to support his family from the sweat of his brow."

"Now you're talkin'." The working man dug in his pocket for change. "I sweat me brow every day and still the childer go to school with patches on their clothes. Here!" He handed over sixpence and walked off carrying the pamphlet. Then he turned and came back.

"Do yous think it's right that half the population of Ireland has to go to England – the ould enemy and all that – to find work? Where's your social justice there?"

He had touched a raw spot in the national psyche. Emigration was the safety valve that protected Ireland from the revolt of the unemployed. As many as forty thousand were leaving the country every year to find work. So I parroted to him the wisdom of Firinne: "If the State would only follow the teaching of the Popes regarding social justice we wouldn't have the emigration problem we have."

"I'll read what the Pope says so." He walked away again; this time he kept going.

A young woman came by another night, looking distracted.

She ran a hand along the pamphlets, then came around to me. "This is a religious thing you have here, isn't it?" She pointed to the barrow.

"Yes." When she came closer I saw that she had been crying.

"Listen. I just lost my baby. I couldn't afford to go to the hospital and –" She broke down.

"Sorry to hear that," we both said, while the woman cried into her hand.

She recovered and glared at us. "And do you know why my baby died?"

We shook our heads. "Are we supposed to know?" Jimmy asked.

"Remember Dr. Noel Browne?"

"Ah, Dr. Browne!" As Minister for Health in the last government he had introduced a bill to provide health care for expectant mothers and their babies. John Charles galvanized his fellow Irish bishops into condemning the idea because, he said, such a bill was part of a Socialist-Communist medical philosophy that would interfere with the God-given right of the father of the family to provide for his children. Despite the best efforts of Dr. Browne, the Archbishop prevailed, the bill was killed, and the government was forced to resign.

"Well," the woman pointed an accusing finger at us, "if your fooking Archbishop hadn't butted in and stopped him, Dr Browne's law would have let me go to the hospital for free and my baby would be alive today." She stalked off.

"But the AB was right," Jimmy said. "It was Communist philosophy."

"Right." But I had a vague guilty feeling inside me for the rest of the night.

I was by temperament a do-gooder, and the implementation

of the Church's social doctrine appealed to me as having the potential for doing the most good to my fellow human beings. But though I had read what the popes and Father Fahey had written about the last of the Six-Point Plan – the one about money and the Catholic Church's approach to its use and abuse – I still felt unprepared whenever someone raised the subject at the barrow. Like the well-dressed fellow who came by one night and barely glanced at the pamphlets before throwing out a casual question.

"I hear you fellows are spouting some very weird stuff about the Roman Church and the monetary system."

"Are you a Proddy?" Jimmy asked, in that friendly-hostile tone he had perfected.

The fellow arched an eyebrow. "I'm a Christian, young man, though not of the Roman persuasion. I'm also a Trinity College Economics Professor. I'd like to know more about Rome's theories on money and its uses. I hear they're rather quaint."

Jimmy knew the Divine Plan by heart and he rattled off point number six as Father Fahey had enunciated it: "*As money governs the supply of the life-blood to the entire economic body, the Catholic Plan for Social Order demands that the monetary system ought to be so arranged as to facilitate the production, distribution, and exchange of material goods and services in view of the virtuous life of members of the Mystical Body of Christ in contented families.*"

"Bravo!" The Professor clapped his hands. "You've learned your catechism well, young man. But do you have any idea what it means?"

"Of course I do," Jimmy began. "It –"

" – It means," I jumped in, feeling I had the answer in common sense terms, "that money is meant to be a tool to serve the welfare of all the people."

"Of course it is," the Professor agreed. "But isn't it doing that right now?"

"Freemasons and Jews have turned it into a mechanism for enriching themselves at the expense of governments and peoples," I blurted, remembering what I had read in Father Fahey's book, *The Mystical Body of Christ and the Reorganization of Society.*

"Thank you. Very interesting." With another disdainful glance the Professor moved on.

"He's taking those lads to his soup kitchen." Jimmy pointed to a man in a Salvation Army uniform who passed by followed by two down-and-out-looking men. "He'll feed them if they join him in saying some Proddy prayers." Jimmy threw up his arms as if in a plea to heaven. "As Fluther Good says, *the whole counthry is in a state of chassis.*"

A Discussion at Work

On being hired into the Civil Service I was appointed to the Office of the Comptroller and Auditor General. From there I was assigned to a group of five people whose principal job was to audit the accounts of the Postal, Telephone, and Telegraph, Services. The group occupied a single large room in the GPO building on O'Connell Street. Our Civil Service rankings varied, from my own, the newest Clerical Officer, to Gerald the Senior Auditor, who was our boss. It was a pleasant place to work. Hours were from nine-thirty to five with an hour and a quarter for lunch, which allowed me time to cycle home to the hot meal my mother had ready each day. And the work wasn't very strenuous: Gerald was due to retire in a couple of years and he was coasting. Which meant he did the minimum amount of work needed to stay out of trouble, and he spent a good part of each day chatting and reminiscing with his staff. This wasting of my work time, which I couldn't help since Gerald addressed much of his chat at me, caused me some scruples: the seventh commandment required an honest day's work for an honest day's pay. However, not all the chatting was wasteful. One day when Gerald was absent Bill, a senior Clerical Officer, said to me,

"I was down O'Connell Street last night and I stopped at the Firinne barrow. That's your crowd, isn't it?"

"Yes." Although I didn't talk about my Firinne activities at work I had met Bill one Sunday morning when selling Fiat outside a church, so he knew about my connection with the organization.

"I browsed a bit at the barrow." Bill grimaced. "Some pretty weird stuff you have there."

"You think so?" I sensed an argument in the offing. "Do you have anything particular in mind ?"

"I read a leaflet on your aims – the divine something or other."

"The Divine Plan for Social Order," I corrected, feeling my tone was a bit priggish. "That's what we're all about."

"I was reading the bit about marriage; I must say that shook me."

By this time I had done my study well and recited the relevant passage by heart. "The third Point of the Plan says that *The Unity and Indissolubility of Christian Marriage ought to be most carefully maintained, as symbolizing the union of Christ and His Mystical Body.* Is that what bothered you?"

"Jesus! Would ye shut up and let me do a bit of work." Tim was a hard-working assistant auditor whose desk was across from mine.

Bill smiled maliciously and ignored him. "Tell me this:

54

why doesn't Ireland allow divorce, like every other country in the world?"

"Why are you worried about divorce, Bill?" Miss Ramos, a late-fifties spinster, was the only woman in the group. "You're not even married." Her smile was benevolent, though a bit roguish.

"And I won't be, either," Bill retorted. "I'm not getting myself into something I can't get out of."

"The Constitution of Ireland doesn't allow divorce," I said. "It says that no law shall be enacted providing for the grant of a dissolution of marriage."

"And a good thing, too." Tim raised his head. "Look at America! Half the people over there are divorced. Including a lot of the Catholics." He went back to studying his ledger.

"I think the Church is making a lot of the stuff up," Bill said.

"What stuff is that?" Mis Ramos asked timidly. She was a shy woman, and also a Protestant.

"All that stuff about sex. You can't even give a girl a decent kiss and a cuddle, for Christ's sake, without going to hell." Bill seemed angry.

"We Protestants are more liberal in those matters, "Miss Ramos remarked with a hesitant smile.

"Get married, Bill!" Tim raised his head. "Then you can do all the kissing and cuddling you want."

Bill snorted and went back to his work.

"Why doesn't your Catholic Church allow divorce?" Miss Ramos asked me, ever so sweetly, just as I was trying to concentrate on my work once more. "England is a Christian country, and it allows it."

I turned to face her – her desk was behind me, by a window that looked out on the courtyard – wondering how to respond: she was the nicest person, and she was older than my mother, and she was a Protestant, so I must not offend her. "The Bible doesn't permit divorce." I knew Protestants read the Bible.

"The Old Testament does," she countered.

She had me there: Catholics were not encouraged to read the Old Testament and I was totally ignorant of what it said about divorce. "But not the New Testament," I parried.

"Listen," Tim looked up at us. "The Pope and the bishops and the priests do a lot of spouting about sex and marriage. But they don't know a damn thing about it, since not one of them is married. My advice to you young fellows," he looked across at Bill whose head was up, listening to him, "is to use your common sense and ignore whatever the clergy say that doesn't make sense to you."

Bill nodded vigorously in agreement and we all returned to work. I tried to focus on the wages of postmen but I was horrified at Tim's cavalier dismissal of Catholic moral teaching. Firinne, aware of what had already happened in the godless world outside Ireland, wanted to preempt such a disaster with its Third Point proposal against a divorce law in Ireland. Sex, according to Catholic teaching – and Firinne was strict in following Catholic teaching – had to be corralled inside the narrowest of moral fences: allowable only within the confines of Holy Matrimony. As I continued to add up numbers in my ledger I was thinking about the heresy Tim had uttered and decided it would be cowardly of me not to defend the Church.

"I think you're wrong, Tim," I blurted, without knowing what I'd say next.

Tim looked up. "Wrong about what?"

"About the pope and the bishops not knowing –"

" – Listen." Tim put down his pen. "I volunteer with the

Vincent de Paul, and I visit homes of the very poor every week. And I get to see the results of what the Church says and does about sex outside marriage. The thing is, people do it and they'll always do it. But when pregnancies result, the women are stigmatized and punished by the Church." There was passion in his tone. "A pregnant woman here can either run off to England and stay there and end up as a prostitute to make a living for herself and her baby, or else she can stay here in Ireland and go into a Church-run so-called charitable institution for so-called fallen women where celibate nuns will tick her off about the errors of her ways. And then they'll take her baby from her and give it up for adoption, or else they'll dump it into an orphanage where God knows what will happen to it or where it will wind up."

"That's awful, Tim," Miss Ramos said. I turned to look at her; there were tears in her eyes.

"And something else I see, too," Tim said. "Catholic teaching, by condemning divorce, makes women stay in marriages even when they're abused; and their health and their children and their lives are put in danger from husbands who beat them up."

What could I say? I put my head down and went back to counting numbers.

Falling in Love

A Social Life

Firinne had radically changed my social life. Before I joined I was wandering lost in an adult world, having left school to work in the Civil Service and having almost no peer friends. Now I was a young man with a Cause that I found worth pursuing, and with friends of like mind. And though I was still tortured by the fear of hell – nature continued to rebel against the Church's strictures on sex – I alleviated that fear with daily mass and communion, daily prayers, and weekly confession. On the bright side, I had money to go to the cinema and to dances: I bought tickets for Seamus and myself to hear Jussi Bjorling and Joan Hammond sing at the Theatre Royal, and I went to the Gaiety Theatre with Jimmy when the opera season came around. Seamus and I went to Croke Park on Sunday afternoons to see all the major football and hurling matches; we went to Landsdowne Road for the Rugby Internationals, and to Dalymount Park for the big soccer games.

My happiness wasn't complete, however: as with most

young fellows of my age I was constantly on the lookout for the girlfriend, that special one who would became my life companion. Shortly after I joined Firinne I met and set my sights on the sister of one of the members. Una, who was a year older than I, combined an ethereal beauty with an aloof personality that convinced me she was the One. I shamelessly befriended Bridgie, her plain-faced friend, in order to get close to her. But all I accomplished was to make Bridgie feel I was attracted to her: Una showed no interest whatever in me and I was left with the unpleasant task of disillusioning Bridgie. However, I didn't give up: Bridgie informed me that the adored one was an aspiring actress and was rehearsing a part in an amateur production of an Agatha Christie play. I joined the group to be near her and got a one-line part in the play. To no avail; I was a terrible actor, and though I managed to mouth my line and exit without disgracing myself, Una made it wordlessly clear that she wasn't interested in me. So I gave up.

Firinne provided not only a Cause for its members but also

Bottom right, at a Firinne party, 1955

a vibrant social life. It was this that made me persevere in the organization until the doctrine seeped into my psyche and held me captive. The members didn't at all resemble the stereotype of fanatical cult plotters: they were mostly outgoing, sociable, and fun-loving – within the bounds set by Catholic morality. We had outings to the seashore in summer and musical evenings and soirees at other seasons. Even Branch meetings were social occasions as well as times of prayer and discussion. And Forte's café was an unofficial meeting place where members were to be found any night for a chat and a cup of coffee. The Civil Service allowed me two weeks vacation in August and I made the most of them socially. In my first year I spent a memorable vacation with my sister Mary and her girlfriends at Salthill. The following year I visited my brother Tom who was then working in London. Another year, Brennan and I hitch-hiked to Donegal, where we pitched a tent and played golf.

My football-playing career, however, was seriously affected by the religious direction that Firinne was taking me. A Gaelic footballer from the age of seven, I was on the St. Vincent's Minor team when I joined Firinne. From there I moved up rapidly to the Juniors, then quickly graduated to the Intermediates and, just after my nineteenth birthday, was given a try-out on the Senior team. I felt then that I was headed for football stardom since at that time St Vincent's supplied almost all of the Dublin County team.

Then Scruples, the ogre that dwelt in my conscience – inspired no doubt by Firinne, though no one in the organization ever pressured me – raised his fussy head and told me that I was about to let my desire for worldly success take precedence over my duties to God. Was I going to spend time training for football honors that I ought to be devoting to His Holy work? I took that

60

argument to heart, abandoned St Vincent's, and joined a team that was local to where I lived and that was just getting under way. Playing with them would be less demanding of my time, and less a source of pride.

Marjorie

I had now many good friends in Firinne, both male and female. I was nineteen, had given up on Una, and was looking once more for the perfect woman. And was surprised when I found her, because she was a Firinne member whom I had known from the time I joined. Marjorie was five years older than I and was beautiful. So beautiful that I and the lads I palled around with were afraid to approach her in a romantic way. She was like the eponymous beauty in Percy French's song, Eileen Oge ... *her beauty made us all so shy,/not a man of us could look her in the eye*. Then, at a social event one Sunday evening it happened – in a manner so corny as to be laughable. We were both standing around in a chatting group when I glanced at her and found her looking at me with a gaze that was ever so tender. I was instantly bowled over, head over heels, bewitched, struck by cupid's arrow. And I sensed from her gaze that she felt something special for me.

After that evening I wanted her so badly; all the pent-up emotions of my young life roared for release at the very sight of her. And those sights were frequent since we both were members of the same Firinne Branch and we distributed Fiat at the same churches on many Sunday mornings. However, I had no idea how to go about declaring my love to her. Much of our knowledge of social behavior comes from observing the actions of our peers, and I had no guidance from my peers about how to romance a woman. Most of my men friends were unattached; it appeared that the terrifying wall of fear which the Church had built around amorous attachments had made them, too, afraid of involvement. The few who had girlfriends didn't bring them into our company or talk with us about them. So, being utterly unschooled in the conduct of romantic love, I had no idea what I'd do even were she, *per impossibile*, to throw her arms around me and say she was mine.

Nevertheless, and despite my ever-present terror of hellfire, I was determined to engage with Marjorie: I had found my true love and I was not going to lose her. Though still smarting from being rejected by Una, I was now so infatuated with Marjorie that I was willing to risk an equally ignominious fate at her hands. I would overcome whatever obstacles stood in the way of my winning this peerless woman. And there were, I recognized, serious obstacles. Our age gap of five years presented no problem to me but it might well stymie my suit with her: would a twenty-four year old elegant woman take a nineteen-year old country lad seriously? There was also the matter of shyness: I was no different from the other lads in being bashful before her beauty. I had always been somewhat shy anyway: raised in an environment where children were expected to be seen but not heard, I was deficient in the art of conversing with women.

Another barrier, more difficult to overcome than shyness or age or sophistication, was the Catholic teaching on sex and marriage. I'd need to be sure it even permitted me to date her. As a scrupulous Catholic I should have consulted a priest about that and abided by his decision. But I feared his answer and thrashed the matter out with my conscience without clerical assistance. "The Church's doctrine," Scruples pronounced in his priggish way, "states a principle that you know from your school days, which is that marriage is the only institution in which any kind of sexual activity is legitimate."

62

"I know that, but –"

" – So is it your intention then to marry Marjorie?"

"I hadn't really thought that far ahead, but –"

" – Well, you better start thinking about it if you want to date her."

"Why do I have to have the intention of marrying just to do a line? Look around you, for God's sake! All normal young men are courting, dating, doing lines, whatever you want to call it. Are you telling me they must all have the intention of marrying the person they're going with?"

"Certainly."

"But what if I do a line with a girl and find out that I don't want to marry her?"

"That's all right. The purpose of doing a line is to find out if you want to marry each other, isn't it? But the rule is, in order to start doing a line you must have a serious intention of looking for a suitable person to marry."

"All right; I'll ask Marjorie out, with the intention of exploring the possibility of our getting married some day."

"Not so fast. Aren't you forgetting another rule?"

"Ah Christ! What now?"

"You know about it; you've heard it in classroom and from pulpit. It's not enough to have the intention to marry, you must also be in a position to get married in the relatively near future."

"Shite!"

"Right."

"Why must I be in a position to get married soon?"

"Those celibate theologians aren't dumb, you know. The 'near future' bit forestalls any procrastinating in what is clearly a dangerous occasion of sin."

Being & Becoming

Doing a Line

I was stymied, wasn't I? I could rustle up an intention easily enough, but on my Civil Service pay I had no hope of being financially able to marry in the reasonably foreseeable future. I was nineteen years old and my salary was too small to support a wife, and would still be too small for another ten years. Not to mention the cost of children that Catholic teaching would expect me to accept if they came along, birth control being verboten. And, although Marjorie had a decent job now, she would have to stay home then: women were required to resign from most jobs, including hers, when they married.

Still, I was not about to give up; *love is as strong as death*, the Scripture said. So despite Scruples, or perhaps because of him, I plunged into a labyrinth of casuistic argument to justify dating Marjorie. It wasn't easy: the moral theologians were thorough and left few loopholes. But eventually, after much tortured self-searching and arguments with Jesus, in which I promised Him I'd avoid any and every occasion of sin, I concluded that I might approach her. I wriggled out of the impediment of being unable to marry in the near future by assuming God would provide: after all, Jesus did say we should consider the birds of the air who neither sowed nor reaped but whom the Heavenly Father fed anyway.

Having overcome the moral objections, I now had to ask Marjorie out. She, like me, would be aware that deciding to do a line was a grave moral choice which should not be made lightly. So unless she considered me a serious prospect for marriage she'd be obliged to turn me down. But I was not deterred: Scruples might make a coward of me but I had conquered him for the sake of love. So I'd screw up my courage to the sticking place and ask

64

her out. All I needed was the opportunity.

That came soon after when my new football club announced that it would hold a New Year party, to which we were expected to bring dates. On a cold December night when I stopped by the Barrow for a chat with fellow members Marjorie came along. I seized the opening and invited her to be my date at the party. To my delight she accepted, and we continued to date after the party. We lived at opposite ends of the city, I on the unfashionable North side, she on the more elegant South. We'd meet at the Metropole, a restaurant-cinema-ballroom complex in the center of O'Connell Street and a popular meeting place for dating couples. We went to films and dances, including several dress dances, and took occasional summer strolls along the strand. But we never engaged in kissing or even hand-holding, for to my scrupulous conscience – and perhaps to hers, though we never discussed the matter – such activities would present immediate occasions of sin. Though we were obviously in love, it was equally obvious that we couldn't afford to marry. Bizarrely, we never discussed the subject, so the entire courtship was a trip to nowhere that in my saner moments I recognized but could not bear to end.

When my male friends in Firinne discovered that I was doing a line with Marjorie, I had to endure much teasing, most of it good-natured, though some more serious. The serious stuff came from a man who was jealous because Marjorie had rebuffed his own overtures, and from others who recognized that since I had no hope of marrying I was placing my soul in jeopardy. But I didn't care: I was in love, and Marjorie reciprocated my love, so I was too happy to worry about jealousy. Or the future.

With Marjorie at a dress dance, 1955

Vocation

Epiphany – the Call

Our idyllic state perdured for almost a year before the serpent of reality whispered to me in earnest that our Eden was but a fantasy. I tried to ignore the beast but eventually I couldn't keep up the pretense. For while my attachment to Marjorie grew, my devotion to religious practices had grown even stronger. For three years as a member of Firinne, and spurred by the organization's urging that we strive for perfection in our spiritual lives, I had become ever-more immersed in a God-centered existence. I read, and learned much from, the *Introduction to the Devout Life,* the work of St. Francis De Sales, a seventeenth century bishop, that was considered one of the most important guides for lay people who wished to devote their lives to the service of God. In light of my future vocation it is also interesting that I read *The Priesthood and Perfection* by Garrigou-Lagrange, a contemporary theologian. I went to mass and communion daily, said the Rosary every day, joined the Third Order of St Francis – an associate membership of the Franciscan Order in which deeper piety was fostered – and studied Catholic social teaching. As always, I struggled with the temptations against Holy Purity that nature and women, and Marjorie in particular, posed.

One weekday morning in November of 1955 I got on my bike after attending seven o'clock mass in Corpus Christi church and began to cycle along Griffith Avenue. As I pedaled towards Glasnevin and home to breakfast before going to work, I braked suddenly, pulled into the curb, and stopped. An argument that I had with myself more than three years earlier when leaving school, and which I thought had been settled forever, returned at that moment with the force of a tornado, bowled over my resistance, and forced me to reverse my decision. At that moment, while I sat on my bike with my foot on the curb, I accepted that I was going to become a priest.

It seems melodramatic that the decision should occur like that. But it did so occur. It was not as spectacular as Saul's conversion on the road to Damascus, but it gave me equal certainty that I had received a call from God. The most startling aspect was that I felt such ineluctable sureness of a vocation in the instant. Although I had decided when leaving school that the priesthood was not for me, I did occasionally have stray thoughts that maybe I ought to pursue a vocation. However, with the advent of Marjorie such thoughts floated away like morning fog. So I was taken totally by surprise when on Griffith Avenue that morning I presented myself with a fait accompli, not only without serious discussion but without even a warning of its imminence.

It turned out to be no mere reckless decision, nor an impulsive reaction to my despair at not being able to marry the woman I loved. I was unable to overrule it when reason returned to its abode. For a whole week I told no one, not even Marjorie, while I waited to see if my resolution held up under the pressure of time and the real world in which I lived. After all, it might have been the result of a particularly devout mass-and-communion experience, which would dissipate with my immersion in daily routines. But it wasn't and it didn't. The determination to be a priest stayed with me all week and didn't buckle under when I thought of what I'd have to give up. It even withstood a date with Marjorie.

In retrospect, though my sudden resolve came as a total surprise, it ought not to have. I had made my own the thesis that since this life is but a preparation for the life to come one should devote oneself entirely to that preparation. So it was logical for me to decide now that I'd forsake the things of this world, which at best could bring only temporary happiness, and focus on eternity. By becoming a priest my life would be devoted completely to God, and so ensure my eternal happiness.

The belief in a distinct vocation to the priesthood is as old as the Jewish religion. St Paul said in his epistle to the Hebrews, *every high priest taken from among men is ordained for men in things pertaining to God. ....no man takes this honor unto himself but he that is called by God, as Aaron was.* After my epiphany on Griffith Avenue I was convinced that I had received such a call. And although, unlike Saul, I never actually heard the divine summoning Voice, I felt an inner compulsion, a terrifying conviction, that I must answer that call. Regardless of my own desires, I had to give up everything that stood in the way of my becoming a priest and dedicating my life to God.

And I now had much to give up. After the restrictions of childhood and school, I was enjoying the freedom of being relatively my own master. I had friends and a social life, I had a little money, I was able to go on vacations. And above all I had Marjorie with whom I was in love. Nevertheless, the thought of giving up all this, which had heretofore prevented me from taking the idea of a vocation seriously, no longer possessed its restraining force. I felt now that I could and would leave all to

69

follow Jesus.

Enamored with the glamor of giving up all for Christ, I refused to acknowledge what was perhaps my strongest driving force towards the priesthood: the bleakness of my otherwise future life. I was now twenty-one, desperately in love, but locked into a job that would not provide me the means to marry for many years. Civil Service pay was based on time served in grade, Clerical Officer pay was abysmally meager and grew only in tiny annual increments, regardless of merit. Promotion to a higher level was based entirely on seniority in grade: it would be thirteen years, I calculated, before I reached the top of the list. To find a better paying job I'd have to emigrate, join the thousands of my fellow Irishmen who left the country every year in search of a better life. And emigration would separate me from Marjorie anyway. So, given my dedication to religion, and with a married future stymied, the priesthood proved an irresistible attraction. And a completely selfish one, though I would have been horrified had that subconscious thought become conscious.

Crossing the Rubicon

Just one week after I felt God's call I crossed the Rubicon of making definitive my response by announcing my intention to others. Naturally, I told Marjorie first. I was still very much in love with her: the very sight of her thrilled me; I virtually purred in her presence. And it was clear to me that she reciprocated my feelings: her eyes and her smile and the warmth of her presence left no doubt about that. Yet she was as undemonstrative in her affections as I was, which was not surprising since she was subjected to the same indoctrination on the dangers of sex. When I told her of my decision to become a priest she gave no indication of hurt or disappointment: she was happy for me, she said. We agreed to keep my decision a secret for the time being, and to continue our relationship as before, except that now she was free to date others if she so chose.

Next, I told my family. No one expressed the slightest surprise. My father thought I should become a lawyer, since I loved to argue so much. He and I regularly engaged in good-natured disputes about many topics, mostly concerning politics and religion. My Dad was still not a particularly religious man, though he continued to makes it to a late mass on Sundays and still did his 'Easter Duty'. Mammy, equally tepid in her practice of religion, said it was my life and my choice to make and that she was happy for me. Tom said his only surprise was that I hadn't gone to the seminary long before. He himself had been expected by the Roscrea monks to become a Cistercian upon leaving their school, but he decided otherwise.

Before making a public announcement to the members of Firinne I decided to choose the particular path I wished to take to the priesthood. There were many options. I could enter a diocesan seminary if I wished to be a priest in an Irish diocese. Or I could study in an Irish seminary and be ordained to work in an American diocese. Or become a missionary priest in a foreign country by joining one of the numerous Irish Missionary Societies that labored in countries in Africa, South America, and Asia. Alternatively, I could become a priest in a Religious Order. And there were so many of those that I'd have to choose a category first. Did I want to be a contemplative monk like the Cistercians in whose school I had been? Or a religious priest working in so-called pagan countries? Or a Jesuit, ready at the Pope's command to perform whatever duties were asked of me.

I excluded the diocesan seminaries when I discovered they would require me to pay for my education; I didn't have the wherewithal for that. I had no difficulty in deciding that the contemplative life was not for me: at boarding school I had seen and admired the Cistercian monks, but shuddered at the thought of becoming one of them. I ruled out the Jesuits when I discovered that the average Jesuit student spent fifteen years preparing for the priesthood; I'd be thirty-six by the time I'd be ordained – an impossible length of time for a twenty-one year old to contemplate. Which left me with the missionary priests, both secular and religious.

I had often said to family and friends that I would never emigrate; this at a time when as many as forty thousand fellow Irish men and women were leaving the country every year in search of work. However, I had no difficulty now imagining myself going forth from Ireland to conquer souls for Christ. So I chose the religious missionary order that I was already somewhat familiar with: Father Fahey belonged to the Congregation of the Holy Ghost, whose priests went mostly to countries in Africa.

I talked to a Holy Ghost priest who was also much involved with Firinne. Father Barry – the Cap, as he was known to generations of Blackrock College students – was a rather unusual priest. He had been involved in the Irish fight for independence, talked like a military man, and used military jargon when talking of The Cause – we must fight for the rights of Christ the King, etc. In poor health when I went to see him at St Michael's College, he was in pajamas having supper in bed. He put me in touch with the Master of Novices for the Irish Province of the Holy Ghost Congregation, who in turn told me that since I hadn't already taken the Leaving Certificate Exam I would now have to pass the entrance exam for the University. I passed the Matriculation exam that summer.

It was inevitable when I informed them that my Firinne

friends would mirthfully conclude that I had decided to become a priest because Marjorie had dumped me, or, as my friend Jimmy was wont to say, 'shot me down.' However, when they discovered that we were still dating, mirth turned to confusion. And for Jimmy it even became a cause for reproach: I had no right, he declared, to be 'leading the girl on' since I could now have no intention of marrying her.

But we did continue to date. At the Crystal ballroom I held her in my arms and wished never to let her go. We saw romantic films and knew our romance could never have the happy ending portrayed on the celluloid. I still have memories of being with her at the Gaiety in the springtime for a performance of *Lucia di Lammermoor*. The tragedy of the lovers who were not allowed to unite, set to Donizetti's impossibly beautiful music, created emotions within me that are still vivid after more than fifty years.

When summer came I went on a final vacation with my male friends before leaving for the Novitiate. Brennan, Murphy, and I set out to tour the west coast in Murphy's 1940 Ford. We drove first to Strandhill in Sligo where Brennan's girlfriend was holidaying with her family. I met his girlfriend's sister, a gorgeous young woman for whom I felt an instant attraction – never mind that I was on my way to becoming a priest and was still madly in love with Marjorie. Though I was going to become a life-long celibate nature continued to battle my resolution. I felt a bitter-sweet satisfaction when Brennan told me that the beautiful sister was entering a nunnery the following week.

We continued down the west coast, camping out in our canvas tent, lying on a groundsheet to sleep, cooking meals on a portable stove, washing up in the bathroom of the best hotel we could locate, finding entertainment wherever we could. On Galway Bay we camped in a field at Salthill and went to a dance at Seapoint, a magnificent ballroom whose floor was said to accommodate three thousand dancers. I danced with many women that night and felt the lure of the feminine as never before. Had I not already made a public commitment to leave all for Christ I might well have turned my back on the priesthood in that ballroom. We returned to our camp at about three in the morning to find that a gale from the Atlantic, accompanied by heavy rain, had flattened our tent; so, for the remainder of the night we huddled in the tiny car. I slept little as I tried to restore my standing with Jesus after my near-traitorous behavior on the dance-floor.

We stopped to view the Cliffs of Moher and, with the folly of youth, stood as close to the cliff edge as possible. Stepping out onto a narrow ledge we held on to the wall of the cliff while the wind swept up from below and threatened to blow us away. Most terrifying was returning from the ledge to safer ground: we had stepped over a v-shaped cut in the ledge on the way out without taking notice; on the return, however, I looked down and saw I had to step over a seven-hundred-feet chasm to get back. Yet, despite my vaunted piety I didn't give a thought at that moment to the imminent danger of vaulting the chasm from life to death.

On our return to Dublin two weeks remained to prepare for the Novitiate. I received a letter giving a list of things to bring, mostly items of clerical attire, mainly in black: suit, overcoat, surplice, soutane, hat, biretta, stock and clerical collars, socks, shoes, shirts, underwear; also an umbrella, sheets, pillow cases, towels, toiletries, books, including a daily missal – of which Marjorie made me a present – and a New Testament. The letter warned that any superfluous articles I might bring would be confiscated: the spirit of poverty, it said, was to be inculcated in advance of taking the vow. I had saved some money over the past year and was able to buy what was needed without asking help

74

from my parents.

The most difficult task remained to be done: saying goodbye to Marjorie. Because we had continued to enjoy each other's company the wrench of parting was postponed to the end. For our last date I got tickets to a performance by the London Philharmonic Orchestra at the Theatre Royal two days before I was due at the Novitiate. We agreed to meet this time at the theater. However, on the day I forget about that agreement and waited at the Metropole, our usual meeting place. I waited and waited and was in despair when she didn't appear. At the last minute I remembered our agreement and dashed the quarter of a mile to the Royal. Perhaps my forgetfulness was but another symptom of my reluctance to part from her.

After the concert we went to dinner at a nearby restaurant and I confessed how very difficult it was for me to leave her. She facetiously warned that I better stay in the Novitiate at least a few months so she wouldn't be accused of frustrating my vocation. I took her home on the bus and we said a long goodbye. I never spoke to her again, though I was to see her very briefly one more time. My feelings at parting from her were of complete desolation. Feelings I could not confide to anyone, because in the social milieu to which I belonged one didn't express one's emotions; the British stiff upper lip was the expected reaction to sadness or adversity. Still, more than fifty years later, I have not forgotten the joy, and sadness, that Marjorie brought to my life.

Religious Life

Settling in

My family was dispersing. Tom had become a Customs Officer and was stationed at Pettigo in County Donegal. In July of 1956, just six weeks before I went to the Novitiate, my two sisters, Mary and Bridie, went to live with relatives in New York. So when I left for the Novitiate, only my parents and Seamus remained at home.

Tom, who now owned a car, came home to drive me to the Novitiate. Both our parents came along. I dressed in my new black suit and black tie. The Novitiate was located in the townland of Kilshane in County Tipperary, on the road between Tipperary town and the village of Bansha. The setting was beautiful, not far from the Glen of Aherlow and the Galtee mountains. A half mile driveway through pleasant meadowland led from the road to a big Victorian house with attached conservatory. The lawn was immaculate with flower beds and neatly-cut grass. I paid no attention to the buildings on the side, which, I soon learned, housed the novices and contained the

76

Kilshane Novitiate: main house and conservatory

novitiate chapel.

The front of the house bustled with smiling young men in black soutanes, two of whom introduced themselves as the 'old' novices immediately I got out of the car: they were completing their Novitiate and welcomed their successors. Other prospective novices were arriving at the same time and were similarly greeted. The 'old' novices ushered us into the parlor of the big house where yet other young men in black waited to serve tea and biscuits. Two priests, one grey-haired and tired-looking, the other young and gaunt, both wearing black soutanes and capes, introduced themselves as the old and new novice-masters.

My family departed with their usual non-demonstrative goodbyes, and with the promise to visit me after Christmas – the first occasion on which, the new Novice Master informed us, a visit would be permitted. Having already spent two years at boarding school I didn't find it wrenching to leave them again. Besides, for the past four years of working and dedication to Firinne, I had regarded home as mostly a place in which to sleep and eat.

During our first week we postulants, as we were called, wore the black suits we arrived in, and learned the practices of the novitiate from the 'old' novices. At the end of the week we were formally admitted into the Congregation in a chapel ceremony by being clothed in the robes we brought with us – black soutane, Roman collar, and a black cincture with tassels that was presented to us. Next morning in the chapel the 'old' novices made their Profession, taking vows of poverty, chastity, and obedience for three years. Then they left immediately by bus for the Scholasticate in Dublin to study philosophy and theology.

The following day we were each examined by a local doctor who came to the Novitiate for that purpose. I had only two medical exams in my life before this: one before going to boarding school, the other before being employed in the Civil Service. In neither did the doctor check my genitals, as the Novitiate doctor did now. Years later when studying Canon Law I discovered the likely reason for this testicular exam: Canon 968 stated that *only a baptized male validly receives sacred ordination*. So in the Novitiate were we already being checked to verify that we were indeed males? Had there been female imposters in the past? Including Pope Joan?

The Master

"The objective of the Novitiate," the Novice Master pronounced in a musical high-pitched voice and with a stare from deep-set eyes that seemed to penetrate our very souls, "is to rid the minds and hearts and wills, and stomachs, of the novices of all regard for earthly things and to focus them on the spiritual life."

We forty-four new novices were sitting at desks in the

small study-hall, writing down every word the priest – who was to be called Father Master – said. He had made clear at the start that we were to take detailed notes of all his conferences – which was what he called his talks – and to study and meditate on them afterwards.

"So there is both a negative aspect to the Novitiate – weeding out attachments to the things of this world – and a positive one – inculcating a love for the Divine."

It wasn't so much the pronouncements the Master made that bothered me, rather it was a combination of the way he made them and his ascetic appearance that I found disturbing. After only two days I'd already formed an unpleasant opinion of the Master of Novices. Tall and ascetically gaunt with sunken cheeks and narrow shoulders, his manner was cold and aloof. The deep-set eyes appeared to be looking inward towards the divine rather than outward towards the world. He had the aspect of a man who had never let his hair down nor was capable of being chummy – I couldn't imagine him whirling a girl around the Crystal ballroom or arguing raucously over coffee in Forte's café. His smile – which made only rare appearances – always carried a hint of 'gotcha.' Obviously very intelligent, he just as obviously knew it – his decisions were instantaneous and never carried the slightest hint of doubt. He was a man to be admired for his piety and feared for his authority, but not easily loved.

Now, as I listened to him, I wondered if I had made a mistake in coming here. But I immediately dismissed the thought: self-pride alone dictated that I remain for some time at least. Marjorie's facetious warning that I better stay a few months lest she be accused of sabotaging my vocation came to mind. But when images of my beautiful former love persisted I resolutely pushed them from my mind.

"You must replace the natural man with the supernatural

man," the Master continued, while we novices wrote. "Of course there is an implicit assumption that you who have sought out the Novitiate have already a strong desire to leave the world behind and devote yourselves to God." The Master's brief smile was more like a grimace. "The Novitiate is where the work of turning that desire into reality begins."

That work had already begun. We were shut off from all contact with the outside world, alone with the Master, the Sub-Master, half a dozen Lay Brothers who took care of the farm and cooked our meals and maintained the buildings, and a few old retired priests who lived in the main house and heard our weekly confessions.

The Master quickly asserted his authority and set the tone for the coming year. His first step in detaching us from the world was to secure the Novitiate against any and all incursions from that world. Newspapers and radio – there was no television in Ireland at that time – were off limits. We had no access to a telephone. We were not even allowed to talk to the Brothers, since they might give us news of the outside world. We could talk to the retired priests only on spiritual matters. In spite of those precautions, shortly after we began the Great Year, as it was called, word filtered through somehow that an Irish athlete had won the fifteen hundred meters race at the Melbourne Olympics.

Silence was the norm: we were not permitted to speak to one another or to anyone else at any time except during two daily post-prandial recreations. Of course we could always talk to the Master, if we dared. Breaches of silence were considered to be most serious and put the offending novice in danger of dismissal. Even more serious was a breach of the Great Silence, a special period that began after night prayer and continued until after mass and thanksgiving the following morning. During that time our thoughts were to be entirely devoted to God and the things of God.

Absolute obedience to all the Master's commands was a sine qua non, as was observance of the Congregation Rule. Ah, the Rule Book! It contained so many instructions that only a genius could remember all of them, and only a saint could observe them all. They encompassed every waking hour of the day, and determined how much sleep time we should have at night. And, as if the Rule Book were not more than enough, there were additional minute rules peculiar to the Novitiate. Here, our every moment was regulated, our every motion governed by some precept. Gone were the days of freedom that I had so cherished. I was in school again, only more so. And it was disconcerting to be treated like a schoolboy again. During the four years since I left the Christian Brothers I had regarded myself as an adult and was treated as such by my fellow workers and the members of Firinne. Now I had to step backwards with my fellow novices into a form of childhood, where we were told what to do and when to do it. We were even told when to evacuate our bowels – after breakfast. We couldn't take the smallest step outside the prescribed routine without permission from the Master.

The ages of my fellow novices provided another affront to my fragile adulthood. They were all so young! Straight out of secondary school and on average three years my junior; with the exception of one who was my own age and was also considered a "late" vocation. It might seem only a slight age difference, but between a schoolboy of seventeen or eighteen and a 'man of the world' of twenty-one – as I thought of myself – was a generation gap. For them, still schoolboys, the Novitiate was a continuation of the only status they had known. I on the other hand felt that I was an adult demoted to childhood. Of course I accepted the indignity with all the pseudo-humility of the new novice.

Being & Becoming

As busy days followed busy days – there was no idle time: our waking hours were rationed between prayer and study and manual work, with two periods of recreation thrown in – there was little opportunity to analyze what exactly was being done to us in this unnatural environment. It was only years later that I understood the purpose of that Spartan Novitiate with its deprivation of all outside contact: it was to spiritually indoctrinate us, to destroy every vestige of attachment we had to anything that could be considered worldly, to have us put off the old man, as the Master said, quoting St. Paul, and put on the new.

The Daily Routine

Each activity was announced by a handbell, rung by a novice who was called the Regulator. He clanged it before six every morning to shatter our sleep and send us scurrying to the chapel, where we engaged in vocal prayers, followed by a half hour of mental prayer, after which we had mass, Communion, and thanksgiving. At the end of that prayer marathon we adjourned in silence to our rooms to make our beds and tidy things up. Beds and rooms had to be always neat: we were subject to surprise inspections by the Master.

Another bell-clang sent us to the refectory where, after more payers called down God's blessing on our food, we were treated to porridge and bread and butter and tea and boiled eggs. After that we were given time to evacuate our bowels, before the Regulator's bell sent us to our allotted daily functions. Those functions were housekeeping chores to maintain the Novitiate in sparkling condition: each novice was assigned a particular task, ranging from putting away mass vestments to cleaning toilets. In the first term – the year was divided into three terms and functions were changed at the beginning of each – I was assigned the function of third sacristan, a euphemism for polishing and buffing the chapel parquet floor.

When we completed our functions, – or when the bell rang, whichever came first – we re-assembled in the chapel and we better not be late, to recite a portion of the Little Office of the Blessed Virgin Mary as a communal prayer. This was followed by the recitation of the rosary, which we said 'in private', meaning we could say it in the chapel or while walking around the grounds. Prompted by another clang of the bell, we proceeded to the study hall where the Master held classes on various aspects of the spiritual life. Classes included scripture, ascetical theology, liturgy, and the Rule of the Congregation.

At twelve forty-five we assembled in the chapel for the most arcane of spiritual exercises, Particular Examen. That exercise requires an explanation as, outside of professional religious circles, it is not a common practice. It was invented by Saint Ignatius of Loyola, founder of the Jesuits. Before he became embroiled in religion, Iñigo, as he was known then, was anything but religious, being a Spanish hidalgo and a soldier and, in his own words, "a man given over to the vanities of the world." He achieved fame for his heroic defense of the city of Pamplona in the year 1521 against the invading French. A canon ball did serious damage to his leg during the siege and he was forced to undergo a long period of convalescence. During that time he found God and religion and decided that henceforth he would be a soldier in the army of Christ the King. To that end he founded the Society of Jesus, the Jesuits, as an army of soldiers for Christ. He determined that Christ's soldiers should be perfect, and to attain that perfection they must root out the defects that rendered them less so.

To accomplish this feat he devised the practice he called

the Particular Examen. It consists of focusing on one particular spiritual fault at a time with a view to extirpating it. Every day the soldier of Christ should examine his conduct over the previous twenty-four hours in relation to that defect, thumps his craw for any failures incurred, and make a firm commitment to his King to do better during the next twenty-four hours. The procedure is to continue daily until that particular fault has been eliminated. Then another fault is to be pulled from the bag of defects and given the same treatment. After a lifetime of Particular Examens there shouldn't be any faults left. Unless, like weeds, those already rooted out grow back again.

Every day at twelve forty-five we novices assembled in the chapel to undertake the task of extirpating our faults. We prayed aloud, examined in silence, prayed aloud again, then went to the refectory for a lunch of plain food, during which we were regaled by stimulating reading from a spiritual book, read by a nervous novice. We all took turns reading, and were corrected on the spot by the Master for any mistakes we made. Another visit to the chapel followed, to thank the Bountiful Lord for our food, after which we were released to enjoy that most desired of daily events, the afternoon recreation.

Like every other Novitiate exercise, recreation was strictly regulated. When not playing football – an activity strongly encouraged since the exercise was considered to reduce libido; which of course was never said because we were all supposed to be spiritual eunuchs – we were to walk around the graveled recreation paths in groups of three and engage in edifying conversation. The 'groups of three' had a special significance: there were forty four novices and each must be the friend of all but the special friend of none. 'Particular friendships,' as they were pejoratively called – that is, having another novice as 'best' or special friend – were verboten. We weren't given a reason for this prohibition beyond the obvious one that we were to be friends with everyone. However, the rule was that we must never be alone on recreation with just one other novice except when there wasn't a third available. Furthermore, and to counteract human deviousness, we weren't allowed to choose the members of the group to which we'd be attached for any particular recreation period. We were to leave the chapel after the post-prandial prayer with downcast eyes and accept whichever two novices were closest to us upon exiting through the recreation door.

Once a week we left the grounds of the Novitiate to walk in the countryside. For this event lists of three were drawn up by the First Auxiliary – the latter a novice functionary who acted as administrative assistant to the Master. The list was changed each week to ensure that no particular friendships were formed. Despite those precautions, I happened to encounter a novice on my very first walk who was to remain a lifelong special friend. Noel and I hit it off in that peculiar way that friends do, in our case through the ruse of an affinity for puns. Of course, what with the rule of silence and the rule about going on recreation with whoever came along first, as well as the stricture on particular friendships, we didn't often have the opportunity to engage in our outrageous wordplay.

The countryside walks no doubt provided amusement to the local people we met on the way. We were attired in black suits and ties, black hats and black overcoats and, rain or shine, we carried black umbrellas. We were not permitted to talk to anyone we met, nor to gaze on any woman we should chance to pass. What a temptation it was then when, before averting my eyes, I spotted the bare legs of a young lady cyclist beneath her windblown skirt.

Tightening the Screws

Monk Behavior

A discipline, dear to all religious everywhere, is quaintly called 'custody of the eyes.' Because the eyes, religious writers say, are windows to the soul, whatever enters through them will either harm or benefit the soul. So, from the very beginning, we novices were required to practice custody of the eyes. Which meant that not only were we not to look on dangerous objects – such as a lady's bare legs displayed by her windblown skirt – but we had to practice not looking at any object out of mere curiosity. We were to walk around with bent heads and averted eyes; those who were seen to fail in this were liable to be corrected immediately by the Master or sub-Master, who were constantly on the lookout for such faults.

The Master told us early on that we would soon be plunged into what he called the Big Retreat: ten days of even more intense spiritual conferences and prayer and silence and self-examination. In the meantime we were to observe certain practices that would ease the burdens and irritations of living in a community. One of the first practices he imposed, in addition to custody of the eyes, was that of addressing each other as Mr. followed by the surname. So I was addressed by my confreres – since the Congregation originated in France fellow members were called confreres – as Mr. Keady. The theory was that if familiarity begot boldness, formality would beget politeness.

We were also trained to observe proper social etiquette. The sub-Master, a small man with cold eyes and thin lips, had the task of presenting a weekly class on the subject, in which he dealt with proper table manners and other social graces that we, as future priests, needed to practice. Once we learned those approved ways of behaving we were required to put them into action immediately and punctiliously. And we soon found that the Novitiate had a not-too-subtle way of enforcing what I came to call 'rulettes' – behaviors that weren't considered serious enough to demand the dismissal of those who failed to follow them, but which, nevertheless, were to be exercised de rigeur.

The forum in which those behaviors were enforced was called the Chapter of Faults. The Chapter had a very old monastic history, stemming, it appears, from St. Benedict's maxim *nosce te ipsum* – know thyself, which that Father of Christian monasticism borrowed from the pagan Cicero, who borrowed it from the Temple of Apollo at Delphi who – God knows who initiated it. Anyway, the idea of the Chapter was to accuse yourself and others of faults you perceived in you and them, with a view to correcting those faults and thereby bringing everyone closer to God Who, Scripture said somewhere, wanted all to be without fault. In the traditional monastery a separate room, sometimes even a separate house, was set aside for this purpose. It was called the Chapter Room or Chapter House because a chapter from the monastic Rule was read there each time before the character slaughter began.

The Chapter of Faults was practiced in the Novitiate in its own peculiar way. Once a week each novice had to write, on three separate slips of paper, three faults that he had noticed three other novices commit during the preceding week. Faults could range from rattling one's rosary beads in chapel to the distraction of others, to chewing food with one's mouth open, to failure to wear socks, to swinging one's tassel, to finishing a sentence at the end of recreation after the bell for silence had sounded. The list of possible faults was limited only by the imagination of the accuser. Each piece of paper had to contain a description of the fault and the name of the offending novice, but not that of the accuser. It was dropped into a container known as the Chapter Box. The First Auxiliary collated the slips in alphabetical order by names of novices cited and presented the box to the Master. On Tuesday evenings after supper and recreation the novices assembled in the study hall. The Master read aloud the list of faults. The following is an imaginary sample.

Mr. Drohan came to chapel with his soutane not properly buttoned.

Mr. O'Rourke sniffles a lot.

Mr. McDonald used bad language on recreation.

Mr. McGeever was late for Particular Examen.

The list would go on, to the embarrassment of the offenders, who were expected to ask the Master for a penance in order to make reparation for the offence committed against the community. For that purpose a penance box was placed at the back of the study hall and the offenders filled out slips stating their faults and asking the Master to please mandate appropriate penances.

Some novices, good-natured, pious, and kind, but unaccustomed to couth, presented easy targets for their fellows in fulfilling the task – and at times it was a difficult task – of finding Chapter faults. They were likely to hear the Master call out their names several times at each session for easily-avoidable faults, such as slovenliness in dress or deportment. Others, like myself, who had been schooled in the ways of polite behavior in previous lives, were rarely cited.

The Big Retreat

A ten-day event called the Big Retreat, about which the Master had forewarned us, came a month after we arrived in Kilshane. Before they left, our predecessor novices had told us with grim facetiousness that we'd be ironed out by It; the Master had since threatened that we'd be sandbagged by It and, as the days leading up to it dragged slowly by, he continually reminded us of Its awful imminence. But having already endured a month of Novitiate austerity, I felt that I was ready to cope with It, whatever It might be.

The carrot and the stick were long recognized as appropriate measures to move a recalcitrant donkey forward. St. Ignatius realized that analogous measures might move recalcitrant souls forward to serve the Heavenly King, so he devised his *Spiritual Exercises* on that principal. Our Big Retreat was based on the first part of those *Exercises*. The Master treated us to an initial sermon on how God in His goodness created us, and how through the sin of Adam and Eve we fell from grace. But that talk was mere prologue to its counterpart, the fire and brimstone sermon on hell. We must meditate on that awful place, he told us, so that, if we fail to love God enough to avoid sin, at least the fear of hell may stop us. In order to perform the meditation successfully, he said, we must begin by imagining the place itself. We should picture a roaring fire engulfing body-clad souls who writhe in flames that never burn out. We must hear in our imagination the howling, the cries of pain, the blaspheming, of the damned. We must smell the smoke, the sulphur, the stench of evil, that emanates from that horrible place. And we are to imagine the infinite sadness of the damned as they recall how they squandered their precious time on earth in enjoyment of the sinful pleasures that caused them to be condemned to this awful place of torments. For all eternity.

How did the damned end up in hell? The Master told us that to understand the path to infernity we must meditate on the Awful Judgments of the Infinite One: the Particular Judgment and the General Judgment. Each individual soul must appear before the throne of the Almighty at the moment of death – not at St Peter's Pearly Gates, as vulgar jokes about this most sacred occasion allege – and there be judged on the life it has led. At that time – if indeed time can be said to exist in eternity – the soul will be subjected to God's Particular Judgment. If there is the stain of mortal sin on it at the moment of death God will condemn it forever to the infinite pains of hell.

As I meditated on the Master's sermon about the Particular Judgment I couldn't help feeling that there was a potential here for gross unfairness in the Divine Judgment of souls. I visualized a man who spent his entire life blaspheming God and engaging in every type of God-forbidden vice, but who repented at the last moment, called the priest, confessed his sins, received absolution. That man would appear at the Particular Judgment in the state of grace and, although he would very likely spend time in Purgatory to burn off the residue of his sins, he would eventually get into heaven. Then I imagined another man who spent his entire life praising God and doing good works and who never committed a mortal sin. However, just once as he was driving, he was distracted by the image of a naked woman on a billboard, and for a single moment enjoyed that carnal vision; which also caused him to crash into a tree and be killed. That man would appear before the Throne of God with the stain of mortal sin on his soul, and he would be condemned to hell for all eternity for his ever so brief lapse from grace. I knew the theologians' answer to that enigma, having long listened to preachers and teachers of religion: it must all be put down, they would say, to God's mysterious ways which are too subtle for us poor mortals to understand. But though my faith accepted the explanation, my reason – which of course I, as a man of faith, rejected – was embarrassed at such a weak explication.

The Master went on to preach about the General Judgment. At the Last Day the Lord will appear in great Majesty in the clouds of heaven, the trumpets will sound and the dead will arise, their bodies re-assembled from the dust and ashes into which they had disintegrated after death. Never mind the physical problems that bodily resurrection pose, as described in the delightful Yorkshire song, *On Ilkley Moor Baht 'At*, which we in Firinne perversely sang at soirees. God's mysterious ways took care of that problem, too, the theologians said. So all mankind that has ever lived will be judged again, in public this time, in order that, as my National School catechism put it, *the providence of God which often in this life permits the good to suffer and the wicked to prosper will appear just before all men.* God's mysterious ways will be finally revealed.

Therefore, the Master concluded, if even the fear of hell or the fear of death or the fear of the Particular Judgment were not enough to persuade us to forsake our lives of sin, surely the thought of the Last Judgment and the possibility of being shamed eternally before the whole world would deter us from future sin and turn us to God!

Having learned about, and meditated on, our sinful lives and the consequences to which those lives were leading us, it was time to do an about turn, away from sin and towards salvation. The first step in that direction, the Master said, was through the door of the General Confession. We had all been going to confession since the age of six or seven. And we were instructed early on about the necessity of making good confessions – never failing to confess all mortal sins and never failing to express sincere sorrow for those sins, combined with a serious determination never to sin again.

"So," the Master said, showing teeth in the grimace that passed for a smile, "might you not reasonably expect that – assuming you have followed the rules of confession – your spiritual accounts are in good order and no stain of past sins is still sullying your souls?" He looked around for confirmation; novice heads nodded affirmatively.

"Well, maybe yes, maybe no." The Master's grin was even more contorted. "The problem is, you can't be absolutely sure. Also, you are beginning a new life of intimacy with God and it would be best if you made a clean sweep of your entire life up to this point and confessed all the bad things you have done so far and have them forgiven, so that you can start with a clean soul."

He allotted us time during the retreat to make a list of all the sins we had ever committed, at least all the big ones. A disturbing and difficult task, even for young minds with good memories and few opportunities to have sinned seriously. I put together a list of my past mortal sins – all dealing with sexual thoughts and desires – and at the end of the week presented myself to my chosen confessor. The old priest listened with an air of gravity, gave me a little homily, and pronounced absolution while I expressed sorrow for all my sins in the formal prayer of contrition. At the end the confessor told me not to worry anymore about my past life, instead to concentrate on the future.

Easier said than done. The General Confession, by its very nature of casting doubt on the soundness of all previous confessions, was an open invitation for Scruples to attack me on the General Confession itself. Which he did, very soon after the Big Retreat ended.

You may have forgotten to confess a few serious past sins in your General Confession, Scruples opened. I was in the chapel saying the rosary.

Really? I was always terrified at the eruptions of this know-all fear-all inner voice.

Of course! You don't really think you were totally, totally, honest about your past sins, do you?

I was trying to be.

I doubt that. For example, you always gave yourself the benefit of the doubt whenever it was unclear whether you had given full consent to impure thoughts?

Those were always difficult judgments to make.

And you didn't always confess to placing yourself in occasions of serious sin by reading salacious material, or going to films that included scenes which fostered temptations against chastity. Or, even worse, by going to dances.

Maybe. My stomach was beginning to churn.

And several time when you were in doubt as to whether you had committed mortal sins against the Holy Virtue haven't you actually gone to Communion?

Oh my God!

When quite possibly you were in the state of mortal sin at the time? That would be a heinous crime in itself?

At that stage I was sweating. But Scruples sustained his torment, continually adding new items to the list of doubts.

Haven't you very likely made a bad General Confession?
I may have indeed. The only way to deal with Scruples was to give in. *So now what will I do?*

Scruples was inexorable. *So, far from cleaning your soul, you have added sins to it. And, in that state, haven't you taken Holy Communion every morning since your General Confession?*

I writhed in agony.

Your only solution, Scruples pronounced, *is to make another General Confession.*

I remade my list, this time accusing myself of all doubtful matter, and went to see my confessor again. He was understanding and told me again not to worry. Again, easier said than done: Scruples continued to torture me on and off for the next ten years.

Standing Fast

Spiritual Direction

With the Big Retreat over, the Master gave us to understand that we were now fully-fledged novices. At least those who survived the retreat were. Not all survived. A novice went missing, mysteriously, shortly after the retreat ended: one evening he was present at supper, the next morning he had vanished. We wondered what had happened to him, but the rule of silence prevented speculation, and the Master gave no indication that he knew about his disappearance.

The mystery was solved that evening. I was walking around the recreation path after supper with Mr. Walsh and Mr. Dunne when the latter said, "does anyone know what happened to Mr. Burke?"

"I know," Mr. Walsh, a very quiet fellow, said. "He left."

"How do you know?" I had discussed the case of the missing Mr. Burke with my afternoon recreation confreres, but neither knew anything.

"He told me last night. After lights out: he broke the Great Silence to tell me." Mr. Walsh and Mr. Burke shared a room.

"Did he say why?" Mr. Dunne probed.

"He said the Master asked him to leave. Said he didn't have a vocation."

"Jesus!" Mr. Dunne exploded. Then he blushed. "Please don't chapter me for that." He looked pleadingly at us."

During the next week two other novices went missing. One of the *desaparecidos* told his room mate – again, during the Great Silence – that he himself had decided the religious life was not for him. The other told his room mate that the Master had asked him to leave. Those bits of information were passed among the novices, and we wondered who would be next to go. We found out as time went by: nine more novices left at various times during the remainder of our Novitiate year. The Master never commented when they disappeared.

After the Big Retreat the Master increased the pressure on us to achieve a higher level of holiness. He enforced the rules more strictly and gave penances more liberally and with greater severity for a wider variety of offences. Making us kneel in public was his favorite humiliation. For a breach of silence he might award a week of kneeling during meals, which required the delinquent novice to kneel at his place and eat from that position. If the offence was even more serious – though what could be more serious than to finish a sentence after the bell sounded to end recreation? – the offender was asked to kneel in the center of the refectory during meals, or kneel by the entrance to the chapel while the community entered to pray.

Manual labor was also intensified, as a means of testing our obedience and endurance. Picking spuds on a cold October day was a test of fortitude, as was plucking tiny weeds from between stones in a path while kneeling. But those were mere physical endurance tests, the kind that novices who had grown up on farms didn't find particularly difficult. The more serious tests

96

were interior. We were preparing ourselves, the Master said, for entry into the religious life, a life dedicated to God. So we must begin now on the path that led to the perfection of the interior life of prayer and commitment to the things of God. The path to God was through Jesus, who was the Son of God and was both human and divine. And the path to Jesus was through Mary, Mother of the human-divine Jesus. This hierarchical structure might be a little confusing at first, he said, but we'd understand it by degrees if we meditated and prayed constantly on it.

The most difficult part of that spiritual life was that we were supposed to occupy our minds with thoughts of Jesus and Mary at all times. Difficult enough when we were engaging in formal prayer in the chapel, more difficult when we were reading spiritual books – of which we did quite a lot – terribly difficult altogether when we were engaged in non-religious activities like manual labor or doing chores. And most difficult of all when we were playing football or talking to fellow novices at recreation. That focus, however, was demanded of us: to spend every waking moment in the presence of Jesus and Mary. That, said the Master, was the true test of our advancement in the spiritual life. The test wasn't verifiable of course, although the Master did try. Each novice was summoned to his office once a month for what was called spiritual direction, in which the novice was expected to bare his soul to the Master, and be guided by him along the road that led to spiritual perfection. The following is my recollection of such a session.

"How are you doing in general, Mr. Keady?" The Master's gaze said he was sizing me up.

"Fine, Father." I had learned early in life that when responding to questions from authority it was best to be terse.

"Are you fitting in well?" The Master made a note on a pad.

"Oh yes, Father." Whatever that question meant.

"Do you still believe you have a vocation, a calling from God to the religious life?" The Master administered his penetrating stare.

"Definitely, Father." Endeavoring to sound confident.

"Are you practicing charity towards all your confreres?" Making another note on the pad.

"I'm trying my best, Father." That was a treacherous question – anyone could be chaptered anytime for a breach of charity, which was infinitely definable – so I was careful not to claim perfection.

The Master's tone now changed to paternal. "How is your health?"

"Not a bother, Father." That was an easy one.

Then casually, with raised eyebrows, he asked, "To your knowledge, Mr. Keady, are any novices engaging in any practices, or any failure to observe the Rule, that have not been reported in Chapter?"

I hesitated while formulating a safe answer. "Not that I'm aware of, Father."

The Master took my hesitation as an indication that I knew something I ought to divulge. "This is not the time or place to observe the schoolboy code of not snitching, Mr. Keady." His tone was stern. "If you know of anyone who is doing anything that the culprit would not want me to know about, then it's your religious duty to speak up."

"I don't know of anything, Father." Neither God nor Scruples had ever told me I must inform on my fellow novices.

The Master turned to probing the state of my spiritual life. "How is your mental prayer progressing?"

"Fine, Father." Mental prayer was an exercise we engaged

in for a half hour every morning, wedged in between vocal prayers and morning mass. It was a formal exercise with its own set of rules which, if faithfully observed, was supposed to lead one to that intimate communion with God that all religious aspired to. As a formal exercise it had to be carefully prepared, so a time was set aside for its preparation on the preceding evening. First we were to pick a theme that we wished to meditate and pray on, such as a scene from the life of Jesus, or a text from the New Testament or the psalms, or a thought inspired by something we read in a spiritual book. Then we had to break the theme down into points we wanted to think and pray about in such a way that they would improve our spiritual lives. It wasn't easy to pick a new subject every day, and often what seemed like a bright idea the evening before turned out to be a crashing bore the following morning. So the results of my efforts at mental prayer were, at best, spotty. Which I didn't acknowledge now to the Master, fearing that were I to confess that I wasn't doing too well at mental prayer he might place me in the queue for departure.

"How are you faring in Obedience to the Rule?" I felt that the Master was challenging me to confess a fault or two.

"Fine." I could honestly say I'd been pretty faithful to the Rule.

He leaned forward as if to tell me something in confidence. "You are preparing to take the three vows of Poverty, Chastity, and Obedience, so it's terribly important that you be faithful to the Rule in all those respects."

"Yes, Father." I had no difficulty observing Poverty since all superfluous items, such as the new watch my parents gave me on entering, had already been confiscated – to be returned at the end of the Novitiate year – and I had no means of acquiring anything new. Apart from impure thoughts, which football and constant prayer were expected to obviate, I had little chance of breaching Chastity here; only on the weekly walk did I even see a woman, and then I had to immediately avert my eyes; and I still knew nothing about homosexuality or masturbation. As for Obedience, my daily life was one long exercise in that virtue.

Now it was the Master's turn to pass judgment. "You're older than the other novices, Mr. Keady, so I expect you to be a bit more mature. However, you must not take advantage of your age to give your brethren the impression that you're superior to them."

I raised a questioning eyebrow at the implied allegation.

The Master responded aggressively. "I occasionally get the impression that you seem to be putting on the dog."

I understood the expression and felt that its application to me was grossly untrue: I had been careful never to claim any superiority because of my age. "The very idea never occurred to me, Father."

The Master's stare implied that I had a colossal nerve to contradict him. "Well, now that the matter has been drawn to your attention you should refrain from any superior airs in future."

I left the session seething at his unjust allegation, and vainly endeavoring to invoke religious humility to cope with it.

Reading Rodrigues

We engaged in a very quaint daily exercise called 'reading Rodriguez.' Alonso Rodriguez, a sixteenth century Jesuit, wrote a series of books on the practice of the Christian virtues that, Novice Masters had ever since felt, no serious-minded ascetic could afford to ignore. Rodriguez – as he was called in the world of aficionados – had a fascinating way with words and an inexhaustible fund of stories with which to illustrate his homilies.

100

The Novitiate had a supply of his books, and reading them was a daily ritual. At a stated time each afternoon we assembled at the starting point of the recreation walk – when it rained we read indoors – and spent the next half hour walking duck-style around the recreation path imbibing the great writer's words of spiritual wisdom.

Chuckles would often break the monastic silence as novices read the humorous anecdotes which, one surmises, Rodriguez never intended to be funny. For example, there was a chapter in which the author wrote on the Conquest of Lust. We must never trust in our own strength in matters of chastity, he admonished, no matter how long we may have been faithful or how many temptations we may have overcame. To support that dictum he quoted the words of a man who had struggled all his life against the assaults of sexual passion: *always remember*, said St Jerome, *that a woman evicted the tenant of Paradise from his possession*. Rodriguez counseled flight when confronted with lust or woman – between whom no valid distinction could be made, he said. He commanded that no unnecessary meetings or conversations be indulged in with members of the sex of Eve. If such communications must absolutely be held, he cautioned that they be restricted to what was strictly necessary.

Remembering Marjorie, I felt uncomfortable with such stringency: surely a chaste friendship between men and women was possible? Yet the ancient Jesuit's teaching had the authority of Church theologians, and his works were highly recommended for spiritual neophytes. He reinforced his instruction with a story from his *Unfortunate History of Those Who Did Not Follow This Teaching*. The subject of this particular story was a hitherto saintly man known as James the Hermit. A practitioner of the eremitic life, he had spent forty years in the desert, fasting and praying and indulging in various kinds of esoteric austerities. And

101

he had demonstrated his sanctity by working miracles and casting out devils. One day his spiritual children brought to him a young woman whose soul Beelzebub had chosen for his abode. The mighty hermit performed his customary prodigy: he cast out the devil and set the maiden free. Such, however, had been the havoc wreaked in the past by the Satan-infested damsel that her friends, apparently not yet convinced that the bailiff of God had really evicted the demon, refused to take her home. So James, with his Christ-like charity, allowed her to remain with him, forgetting feisty old Jerome's admonition.

The inevitable happened. "Since he trusted in his own strength", Rodriguez lamented, "God allowed him to commit fornication with her". Worse was to follow. In the fulness of time and in the absence of planned parenthood, his partner in lust became pregnant. The horny hermit, with a forty year reputation for sanctity to protect, now compounded his fornicatory felony by murdering his child-bearing mistress and dumping her body in the river – Rodriguez found no incongruity in the existence of a river in an eremitic desert. Then, realizing the enormity of his crimes, and despairing of Divine forgiveness, the now anchor-less anchorite abandoned his life of prayer and drifted away from his desert abode to the world of Sinful Society, where for the next ten years he developed a reputation for debauchery as great as his former reputation for austerity.

There was, however, a happy ending. "Since," Rodriguez concluded, "we must never despair of Divine forgiveness, for the mercy of God is limitless, James was given the grace of repentance. He returned to the desert, and by practicing penance for another ten years he was canonized when he died." Unlike Rodriguez himself.

Persevering

The Novitiate year was long. For me, deprived of the freedom and the social life I had been accustomed to, it seemed eternal. No matter that I was immersed in the struggle for spiritual perfection, the body craved sexual release, the emotions craved friendship, the stomach craved home cooking, the mind craved freedom. I actually thought of leaving. But I couldn't and wouldn't quit. I believed in the Church and I believed in her teaching. It didn't matter that I wasn't happy; all that counted was that I was preparing myself for admission to the eternal joys of heaven. It was entirely logical and totally selfish. The truth was, though I wasn't conscious of it, that I wasn't really in love with God or Jesus or Mary. Though I forced myself to believe I was, I simply wanted what was best for me. And best for me was to be in heaven forever. To get there I was willing to put up with the Spartan life of the Novitiate, to accept its deprivations and tolerate its humiliations.

I never articulated my thoughts in this manner of course. In my conscious mind I believed I was striving for sanctity out of pure love of God. And Conscience kept me on the straight and narrow path of holiness, pulling hard on the reins whenever I accidentally deviated. But whenever I faltered, out of normal human weakness or because of the harshness of the Novitiate environment, my real motivation for being there rose to the surface of awareness, reiterating that I was in the right place: on track for heaven.

My scruples were a concomitant of my real motives, for had I been driven by the love of God I'd surely have trusted Him to understand my fallibility and human weakness. But since I was spurred on by my determination to get to heaven at whatever cost, I didn't trust God; I saw Him, rather, as the Stern Taskmaster

103

Whose rules I had to obey in order to get into heaven. God was just waiting to catch me out, my sub-conscious warned, so He could deprive me of my eternal reward. Therefore I had to make assurances doubly sure by being scrupulously honest with Him Who knew what was in my innermost thoughts. Hence my doubling up on the General Confession.

Feast-days provided minor relief from the dismal everyday rigor of Novitiate life. The Immaculate Conception, Christmas and the week following, St. Patrick's Day, Easter, Pentecost, the Ascension, Corpus Christi, were times of ever so slight relaxation. Meals on those occasions were more interesting, recreation periods were lengthened, we were permitted to sleep a little longer and allowed to converse during some meals. Tiny concessions objectively, but cherished and savored by sensory deprived novices.

Sometime between Christmas and St. Patrick's Day came a major event: on a particular Sunday we were allowed to receive visits from our families. Till then our only connection with home had been the monthly letter that we were permitted – rather commanded – to write, and which the Master reserved the right to read. I was delighted to see my parents and Tom; Seamus didn't come. But I was shocked to learn they were planning to emigrate to New York the next month. I knew my mother had always longed to return to America; she had many times told us of her happy days in that country and of her desire to return. So now that the family was grown and scattered, she was about to fulfil her dream. My absorption with my spiritual life made this new level of separation easier to accept. Detachment from the world, a requirement for those who consecrated themselves to God, meant also detachment from one's family. So I accepted their impending departure with an amount of serenity.

The Archbishop's Egg

Sex and Vocation

Shortly after my parents' visit we had our second ten-day Retreat. Though it lacked the hell-and-damnation terror of the Big Retreat, it was no less intense. Two subjects dominated: sex and vocation. The Master covered the several lectures on sex with extraordinary light brush strokes and with scarcely a mention of the s-e-x word. His objective, of course, was not to titillate us with the profane pleasures of lustful activity but to inculcate in us a holy fear of carnal delight which, he said, we must replace with a sacred love of the Holy Virtue. Practice of this latter, he said obliquely, consisted in not only abstaining from all sexual activity but in possessing a positive abhorrence of even the slightest erotic desire.

It might seem difficult to talk about sex without describing it, but the Master succeeded. Rather than mention the word *sex* he focused on the word *chastity*: the latter sounded positive though it denoted a negative. It was the negative state of not-sex, but with a little word-manipulation it could be made to seem like a positive esoteric activity rather than a denial of an erotic one. A chaste person, the Master implied, was engaging in a positive non-sex act, with its accompanying non-pleasure. Chastity had a positive character, he said, in that its objective was to curb what was inordinate in voluptuous pleasures. He acknowledged that the latter had their place in perpetuating the human race, but, he cautioned, they were lawful only between married persons; and then only when they furthered, or at least didn't interfere with, the procreation of children.

Chastity was called the angelic virtue, he said, because it likened the chaste to angels, who were the very definition of chastity since, the Gospel said, they neither married nor were given in marriage. Chastity was also called the difficult virtue, because it could be observed only by waging a constant struggle against that most tyrannical of our desires, the libido. The Master didn't use the *libido* word, that being Freudian and therefore un-Catholic; instead he used the term beloved of moral theologians, *the passions*.

There were several degrees of chastity, the Master taught. The first and basic was to refrain from consenting to any thought, word or deed that would soil the Holy Virtue. I, well aware of that level, acknowledged to myself that I was still waging my own war there. The next degree was attained when one immediately and energetically expelled any thought or deed that would sully the Holy Virtue. I hoped that by the end of the Novitiate I'd have risen to that level. One had reached the third degree, the Master continued, when one acquired such mastery of the senses that one could deal with questions relating to chastity with magisterial calm. Was that the degree the Master himself had reached? I couldn't imagine the man, with his thin ascetic visage and other-world-searching eyes, having the kinds of unchaste thoughts and desires that constantly bombarded my own imagination.

To attain the fourth degree of Chastity, the Master

concluded, which consisted in experiencing no unchaste feelings whatever, one had to be given a special privilege by God Himself. He gave the example of St. Thomas Aquinas. That great Doctor of the Church decided to became a monk when he was a young man, much against the wishes of his noble parents. To dissuade him from his holy calling his father confined him to his room and sent a gorgeous young woman to corrupt his virtue. But the chaste young Thomas resolved that temptation by grabbing the flaming torch that lighted his room and chasing the temptress from his presence. God rewarded him, according to holy legend, by his never having to suffer temptations against chastity again. Even in my Novitiate fervor I wasn't sure I wanted to attain that degree.

Having delicately disposed of that sensitive subject, the Master turned with greater ease to the subject of Vocation. Each novice was here, he said, because he believed he had a call from God to the religious and priestly life. However, of all present in the study hall, only one, Father Master himself, could be sure he had been called by God. Novices believed they had vocations, and were here in the Novitiate to test their beliefs. But it was only when the bishop called us to priestly ordination that we could be certain we were called by God, not by our own pride.

Scruples raised his head at this new piece of information. *So is it really God Who is calling you?*

Yes! I firmly believe that God has called me. Remember Griffith Avenue?

That could be just your imagination. Scruples was sly.

Could be, but it wasn't. Look at all the obstacles I've overcome to get this far; I couldn't possibly have overcome them if God wasn't helping me. And He wouldn't help me if He didn't want me to be his priest.

Could be just your pride! Scruples never let go. *Remember what the Master said in a conference last week – that pride can be very subtle at times? And after all, here in Ireland the priesthood is the pinnacle of career success for most fellows. When you're a priest you'll be regarded as just a little less than God Himself, a man apart, to be admired by everyone and treated with the utmost respect and reverence. So isn't that what you're really after?*

Definitely not. I want to give my life to the service of God.

So you say. But you didn't have any other real options, did you? You couldn't afford to marry, which was what you really wanted to do.

Look! If God wanted me to marry He'd have made it possible. So therefore He didn't want me to get married.

And you had a rather lowly job in the Civil Service, hadn't you? Scruples was like a dog with a bone: he had to keep gnawing at it. *And you were bored with the work. And you wanted something better for your life. And that was why you chose the priesthood. Your vocation didn't came from God at all.*

That's just not true. I was never interested in worldly glory. I just want to serve God. And go to heaven when I die.

Nevertheless, you now need to make a prayerful examination of your vocation to make sure it's genuine.

To make sure it is genuine! The Master spelled out the indicators of a true vocation. The first, he said, was to have a pure intention, which meant we mustn't be looking for fame or fortune through the priesthood. He stared at us intently as he said this. I felt sure I was blushing, for how could I be certain I hadn't come to the Novitiate to attain the respectability and honor that went with being a priest? Secondly, the Master said, we must be motivated by the love of God. Well of course I love God; that was a given, wasn't it? Everyone here loved God; it was unthinkable that they didn't.

Not so fast, Scruples interrupted. *What does loving God mean? It's easy to say, 'O God, I love you,' as you do a hundred times a day, but does saying it mean anything?*

It means I love Him. Though, to be honest, I'd never really asked myself what it meant.

See! Scruples crowed in triumph. *Don't the saints say – and they're the experts – that you prove your love for God by doing His Holy Will: by not committing sin and by doing the things that please Him. On that basis,* Scruples was sneering now, *your love for Him is more than a bit spotty, isn't it? Because you do commit sins. So, it looks like you don't have a vocation after all?*

However, I shot back, *does one have to be sinless to have a vocation? Because if only the sinless can have vocations then nobody would ever have one; after all, the Church says that all sons of Adam and Eve are sinners.*

Maybe. For once Scruples seemed stymied.

I pressed home my advantage. *So then my sinfulness doesn't preclude my having a vocation, does it?*

Scruples shut up for the time being.

Thirdly, the Master continued, we must be motivated by the salvation of our own souls. Here, I felt, I was on solid ground: I was certainly motivated to save my soul; in fact, keeping my soul out of hell was my principal motive in wanting to be a priest. But then didn't everyone who gave the slightest thought to the matter want to save his soul? So why didn't everyone want to be a priest or religious? For instance, all my Firinne friends went to mass and the sacraments and seemed to be trying to live holy lives, yet I was the only one who aspired to be a priest. Because God was calling me but not them, seemed the only sensible answer.

A vocation from God came only after one had persevered

109

in virtue over a long period, the Master said. Which was one reason why we had such a long training in the religious life prior to ordination. We were still only at the beginning of that training, he warned. After we left the Novitiate hothouse, where the regimen made it relatively easy to be virtuous, we would face more difficult tests to our vocations and even to our faith.

It seemed to me then that perseverance in the religious life would be the best proof of my being called by God. So I was determined to persevere.

"Father Master is a great man, isn't he?" Mr. Griffin, a big fellow with a big voice, said at evening recreation during the retreat.

Though I now looked on the Master as a little dictator, what was I to say? "He is," I mumbled.

"He's inclined to be a bit bombastic, I think." Mr. Leonard was the third member of our group, a no-nonsense lad and a good footballer.

"I like the way he explained that having a vocation requires that one has the desire to help save other people's souls." Mr. Griffin started to swing the tassel on his cincture, then stopped abruptly – tassel-swinging was a chapter-able offence. "I myself decided to become a priest," he continued, "so I could save souls. It's a very satisfying thought, you know."

I thought Mr. Griffin himself was a big bombast, but I said nothing.

"But isn't saving souls the reason we all want to be priests?" Mr. Leonard pointed out.

Mr. Griffin agreed. "Otherwise we wouldn't be here."

I supposed that I, too, wanted to help others save their souls, though I hadn't given much thought to that aspect of the priesthood. Still, I had joined a missionary Congregation and in due course after ordination I'd be sent to Africa or some other pagan territory to harvest souls for Christ.

"Let me ask you both this." Mr. Griffin stopped in the middle of the path, forcing the group following to step around."It's a question that's been bothering me for some time." He paused dramatically before asking, "Do cows have souls?"

Mr. Leonard's laugh was disparaging. "Why would they?"

"Of course not," I said. "Only people have souls."

"Well," said Mr. Griffin, "I think cows have souls, too."

"So," Mr. Leonard scoffed, "are they already in heaven when they're beef on your plate?"

"They can't go to hell anyway," I said facetiously. "They're already cooked enough."

"How do you know?" Mr. Griffin challenged. "See, I think cows have souls, only they're not immortal like ours. I think –"

At that point the bell saved further discussion.

Lent and Easter

Lent, the six weeks of penance and prayer that the Church devotes to preparing for its annual commemoration of the Passion and Death of Jesus and the celebration of His Glorious Resurrection, was observed with grim severity in the Novitiate. The purple mass vestments reminded us each morning that we were in a period of even greater austerity than usual. Manual labor was harder, food was plainer, prayers were longer, even the silence seemed deeper. For me the most severe strain was the fasting: I and one other novice had reached the age of twenty-one, so we were bound by Mother Church's fasting law. That law allowed us only one full meal each day and two collations. The latter were limited to eight ounces each and could not include

111

meat. Since I weighed less than a hundred and forty pounds and had a very hearty appetite – "you eat like a horse and have nothing to show for it," my father used to say – the fast was a serious penance. As a consequence of fasting and the extra manual labor, I lost ten precious pounds during those six weeks.

The fasting rules contained an unintended irony. Lenten supper for novices consisted of tea with bread and butter and a small piece of cheese; however, we two novices who were fasting were allowed an egg at the evening collation, to the envy of our younger brethren. The egg was known as the archbishop's egg because of a decree once issued by the Archbishop of Dublin and subsequently adopted by other Irish bishops. The austere John Charles McQuaid always laid down in minute detail what fasting entailed for his flock. One year, in a fit of extraordinary generosity, he allowed those fasting to have one egg a day as part of their collations. A cloistered Order of nuns in the diocese, renowned for its jejune diet, followed his Grace's instructions to the letter and served a daily egg to each nun as part of the Lenten fast; previously, they hadn't permitted themselves such a luxury at any time of the year. They referred to their unexpected bonus as the archbishop's egg.

The Master selected chapters from the Old Testament for breakfast reading to provide us with background information about the coming of the Messiah and His rejection. One of those readings was the story of the chaste Susanna and the infamous judges who lusted after her. I had never heard the story previously and was shocked at the part about Susanna being watched by the dirty old men while she bathed. Although the story excited my own lusty imagination, I told myself that the impure thoughts it produced could not be sinful since they were caused by the word of God.

The purpose of Lent, the Master told us in his conferences, was to focus on the central tenet of the Christian life: the Passion, Death, and Resurrection of Jesus, the Christ. Our prayers and meditations were designed to make us not only understand that Jesus suffered and died to redeem us from the powers of darkness, but also to allow us feel something of His pain. Fervent novice that I had become, I did so feel each time I meditated on Jesus' scourging, crowning with thorns, dragging the heavy cross through the streets of Jerusalem, suffering the cruel nails hammered through his hands and feet. Kneeling in the chapel with my eyes closed, and deep in contemplation of His awful Crucifixion, I even thought I experienced the rough crunch of nails penetrate my own hands and feet. I told Jesus how sorry I was to have caused Him such pain by my sins, and promised to devote my life to making reparation.

The sadness of Lent and the horror of Holy Week eventually gave way to the joy of Resurrection. The long religious ceremonies that commenced on Saturday night, followed by midnight mass, reflected the new beginning made possible by Jesus's sacrifice and His glorious rising. I felt as if I were born again. We had earthy celebrations, too, to complement our spiritual joy: at two in the morning we were treated to tea and cake, and we were allowed to sleep later than usual. Sunday morning our letters from home, which had been withheld during the six weeks of Lent, were distributed. I had one from my mother in New York: my parents and Tom had joined my two sisters there and were settling into their new home. I also had a brief note from Seamus saying he was still in Dublin and was looking forward to seeing me when I returned to the city.

Lunch on Easter Sunday was what, in Novitiate parlance, was called a 'stodge,' a heavy main course followed by a cream-laden dessert. That night my stomach rebelled at the sudden overload. To my chagrin, the sub-Master, who doubled as infirmarian, put me on a diet of dry toast and milk-less tea for two days till I recovered.

Final Phase

Though we had more than four months still to go in the Novitiate we felt – novices loved to discuss the subject during recreation – that we had already weathered the most difficult part. We hadn't: the Novitiate was designed to became ever more demanding as we progressed through it. The sheer monotony of the life was one of its biggest challenges. The capricious humiliations inflicted by the Master and Sub-Master, in their efforts to assess our fitness for membership of the Congregation, were also a major source of worry and tension. I was subjected to a humiliation of this kind in the early part of summer. My function was that of third gardener and my principal job was to cut the grass on the lawn in front of the big house with a small reel mower. I was also responsible with the other two gardeners for keeping the flower beds weed-free. One morning the Sub-Master came to inspect and, while the lawn and flower beds were immaculate, he found some tiny weeds sprouting between the flagstones in a path that was unrelated to our function.

"Mr. Keady, keeping this path free from weeds is part of your function." The tone was peremptory, the small eyes hostile. "Get down on your knees now and remove them."

All my life I had a detestation of being unjustly accused, so my natural inclination now was to protest that the path was not my responsibility. It spoke much to the success of Novitiate brain-washing that, without protest, I immediately dropped to my knees.

114

Playing croquet, a pastime permitted in summer, provided an unexpected test of monastic self-discipline. The game, we thought, was intended to give us a little diversion during recreation periods. But nothing in the Novitiate was quite what it seemed. Novices hastened slowly to the toolshed at the beginning of recreation – mindful of the rule not to run, with a Chapter fault awaiting anyone who offended – and grabbed one of the four mallets whose possession entitled one to play. But problems soon arose: there were many ambiguities relating to the finer aspects of the game as we were given to understand them. Novices, otherwise polite and disciplined, engaged in heated arguments over the rules, sometimes even losing their tempers. After a few such episodes I decided that croquet was a most dangerous game for a novice, and thereafter refrained from playing it.

Summer weather came slowly, as always in Ireland; the wags said it came only once every four or five years. However, the summer of our Novitiate was fine and we enjoyed helping the Brothers save the hay. Then came the principal summer treat for Novices: the Great Mountain Climb. Galtymore is not a particularly high mountain, a mere three thousand feet or so, but it rises directly from the deep Glen of Aherlow and is quite a steep climb. The base of the mountain is eleven miles from the Novitiate and on the appointed morning we set out in the usual groups of three. The Novitiate car, driven by the Sub-Master and carrying lunch, arrived at the base before us. After the meal we climbed. It was considered a matter of Novitiate pride that all reach the top, and we did. However, we couldn't stay long to enjoy the magnificent view as the Master had set a deadline of eight o'clock for our return to the Novitiate. After a quick snack on descending we raced the eleven miles back to Kilshane. We failed to meet the deadline by about fifteen minutes, for which delinquency the uncompromising Master roundly berated us.

Being & Becoming

By the beginning of August we were looking forward to leaving the Novitiate and moving on to the next phase of our training at the Scholasticate in Kimmage, Dublin. But first we had to undergo a third ten-day retreat, this one dealing with the religious vows of poverty, chastity, and obedience, vows we would bind ourselves to for a period of three years.

On entering, I hadn't given much thought to the vow of poverty. That vow, the Master told us now, would help us overcome one of the great obstacles to spiritual perfection, the inordinate love of worldly goods. It would also impose a sacrifice, for we'd own nothing and must always ask our Superior's permission to obtain anything we needed. Having grown up poor and never having been particularly enamored of material goods, I didn't consider renouncing all external possessions daunting.

The vow of obedience, the Master said, was even more difficult to live up to. We'd have to surrender our will not only to God's will, which of course everyone had an obligation to do, but also to the will of our Superior and to the Rule of the Congregation. The idea of taking a vow of obedience didn't disturb me either. All my life I'd had to obey parents, teachers, priests, employer, and follow all kinds of irritating rules.

The vow of chastity was another matter. Despite my inhibitions and repressions and ignorance in matters of sex, my instincts had told me when I was leaving school that I could not, and did not want to, live without the company of woman. For that reason I had resisted the tug of the priestly life for several years. In some peculiar manner, however, during and after that illuminating moment on Griffith Avenue when the priestly vocation beckoned as never before, I had managed to vault the sex barrier and remain on the other side ever since. Now, faced with making a vow of chastity to God I found that the Novitiate had

116

done its job well: I was so enamored of the priestly and religious life, that the idea of doing without the company of woman no longer dismayed me.

Two weeks after the retreat the new novices arrived and we spent a week breaking them in, as the previous year's Novices had done to us. Then we took our vows in the Novitiate chapel. *In the name of the Father and of the Son and of the Holy Ghost, Amen. In the presence of our Lord Jesus Christ, of the ever Blessed Virgin, of the Patron Saints of the Congregation, and of all the Heavenly Court, I, Walter James Keady, make for three years to God, the three simple vows of Poverty, Chastity, and Obedience, in the Congregation of the Holy Ghost and of the Holy Heart of Mary, and in accordance with its Rules and Constitutions.*

The following morning we boarded a bus for the Scholasticate in Kimmage.

Second row, second from left, with novices who survived, 1957

117

Kimmage

Return to Dublin

"You're a Mayo man," Seamus said. "Like me you were born in Castlebar."

"But I became a Dublin Jackeen at the age of two when we moved up here."

"But you became a Mayo lad again at six when we moved to Grandpa's farm."

"But we moved back to Dublin when I was fifteen, so I became a Jackeen again."

Seamus snorted. "So which are you now, a Jackeen or a Mayo man? Who are you going to cheer for on Sunday when Mayo play Dublin?"

That argument took place before I went to the Novitiate. It was an important pub-social-gathering question because a significant portion of the city's population was born outside of Dublin, and the all-important test of that portion's allegiance was: which county did they cheer for in Croke Park at football and hurling matches? Any *culchie* – pejorative Dublinese for non-

118

Dubliners – who cheered for Dublin was looked on as a traitor to his county of birth. And I belonged to that class: having played football for St Vincent's, Dublin's premier club team, I felt I owed Dublin my allegiance. Besides, I had grown to love the city, somewhat in the way one comes to love a pair of old shoes: it mightn't be elegant or spiffy – the natives called it 'dear old dirty Dublin' – but it was comfortable and I knew my way around it, on foot, on the bike, and from the top of the double-decker.

Now, however, observing the city from the bus as we drove through it on the way to Kimmage, I experienced a dissociation, as if I had been away for a very long time. I had been gone for only a year, yet the streets, the sounds, the people, once so endearingly familiar, now looked coarse and alien. The year in Kilshane had changed my way of viewing life and people and material things; it had turned me into a religious snob, proud of my piety, subconsciously disparaging the great masses who I felt lacked the insights I had gained into eternity. The world of the city could be no longer what it once was for me: a relatively care-free community that I had sensed – despite my religious scruples – was designed for enjoyment. I no longer belonged to that Dublin. It felt foreign because of the brain-washing I had received in Kilshane. It threatened me with its remembered freedom and insouciance and attachment to the world that I had left behind. Its external appearance had become more materialistic, too: its people were better dressed, there were many more cars, fewer bicycles. And there were the television antennae, sprouting like giant weeds from every rooftop; before I went to Kilshane there were hardly any but now they were ubiquitous. And to my narrow religious outlook they were another indication of how decadent was the world I had forsaken.

Kimmage Manor

The Scholasticate

The Holy Ghost Congregation's senior Scholasticate was located in Kimmage, a district in the south side of the city. A large complex, it housed over two hundred Scholastics and forty to fifty priests and lay brothers; it also served as a guest-house for the many missionaries of the Congregation who came by on their visits home from Africa and other *partes infideles*. The place was known to the locals as Kimmage Manor, because it had once been an aristocratic manor house, home of Sir Frederick Shaw, the Recorder of Dublin. Scholastics called the Manor the 'Old House' to distinguish it from the newer buildings in which we were quartered. The latter consisted of three long parallel concrete structures, three stories high, architecturally ugly, and austerely functional. In front of them, the first building we new arrivals saw as we were driven up the elegant driveway, was the Scholasticate chapel, a rather unimpressive edifice on the outside.

A farm was part of the complex, extensively cultivated by

lay Brothers to feed its denizens. It provided beef, potatoes, vegetables and milk, which, in addition to bread, were the staple foods of the Scholastics.

When we got off the bus we were surrounded by a swarm of black-robed Scholastics, led by the former novices we had met last year in Kilshane. They welcomed us with that peculiar greeting – Christ-like but reserved – that was special to religious communities. Then a priest stepped forward to greet us.

"I'm Father John, your Director." He was a medium-sized man with piercing black eyes, the hooked nose of a stern hawk, and tight thin lips that suggested a lack of humor; the black cape of authority covered his shoulders. We had already learned that he was new to his post as Director of Philosophers. He welcomed us to the Scholasticate in the softest of tones, with a smile that was obviously forced, and hoped we'd be happy in our new home. But we weren't fooled: the man's reputation had arrived among us while we were still in Kilshane: a novice, who had been the recipient of his attentions in one of the Congregation's secondary schools, said in a rather shocked tone when he heard the name of the new Director, "that man is a killer."

One of the Scholastics took charge of me by taking my suitcase. "I'm Martin," he said. "If you like I'll show you around." His genuine smile was a welcome antidote to the Director's foreboding grimace. "Would you like to see your room first?"

"Looks great," I managed when he opened a door in the middle of a long corridor. I looked in on a small rectangular bare-walled room, furnished with just a narrow bed and a wooden stand with washbasin and jug. In Kilshane we had to share rooms, so this was an improvement.

"We can leave your suitcase here," Martin said, and took me on a tour. "In case you don't know," he said as we walked along a wide ground-floor corridor with glass walls that looked out on a central courtyard, "the Scholasticate is divided in two: the House of Philosophy and the House of Theology. In the House of Philosophy, we study philosophy of course, though some also go to the University to study other subjects, like English or Classics or Biology."

"Do you get to choose what you want to do at the University?" I'd like to study English.

"Afraid not." Martin said. "And not everyone even gets to go to University. Most Scholastics do their Philosophy courses here in Kimmage; it's called Home Philosophy."

"Do the Theologians go to the University, as well?"

"No. Most study theology here in Kimmage. A few go to Rome and Fribourg to get degrees. Theologians are ordained priests at the end of their third year."

"Father Master mentioned that we wouldn't be allowed to talk to the theologians."

"Weird, isn't it?" Martin made a face. "Members of both Houses share chapel and refectory but otherwise we're kept strictly apart."

"So why can't we talk to them? The Master never told us why."

Martin laughed. "We were never officially told either. So various theories are kicked around. One is that they're afraid the theologians might confuse philosophers with their more advanced studies. Some of the more cynical fellows here think it's to keep the theologians from contaminating us with their tarry attitudes to the Rule."

"Sorry! What does tarry mean?"

Martin chuckled. "You'll have to get used to a lot of Kimmage jargon, I'm afraid. Tarry is a label for someone who's careless about observing rules. Anyway, as no doubt the Director will tell you very soon, the separation of Philosophers and Theologians is a very serious rule. People have been sent away from the Scholasticate for ignoring it."

We walked through a large room with a shiny wood floor, bare of furniture except for folding chairs stacked against a wall. "This is our recreation room," Martin said. "We hang out here during rec when it's raining." He led the way through open double doors at the end of the room. "And this is our study hall; you'll be spending a lot of time in here." The large room was austere and unimaginatively laid out. Rows of desks occupied most of it; the back wall was covered with book shelves; at the front a rostrum rested on a platform. "There are about a hundred and twenty desks," Martin said, "and they're assigned in order of seniority. So you new arrivals will be in the front. The most senior – those who are longest in the House – are at the back." Pointing to the rostrum, he said, "that's where the Director sits when he's giving us conferences. We have one most evenings."

We continued walking. At the end of a long wide corridor we went through a door to the outside. "This is the rec door," Martin said. "Same rule as the Novitiate: you take on recreation whoever comes out the door with you." We walked around a gravel path that circled a football field which he said was the recreation walk. "Do you play football?"

"I play anything that includes a ball."

"Good man. We play rugby, soccer, Gaelic, and hurling here. We also have a sports day in the summer."

Next he showed me the refectory, which was large and airy, with windows all along one wall. A broad aisle ran down the center, with ten-person tables on either side. "The aisle separates Philosophers and Theologians. And the double doors at the end lead into the kitchen where the Scholastics' food is prepared." He pointed to a table on a dais at the other end. "That's where the Directors and teachers eat." A pulpit-like structure stood to the side, in front of the Fathers' table and facing the Scolastics' area. "We read from there during meals," he explained, "and theologians deliver sermons from there during breakfast."

Kimmage Chapel

A visit to the chapel ended our tour. "As you might guess, we spend a lot of time in here," he whispered. The interior was monastic, with facing stalls across the center aisle for the Scholastics, and benches at the back on a raised platform for the priestly staff. For the occasional lay people who came to pray or to attend mass there were transepts on either side of the high altar.

That night lying on a thin mattress in unfamiliar surroundings I felt discombobulated. Kilshane had been temporary and unreal and I was glad to leave it. But this place seemed permanent. My family, except for Seamus, was now in America, and I, abrogating freedom and home, had committed my life to an austere monastic setting. I thought of Marjorie and wondered if I had made a terrible mistake. Then I slept until awakened by the clang of an electric bell outside my door.

The New Director

The previous Director of Philosophers was apparently a genial man whose easy-going ways with his charges did not at all please his superiors. So just as I and my confreres were about to descend on Kimmage he was replaced by Father John, the man with the hawk-like face, who was given the mission of restoring the House of Philosophy to pristine austerity. The new Director lost no time setting about the task of weaning the Philosophers from the slovenly habits they were said to have acquired under the previous regime. And since the newly arrived were not guilty of those habits, he decided to enlist our help in his crusade.

His chosen weapon for commencing reform was our old nemesis, the Chapter of Faults. We learned to our dismay on arrival that we hadn't left that odious monastic practice behind in the Novitiate: weekly Chapter was also part of the Kimmage Philosophers' regime, though its format was somewhat different. Each week the Director would call on a number of his charges, starting with the most senior and working down to the most junior, and order them to stand and make one critical remark each about the behavior of a confrere. In the previous regime, in order to maintain good relations with one another, Philosophers had agreed among themselves to make only innocuous remarks, such as 'the confrere has a habit of swinging his tassel' or 'the confrere makes rude noises eating his porridge.' They had also agreed that no one would ever make a remark about a confrere more senior than himself.

Enter the new Director intent on reform and a new batch

of uncontaminated Scholastics fresh from the Novitiate, and the stage was set for a confrontation between the Director and the older Philosophers. Engagement did not occur immediately, however. The first few weeks of Chapter proceeded in traditional fashion: the senior men commented harmlessly about their juniors and the juniors made similar comments about their juniors. The newly arrived, the most junior of all, bore the brunt of the remarks, all of which, however, were trivial. The Director railed in vain each week against the insignificance of the remarks being made. Rules were being ignored and silence was being broken, he thundered from the rostrum. Why were those serious faults not being brought to the attention of the guilty? The older men paid him no mind, but they grew extremely nervous as the time for the new men's turn approached.

Since our arrival we had acquired a reputation as strict observers of the Rule. So the older men warned us at recreation not to break with tradition: we must make only innocuous remarks and confine them to the members of our own year. To us this pressure was unfair and contrary to the concept of holy obedience that the Master had inculcated in the Novitiate. So when one Tuesday night our turn came and the Director demanded, in the name of Holy Obedience, that we do our duty and point out the faults of those who committed them, each new Philosopher stood when his name was called and, almost to a man, pointed out a significant fault committed by a more senior Philosopher.

The result was quiet pandemonium. The Director was pleased. Those whose faults had been called out were furious. Most of the older men were annoyed. We new men felt justified, even sanctimonious. But the consequences were serious. For weeks after that particular Chapter a sense of crisis hung over the

126

House of Philosophy. A small number of older Philosophers were rude to the new men, paid even less attention to the rules, and shortly thereafter disappeared. Eight Philosophers left in a single month. As in the Novitiate, no official announcement was made about their departure.

Some of the older men blamed us new fellows for their leaving. The departed were good lads, they said, who had been hounded out by the new Director, abetted by overly zealous newcomers who didn't yet understand the Kimmage Zeitgeist. The newcomers needed to take it easy, they admonished; later, when we became a little tarry we'd fit better into the community. The older men labeled us 'strict observers,' and dubbed as 'pallbearers' those who sported sober expressions of piety.

Scholasticate Life

Getting Started

The Chapter crisis took place against a backdrop of serious intellectual studies. On arrival in Kimmage we were assigned to take philosophy classes either in Kimmage, called Home Philosophy, or at University College, Dublin. I and four others were assigned to the University. However, since those classes didn't commence till mid-October and Home Philosophy classes started at the beginning of September, we were ordered to attend the latter classes in the meantime.

On the morning of our first Home Philosophy lecture we were assembled in a classroom when the professor, a pale young priest sporting a wooden expression, walked in, strode to the rostrum and, without so much as a glance at us, commenced, poker-faced, to lecture on Greek philosophy, in Latin. To the amusement-turned-consternation of his students, who thought at first that he was joking, he continued the lecture in Latin for forty-five minutes. We had all taken five years of Latin classes in secondary school so none were unfamiliar with the language.

128

However, we were not yet able to understand an introduction-to-philosophy lecture delivered in the official tongue of Holy Mother Church. We learned later that the professor had no choice of language: the Vatican had decreed that all philosophy and theology courses in seminaries were to be delivered in Latin.

A week after Home Philosophy classes started, the Director told me to report to Blackrock College, a secondary school run by the Congregation in Dublin, to fill in as a substitute teacher until the University opened. As Holy Obedience dictated, I said 'yes, Father,' although I had never taught a class in my life nor had I ever received any teacher training. So for a month, until the University opened, I stumbled through, teaching classes in English and Latin to first year students whose parents were paying significant fees for the privilege.

In mid-October University classes began. On the morning of opening day we Scholastics who were assigned to attend – in subjects ranging from English and Classics to Philosophy and Biology – donned black suits and black hats, fastened the ends of our trousers with bicycle clips or, if we didn't have clips, tucked our trouser ends into our socks, mounted our Kimmage bicycles, and pedaled forth, in twos, to one of the great centers of Irish learning, located in the city center four miles away.

The Kimmage Bike

Over the years a number of bicycles, mostly second-hand, had been donated by mission-conscious people for the use of Scholastics. By the time I arrived in Kimmage in 1957 those cycles were an aging set of machines that their riders said, only half jokingly, were held together by prayer, candle-grease, and string. Scholastic bike functionaries did their best to keep them in repair and somehow or other, though not without many a forced walk home due to break-downs, the bikes managed to transport Scholastics to and from the University.

There were other bikes in the shed in addition to the Kimmage crocks; machines that were much admired and not a little envied. Those were private bicycles, loaned by parents to their Scholastic sons for their sole use. Private bikes were mostly sleek new machines, complete with multiple gears – Kimmage bikes had only one gear – saddle covers, and lamps. How this practice accorded with the community vow of poverty was never questioned or explained.

Special rules were laid down for Scholastic cyclists. The dress code demanded that we always wear black suits in place of the soutanes and cinctures that were our normal in-house garb. Hats were de rigueur: a Philosopher who was reported seen outside the Scholasticate not wearing his black hat was subject to a severe admonishing by the Director. An even more serious reprimand awaited the culprit should he be reported to the Archbishop for committing such an egregious offence: his Grace required that all clergy in his diocese wear appropriate dress in public on all occasions, including hats. Fortunately for the Kimmage miscreants who were occasionally sighted *sans chapeaux* and reported to his Grace, the reporting spy was never able to identify them by name, so the reprimand delivered to the Kimmage Superior was diffused-diluted among all the bike-riders of the Scholasticate. Other breaches of the clerical dress code were equally frowned on and duly noted. On one occasion, a Kimmage Scholastic was reported to the AB – as the Archbishop was, not so affectionately, known – for cycling through the center of Dublin with trouser ends tucked inside yellow socks. The shock waves of his Grace's anger over that outrage reverberated throughout Kimmage during a whole week of chuckles. Happily

130

the culprit was never identified; no doubt he jettisoned the offending socks via the toilet or other safe method of evidence disposal.

Kimmage applied additional rules to Scholastics attending the University. We were permitted to attend only those lectures in which we were enrolled. We were not to dally after lectures ended but were to return immediately to the Scholasticate. We ought not engage in lengthy conversations with other students, even with those – the majority in philosophy lectures – who belonged to seminaries or other religious Orders. Under no circumstances were we to talk to persons of female persuasion. And we were to ride to and from the University in pairs.

Observance of the latter rule wasn't always possible because of lecture schedules. Once when returning solo to Kimmage after morning lectures I saw Marjorie, who lived in the neighborhood of Kimmage, coming towards me on the sidewalk, accompanied by her mother. The shock – for a moment I thought I must be hallucinating – almost cost me my balance. I had not seen her since I went to the Novitiate, and my commitment to God prevented me from even voluntarily thinking about her. With the passage of time and the intensity of my new life she had been slowly fading from my thoughts. But the sight of her now, so close that I could reach out and touch her, sent feelings sweeping over me that I had thought consigned to the dustbin of memory. My whole being cried out to greet her, even though I was aware that the Rule forbade it. I quickly argued with myself that to stop and say hello would be the Christian thing to do, that even the Rule couldn't supersede the law of charity. She, however, was engrossed in conversation with her mother and didn't see me. The almost-encounter was over in seconds as I pedaled by, continuing to argue in favor of saying hello. For weeks afterwards I felt emotionally traumatized. I never saw her again.

131

University Classes

Nothing in my intellectual life heretofore had prepared me
for the study of philosophy. In all the reading I had undertaken as
a member of Firinne I never delved into this most arcane of
subjects. During the week that I attended the Home Philosophy
classes I was too engrossed in trying to understand the professors'
Latin to pay much attention to their subject matter. So the initial
philosophy lectures in English at the University – on Metaphysics
and Cosmology – were to me and my confreres a bewildering
jumble of meaningless words and expressions. We'd cycle back
to Kimmage after lectures astounded, wondering out loud if we'd
ever comprehend such abstruse subject matter. The lectures in
Logic, on the other hand, which was also a new and challenging
subject, were intelligible, as were those in Ethics and Politics and
Psychology.

As First Arts students we had to take courses in English
and Latin as well. The English course was delightful, and I and
my Kimmage confreres relished it. We particularly enjoyed a
young lecturer named Denis Donoghue, who was new to the
faculty. Classical Latin, however, was a different matter.
Professor O'Meara informed us on the first day of class that
passing his exam in Latin at the end of the year was a requirement
in order to continue on to Second Arts. Having got our full
attention with that statement, he informed us that in the previous
year more than fifty percent of those who took his Latin class had
failed. However, there was an alternative to taking that very
rigorous Classical Latin class: those who felt they might be
somewhat weak in the subject could opt for a simpler course that
dealt with Roman History. That course, he added with a touch of
disparagement, which was also known as 'Baby-Latin,' was

132

conducted in English.' But by passing it, Arts students would satisfy the requirement to pass in Latin, and thus be able to continue into Second Arts. Terrified by the Professor's grim warning, more than a hundred and fifty of the two hundred or so students present, including my Kimmage confreres, opted for 'Baby Latin.' Since I had grown to love the language in secondary school I took my chances with the Classical Latin class.

Food

I had always found that preoccupation with food leaped to the forefront of my attention whenever its sapor was insipid. I enjoyed home cooking because, though the ingredients were plain, my mother managed to make tasty meals after we left Grandpa's farm. I was food-obsessed at boarding school and in the Novitiate because in both institutions the quality of the food was significantly less than my mother's cooking. And in the Scholasticate it became an obsession again. But whereas in the Novitiate we were forbidden to discuss the subject, in the Scholasticate we weren't. So in Kimmage food was the subject of much critical discourse. It wasn't that the food was unwholesome or insufficient: we had three substantial meals a day as well as an afternoon snack. But the cuisine was unappetizing and the menu rarely varied. For breakfast there was porridge followed by a boiled egg, bread, butter, and tea. During the winter months fried bread – thick slices deep fried in beef fat – replaced everything except the tea and porridge. Lunch-dinner consisted of potatoes, meat, and vegetables, the latter steamed too much, the former – meat was always beef except on feast-days – boiled to death. The only dessert that was popular was a bread pudding with raisins and served with hot custard. Afternoon snack was bread, butter, and tea. Supper consisted of more bread and butter and either an egg or cheese. I looked forward to feast days more because of tastier meals – chicken for dinner and a creamy dessert – than because of any spiritual gain.

Our meals were prepared in a huge kitchen presided over by an imperious lay Brother and cooked by a lay chef and staff. The chef was a Dublin wag who was much given to malapropisms: he worked in the cemetery up in Kimmage; at mass he sat in the transcript; he loved the Mozarts on the walls; once when he broke his arm 'they plastered me Paris'. On feast days the Brother gave him a bottle of sherry to use in cooking; once when I was on kitchen duty I spotted him putting equal swigs in the pan and down his throat.

The menu for the 'Fathers' – the Directors of Philosophers and Theologians and members of the teaching staff, was quite different from that of the Scholastics. Their food was cooked in a separate kitchen by a different chef and was more varied than ours. But the Director never explained how such a difference could be harmonized with our common vow of poverty.

Meals were conducted in silence except when a colloquium – permission to speak – was granted by the presiding priest on some special occasion, as when a visiting missionary joined the Fathers' table. Dinner and supper were accompanied by the reading of a spiritual biography or other pious work, Dinner reading always concluded with the reading of the day's entry from the Roman Martyrology – the official listing of the Church's saints – which always ended with the sentence that was forever engraved in my memory: *et alibi, aliorum plurimorum sanctorum, martyrum et confessorum, atque sanctarum virginum.* Which may be translated as "and elsewhere many other saints, martyrs and confessors, and holy virgins."

134

Intellectual and Spiritual Life

Indolence was not permitted in Kimmage. Our days were taken up with prayer – totaling about four hours – classes, study, spiritual conferences, compulsory recreation. And sleep, of which we were allowed seven hours and fifty minutes per night. There was never enough time for study. Philosophy classes at the University consisted of forty-five minute lectures, delivered without opportunity for questions or discussion. And while there was a lot of required reading on each subject there were no course textbooks, so students had to take copious notes. My handwriting, never great, deteriorated so much under the pressure that I was scarcely able to read my notes afterwards. Since those notes contained most of the future exam material, I re-wrote them on return to the Scholasticate.

The Kimmage library was inadequately stocked with the books we were expected to read, so we requested others from a city Central Library, a request that could take a week or more to fill since the Scholastic librarian was allowed to visit that library on Saturdays only. Once, when I had the Central Librarian function, my list included a request from the Director for Simone de Beauvoir's *The Second Sex,* which had been published several years earlier. When I delivered the book, the Director sheepishly told me that despite the provocative title it was a serious work that people in his position needed to read. However, he admonished, I was not to mention to any of the Scholastics that their Director had borrowed it lest its title scandalize them.

It had taken my confreres and me most of the first term to even begin to understand what philosophy was all about. When we finally did we relished the subject and discussed its complex problems with each other. I loved the intellectual challenges presented, and devoted as much time to their study as religious

135

duties made available. But I never thought about transferring to my religious faith the rigorous logical thinking that philosophy imposed in discussing its problems. Faith – intellectual assent to what could not be proved rationally – governed my religious beliefs, and faith required that those beliefs never be questioned. When proofs from philosophy were applied to matters of faith, as they were regarding the existence of God and the immortality of the soul, I accepted those 'proofs' without challenge, since they simply corroborated what my faith already taught.

High Mass, perhaps the most resplendent of all Catholic ceremonies, was celebrated every Sunday in the Scholasticate chapel. It was conducted by members of the House of Theology, with full attention to liturgy and rubrics. Fourth year students, who had been ordained priests at the end of their third year, took the parts of celebrant, deacon and subdeacon; the lesser functions were performed by other Theologians. A rehearsal was conducted during the week to ensure that all were properly prepared. Participants took every rubric seriously, for this was the worship of God. They also knew that any gaffe committed would not only be subject to reprimand by their Director, but might also be the topic of Scholastic amusement. Nevertheless, there were mistakes and Scholasticate chuckles, as in the case of the celebrant who couldn't sing. Father Gus was tone deaf and, unable to pick up his note from the organ, 'sang' his part in an off-key monotone. The initial reaction from the Scholastics was smiles, but chuckles soon became audible as his 'singing' continued, then guffaws, accompanied by body movements as Scholastics bent over in agonies of mirth. Even members of the staff were seen to smile.

Not all who laughed were themselves warblers of note,

Third row, second from left, with Kimmage Choir

though all were expected to sing at liturgical functions. The Scholasticate had three recognized categories of singers. The 'common man' comprised the largest and least musical body, and was composed of all who didn't qualify for either of the special categories; they sang, or rather bellowed, the 'common' sections of the High Mass in Gregorian chant. The second category was the choir, a select group of Philosophers and Theologians who practiced twice a week during evening recreation and sang multi-part harmony or polyphony at some High Masses and on other special occasions. The *schola cantorum*, the third category, was the elite group; its specialty was singing the 'proper' parts of the High Mass in Gregorian chant. I was inordinately proud of being part of this group, especially since other Scholastics who I knew were much better singers than I were not included.

Periodically, the Director met with each Philosopher individually to discuss the latter's progress. Unlike such sessions with the Novice Master, the Director of Philosophy did not discuss our spiritual progress with us: that function belonged to the Spiritual Director, whom we chose individually from among the priests on the staff and retired missionaries. The session with the Director was known as 'going on direction,' and Scholastics did not look forward to it. The Director, to put it mildly, was not much liked by us, for we felt that he regarded us as enemies to be conquered rather than trainees to be coached. So those sessions were, for most, jousts to be endured and survived with as little damage as possible. Jack, an otherwise fervent Scholastic, regaled us on recreation with a description of his latest 'direction' encounter. In his telling it went somewhat like this:

Director:	*Mr. Doyle, how would you describe your attitude to the Rule?* The Director's hawk-like eyes staring without blinking at the Scholastic.
Jack:	Trying hard not to make eye contact. *I think I'm observing the Rule to the best of my ability, Father.*
Director:	Making a note. *How are you doing with your studies?*
Jack:	Sounding positive, even friendly. *Oh, I'm studying very hard, Father. Very hard indeed.*
Director:	Picking up a pencil and running his fingers along it. *How do you feel about those who habitually flout the Rule?*
Jack:	Feigning bewilderment. *What do you mean, Father?*
Director:	Holding the pencil by the ends and turning it slowly, while fixing his gaze on the Scholastic's face. *You know and I know that a few Scholastics*

138

	are deliberately flouting the Rule in many areas.
Jack:	Lowering his head, speaking to his lap. *No, Father, I don't know anyone who is deliberately flouting the Rule.*
Director:	Spinning the pencil between his fingers. *But don't you agree that, for instance, some Scholastics habitually make light of the rule of silence?*
Jack:	For the first time looking at the Director. *No, Father, I don't think any Scholastics are making light of the rule of silence.* Holds the Director's eye defiantly.
Director:	*I see.* Puts down the pencil, picks up a pen and writes on his pad. *Do you sometimes take steps not to go on recreation with confreres you don't particularly like?*
Jack:	Feigning shock. *Absolutely not, Father.* Shifts in his chair. *I like everyone.*
Director:	Putting down the pen and staring at the Scholastic. *And you feel you are making good progress with your studies?*
Jack:	Looking the Director in the eye again. *Yes, Father, I'm making good progress with my studies.*

"I swear the fecker was trying to hypnotize me with the bloody pencil," Jack concluded.

I chose as my spiritual director a wonderful old man who was retired from the African missions, a pillar of common sense that I so needed at the time: I was still a victim to Scruples, constantly worrying about the sinfulness of impure thoughts that were impossible to keep at bay even in the monastic sex-vacuum of the Scholasticate. I endured mental torture every morning as

139

Communion time approached. On more than one occasion after the start of mass I bolted to the confessional at the back of the chapel, where a priest was always on call, no doubt for the express purpose of alleviating the anguish of scrupulous Scholastics like me. Father Phil, my spiritual director, helped to ease somewhat the burden of my scruples. When I told him of my fears he asked, "were you ever tempted to run away with a woman?" Which made me laugh, for no such thought had ever entered my head, not even after that almost-meeting with Marjorie. He was making the point that if I wasn't tempted to abscond from the Scholasticate with a woman I didn't have any real sexual problems. Though that gave me short-term solace it didn't rid me of Scruples.

Holidays

Visits

Christmas brought a respite from studies: we had a week away from the University and free time to go on walks and engage in visits outside the Scholasticate. Since my brother Seamus was still living in Dublin, I wrote to him in advance advising that I could visit him the day after Christmas. We met at a restaurant: he was living in digs since my parents went to America. I, who had roamed the city so freely on my bike for years, now felt like a bird released from its cage – but with a string attached to make sure I returned.

Seeing Seamus again combined pleasure with nostalgia. In age just a year apart, we had always been very close, played together, fought each other, went to school together, and enjoyed the same music and films and sports. Though I refrained from asking, he told me now about current events. I particularly remember him telling me about the popular new American phenomenon, Elvis Presley, whose music had just arrived on the Irish scene. Elvis the pelvis, they called him, Seamus said. We had a delightful afternoon together, but I was saddened when he told me that he'd soon be heading for New York; he'd be leaving next month. There was no future for him here, he felt, and he missed the family. But he promised to come back periodically to visit me. He kept that promise.

We had permission to visit relatives or friends at Easter as well. By then Seamus had emigrated to New York so I visited an old friend from Firinne. Ernie had recently married and he and his wife exuded an aura of sacredness about their new state, a radiance that I attributed to the extraordinary sanctity with which they regarded Christian marriage. They treated me with the kind of reverence that Irish people usually reserved for priests. Renewing acquaintance with my friend brought back memories of my life as a member of Firinne. But just memories: I no longer felt the fervor that I once had for propagating the Divine Plan for Social Order. Kilshane and Kimmage had re-focused my life towards personal and priestly sanctity.

Scholastics were permitted to receive visitors once a month on a Sunday afternoon in the parlor of the Old House. Not long after Easter my favorite relative, Aunt Mary, paid a visit. Married to my Uncle Walter, my father's eldest brother who was also my godfather, she was his second wife – the first having died, leaving him with three young children. Aunt Mary had two children from her marriage to my uncle. As a boy I had spent several summers at their home, where Aunt Mary always made me feel part of the family; so much so that I had come to look on her as a second mother after my family went to America. She wrote regularly to me in Kimmage and sent me cakes for all occasions – she was an outstanding cook, having taught home economics in a girls' school during her early years as a nun. Meeting her in the parlor brought back memories of an earlier happy life, as well as twinges of regret that the life I had known then was gone forever. Aunt Mary reminisced about our Saturday evening trips to Tuam to do

At right, with Uncle Walter, Aunt Mary, and family, 1947

grocery shopping, a routine that was both delightful and invariable. Uncle Walter would drive us to town in his Ford. In Tuam he would disappear to a pub after arranging with Aunt Mary to be back at a certain hour. She and I would walk to the Mercy Convent to visit my father's sister, Mother Carmel, Aunt Mary taking with her a basket of eggs to give to the nuns. We'd be greeted like long-lost children by Mother Carmel, the eggs would be sent to the kitchen, and the guests ushered into the parlor where the gossip between Aunt Mary and Mother Carmel would flow like drink at a wedding. A young nun would look in the door and ask if we'd like a spot of tea, Mother Carmel would say of course they would, the nun would vanish and return in a few minutes with a tray containing china, a pot of tea, and slices of cake. Mother Carmel would do the honors, and I would be urged to have several pieces of cake while the women continued to chat. As soon as we finished Mother Carmel would stand to indicate the visit was over and Aunt Mary and I would walk across the convent grounds to the Cathedral where we'd go to confession. Then we'd shop for the groceries and return to the car, where we'd have to wait for Uncle Walter, who on returning would look happy and, though not inebriated, would be much more loquacious than was normal for that taciturn man.

Aunt Mary's visit to the Scholasticate ended, like every visit I ever had with her, with her tears flowing as if we'd never meet again. She promised she'd come back to see me soon again. Which she did, despite the hundred and forty mile trip by train: she did not drive and Uncle Walter was set in his ways, which ways didn't include driving to Dublin to visit his priest-in-the-making godson.

Summer Activities

Summer came and with it an end to classes. My confreres and I passed First Arts exams. Kimmage swung into holiday mode in which recreation periods were lengthened, the Philosophy swimming pool was opened, and we had a sports day that included a slew of track and field events. There were outings to the strand at Portmarnock, which brought new temptations to chastity: young women in bathing suits seemed to be everywhere we looked, and custody of the eyes was never more difficult.

The second Sunday in July was Ordination Sunday. Theologians who had completed their third year of studies became priests on that day. Ordinations took place in the Chapel of the Dublin diocesan seminary at Clonliffe College, to which we were not invited. I wondered why Holy Orders were not conferred on our fellow Scholastics in the Kimmage Chapel, since our conferes comprised most of the ordinands that day. It appeared that the Archbishop, himself a former Holy Ghost Father, chose not to do so, thereby depriving Scholastics of the joyful experience of seeing our fellows achieve the goal we all aspired to. As it was, we Philosophers were scarcely aware that this was Ordination Sunday: the Director did not inform us, and we were alerted to the event only on noting that the third-year Theologians were missing from morning prayers.

Ordination day in my first year in Kimmage was memorable for a sad event. Despite the invisible wall of separation between the two Houses of Study, Philosophers heard around midday that one of the Theologians scheduled for ordination that morning was not allowed to go forward. He suffered what was called 'a nervous breakdown' the previous night and was declared by his Director to be unfit for ordination. We speculated on what would happen to him next, and soon found out. Since he had been ordained a sub-deacon, which carried with it the obligation of perpetual celibacy, he could never be reduced – in Vatican-speak – to the lay state. So, never after declared fit for ordination, he remained in the Scholasticate, in a twilight zone between Scholastic and priest, maintained by the Congregation but never permitted to leave legitimately. He was not the only confrere in that predicament: soon after arriving in Kimmage I noticed a much older man seated among the Theologians in the refectory. He, too, had once been a Scholastic en route to ordination, but for some reason was not ordained a priest after receiving the orders of sub-Diaconate and Diaconate. Those two men were grim reminders of what could happen to any Scholastic on his way to the priesthood.

It had been customary to allow Scholastics to spend the month of August at home with their families. The arrangement was deemed good for Scholastics and their families, and it saved Kimmage the cost of supporting us for the month. The Vatican, however, decided that henceforth it would be dangerous for

Scholastics to be let loose in the bosom of their families. Young religious, for their spiritual welfare at this precarious stage of formation, must from now on take vacations in their Scholasticates, or in some other religious house. Fortunately for us first-year Philosophers, our religious superiors dared to allow common sense supersede Vatican regulations and decreed that those who hadn't a vacation last year should be allowed to spend the month of August this year with their families. I, since my family was too far away – Congregation largesse did not extend to a vacation in New York – was permitted to spend the month with my second family, Aunt Mary and Uncle Walter. I wrote and got their permission, and took the train to Galway on the first day of August, 1958.

During the first week I felt a stranger to a milieu that was now foreign to me. For two years I had been confined to religious institutions. Brainwashed during the first year, and subjected to full monastic discipline during the second, it took me some time to readjust to a world inhabited by non-monks. However, my relatives' placid acceptance of the black-suited, Roman-collared cleric among them eased my re-entry into that world. I became a member of the family again. Aunt Mary remarked that she and I would be deprived of a pleasure we both used to enjoy, that of breakfast in bed – she of presenting, I of receiving. Since I was not dispensed from my spiritual exercises while on holidays, I had to rise early to go to mass. Indeed, morning prayer, meditation, mass and thanksgiving, were to be performed in the local church every morning. Particular Examen, the rosary, and the Little Office, as well as spiritual reading and night prayer, had also to be fitted in with each day's activities. "You don't cease to be Scholastics when you are on holidays," the Director had lectured us before we left.

A neighboring parish priest came to visit my uncle one Sunday evening. They were old friends, and they settled down in the parlor with a bottle of whiskey and chatted for several hours. I sat with them because I was invited to, though I didn't take part in either conversation or whiskey. Part of their discourse went something like this:

Uncle Walter: I suppose you heard that Jack Mangan died.

Parish Priest: I did, the poor man. I heard the sad news an hour after he died. The sister rang to tell me. He was young, the Lord have mercy on him. I knew himself and the mother well when I was a ladeen.

Uncle Walter: He wasn't that young, mind you. Sixty four, they said. Over in Cloughkane the mother lived, wasn't it?

Parish Priest: Ah no, no. They used to live in Cloughkane all right. You see, the mother married into a house and land there. But when Jack's father died didn't he leave the place to a nephew: he had a falling out with Jack and the mother, you see. Something to do with a girl Jack was courting, they said. The nephew was a young man, too, when he died. Killed by a bull, no less, gored to death when he went into the field his own bull was in.

Uncle Walter: I always say you can't be too careful with bulls. They'll turn on you in a minute no matter how well you think you know them.

Parish Priest: They will. They will indeed. Anyway, Jack and the mother had to go and live in Ballycurran with the mother's sister who was a spinster and had got the place from their father when he died. She was the only one left at home at the time, you see. The

> *brothers had all gone to England.*
> *Uncle Walter:* *But wasn't that a terrible thing to do? Putting his own wife and child out of house and home like that. I hadn't heard of it before, mind you.*
> *Parish Priest:* *There was great ri-ra over it at the time, God help us. Jack took the nephew to court claiming he exercised undue influence over his father. The case got great coverage in the Western People.*
> *Uncle Walter:* *Faith, it didn't make it into the Tuam Herald or I'd have seen it. I suppose that's why I never heard of the row.*
> *Parish Priest:* *Newspapers are funny like that. You'd have to read all of them to get all the news. I remember one time ......*

The conversation went on like that for hours. They discussed who in the parish was related to whom, who got married recently and to whom, who died and what land they left to whom. Uncle and priest knew everyone in all the parishes around, and they discussed not only the living but also their ancestors, and they discussed people's successes and failures and those of their kin. There was no malice or backbiting in the conversation: felonies and misdeeds were talked about with the same dispassionate calm as were stories of wealth and good fortune. It seemed that persons, their lives and their fates, were the only topics of interest to both priest and farmer. Not for them discussions of philosophy or theology or morality or politics. Life and those who were living it and those who had left it, were their subjects of discussion.

But neither God nor religion were ever explicitly mentioned: Irish people of their generation, though they were considered by the world to be the most religious of people, never discussed religion directly in their everyday conversation. Even in Kimmage where we were religious by profession, we Scholastics never exposed to each other our personal feelings in relation to Jesus or Mary or the Blessed Trinity; we talked about them in the abstract as budding theologians, but never in a personal way. We treated our relationships with the Deity somewhat like sexual relationships: private and personal and not to be aired in public. Or perhaps as if we understood that our God was a very private God who didn't want to acknowledge to others His friendship with us.

Two More Years

Second Year

All too soon vacation ended and I was back in Kimmage and immersed in the routine of Scholastic life. At the beginning of September the new first-year men arrived from the Novitiate and my class became second-year Philosophers. The Chapter of Faults was abolished, quietly, without announcement: it had been halted after the earlier crisis and was never convened again. Our secretive Director continued to give the impression that he didn't trust us to understand any difficult decisions he made, or even to behave as professed religious unless he continually prodded us on. And he obviously felt that we must be protected against the world: we never got any news of what was happening outside our monastic enclave. Because of this seclusion we remained oblivious to momentous happenings in the world beyond. We heard nothing about the Boeing 707 jet airplane that commenced service, or the birth of Barbie Doll, or the coming to power of Fidel Castro in Cuba, or Cypress gaining its independence from Britain, or Nixon and Khrushchev debating in the kitchen, or the

150

Dalai Lama fleeing Tibet, or The Sound of Music opening on Broadway, or IBM shipping its first transistor-based computer, or Xerox its first copier, or Charles De Gaulle returning to power as President of France. Our Director also chose with great care the occasional films he permitted us: one of the conditions of suitability seemed to be that it contain no female characters.

My mother wrote – she was a sporadic letter writer – to tell me that my sister Mary had married. Later she informed me that she was planning to come over in the summer and that I was to rent a car for the month of August. At this time I had never driven a car and didn't know how. Brother Tom came to visit at Christmas; he was now working for Aer Lingus in New York and had free travel privileges. I was permitted to spend an afternoon and evening with him, and when he took me for a drive in his rented car he gave me a half-hour driving lesson before treating me to dinner at the Gresham. He also introduced me to the family of his fiancée in Ringsend, an introduction I was to value a few years later.

On the University front, I fell ever more deeply in love with philosophy and philosophers from Zeno to Ayer and, since there were no exams at the end of Second Arts, I was able to focus on understanding philosophical concepts rather than on cramming exam material.

Then it was summer again and the end of the school year. When vacation time came round, we second-year Philosophers were told we wouldn't be allowed home this year: as required by Vatican decree we were to be sent to another house of the Congregation for the month of August, where we could relax and renew our spiritual energies while remaining protected from the pernicious influences of family life. In panic I went to the Director and explained that my mother whom I hadn't seen for two and a half years was coming all the way from New York to visit me. To my surprise and delight, the Director displayed a hitherto hidden streak of humanity and allowed that I could spend the month of August with my mother.

She arrived in Dublin on the first of the month. I managed to rent a car. However, fearing that if the rental people saw my efforts at driving from the lot they might not allow me to leave, I arranged for them to deliver the car to Tom's future in-laws house, where my mother was staying. On the second of August we put our luggage in the boot, said our prayers and, lurching and stalling and bucking and braking as I tried to balance clutch and pedal, left the city and drove a hundred and sixty miles across the country to Castlebar, the town of my birth. I was terrified throughout the journey and would gladly have abandoned the car, while my mother sat as calmly in the passenger seat as if I were an experienced driver in whom she placed perfect trust.

She had arranged that we'd stay with her sister-in-law who owned a shop in the town. Margaret welcomed us warmly and took good care of us. Unfortunately for me, both she and my mother wanted to tour the beautiful west coast of Mayo and Galway and I was their designated chauffeur. Heart in mouth and with many a bounce and not a few stalls I drove them through some of the most gorgeous scenery in Ireland. Though, with my eyes glued to some of the worst roads in the country, I didn't get to see much scenery myself. Mother and aunt enjoyed the tour, however, seeming oblivious to the constant danger they were in as they rounded hairpin bends and drove along cliff edges in the not-at-all capable hands of their novice driver. Only once did they poke a little fun at my ineptitude – when returning to Castlebar after a day's outing and we found ourselves at the end of a long funeral procession. I was driving well until we came within a couple of miles of Castlebar, at which point traffic slowed to stop-and-go mode. As I still hadn't mastered the pedal-clutch maneuver, each time I had to pick up speed I managed to make the car kick and stall like a bucking bronco in a cowboy film.

The church in Castlebar was about a mile away from my aunt's house so I drove there each morning for mass and communion. The street by the church was narrow and cars were parked on either side. One morning on my way home I made an error of judgment and grazed the end of another car, smashing one of its rear lights as well as the front light of my rental. In panic I drove on and didn't inspect the damage to my car till I arrived at my aunt's house. One headlight was hanging loose and had to be repaired, the cost of which my mother had to pay. I discovered later that the car I hit belonged to the parish priest of Castlebar. But I didn't own up to my guilt: apparently religiosity and honesty didn't necessarily go hand in hand.

At the end of August we drove back to Dublin without incident and my mother returned to New York. I went back to Kimmage and discovered that my vacation was tame compared to what my second-year confreres had enjoyed at Blackrock College. Those young men, who hitherto had been noted for sober piety and strict adherence to Rule, had apparently transmogrified during the month of August into loud-laughing fellows who showed little regard for Rule or monastic reserve. Their innate high spirits, suppressed for three years in Novitiate and Scholasticate, suddenly broke free in the holiday atmosphere. I gathered, from the tidbits of information they released over the next month about their near-bacchanalian behavior, that they had eschewed the vacation rules set down by the Director, leaving the premises at will without permission, and accepting money from their families, which they used to visit places and buy things and see films that the Rule did not allow. Scholastics were even seen sneaking into the College after midnight. But all was done so

153

surreptitiously that the Director did not become aware of their nefarious activities till the end of the month.

Third Year

During my third year in the House of Philosophy I had to focus on two life-changing events, final University exams and taking perpetual vows. University lectures ended in June and exams for Honor degrees were scheduled for September, leaving students the entire summer to prepare for them. I had done very well at my philosophy studies and was being confidently tipped by my confreres for first-class honors. However, the three months study time was theoretical only since other events would significantly disrupt the period.

The three-year temporary vows that my confreres and I took before leaving Kilshane would expire in September. Most Scholastics were asked to renew them for another three years while a few, including myself, were offered the 'privilege' of taking perpetual vows in September. I accepted the offer because I felt sure of my vocation, and also for another reason. The next step for most Scholastics was two or three years teaching in one of the Congregation's secondary schools, but because I was considered a late vocation – twenty-one on entering the Novitiate – I was allowed to skip the teaching and to go straight to the House of Theology. As a result, in less than three years I'd be eligible for ordination. Since I'd have to have taken perpetual vows in order to be ordained, I needed to take those vows now: for some reason vows had to be taken at three-year intervals.

To prepare for the step of taking for life the vows of poverty, chastity, and obedience, Scholastics were obliged to undertake a thirty-day retreat during July. Father Mac, an experienced missionary, was appointed to conduct the retreat. Ah, Father Mac! Our superiors must have considered him a holy man to assign him to that exacting task. And he spouted all the correct spiritual jargon to inspire us young religious with the fervor we needed to shoulder the burden of perpetual vows. However, the good priest seemed obsessed with sex, or rather with the fear of it. He slid quickly through the material dealing with the vows of poverty and obedience, and his primary focus for the greater part of those thirty days was on chastity and the dangers we'd encounter in preserving our vow. He told us lurid stories of priests who seduced, and were seduced by, sirens masquerading as pious women. Since none of his hearers had any first hand acquaintance with such femmes fatales we found the stories simply funny and titillating, but too remote from our life experiences to be what Father Mac intended: sober warnings of what lay in store for us.

When the retreat ended we were permitted a holiday with our families. I spent August again with my uncle and aunt in Galway. Cousin Marian, for whom I had a strong brotherly affection, was home on holidays and we spent a good deal of time together: we rigged up a net on the front lawn to play tennis and spent hours discussing Irish and American politics. At the end of August I returned to Kimmage, took perpetual vows, and settled in to spend the two remaining weeks cramming for final University exams. Then the strain, of taking vows and worrying about exams, caused me to almost lose my mental equilibrium.

I was unaware of the nature of stress and how it could affect my life. One night I went to bed as usual after a day of intense study, fell asleep as usual, but woke shortly after in a state of physical and mental turmoil. I felt I wanted to climb out of my body but couldn't, undergoing what I later believed was a panic attack, though at the time I didn't know what was happening.

Getting out of bed I stumbled into the corridor and jumped up and down in an effort to expel whatever demon was causing me such distress. When the agitation persisted I felt a need to get immediate help before I lost my mind, so I went to the door of my friend Noel to wake him. My hand was raised to knock when I stopped. Above the cacophony of panic a voice told me that if I sought help now for my predicament I'd be declared unfit to continue my path to the priesthood. Recollection of the theologian who was overcame the night before ordination brought instant fear that I'd join him as a permanent Scholastic: I had, after all, just taken perpetual vows. I retreated to my room.

Eventually, the disorienting feelings passed and I was able to return to bed and sleep. But the effects of that night remained with me for years. I suffered panic attacks without warning on numerous occasions, attacks that I learned to suppress. Though I couldn't restrain them entirely. For years to come I, who had hitherto never feared heights, dared not stand near a precipice or ledge for fear of jumping off. Worse was my inability to control a tremor in my voice whenever an attack came on while I was engaged in public reading or speaking. As a Theologian I had to take my turn reading night prayers for the community in the chapel and reading from the refectory rostrum during meals. I was never able to perform those duties without a tremor shaking my voice. I feared that my superiors would notice my distress and try to determine the cause. They never did.

In the final University exams – we were tested on the last two years of work with fifteen hours of essay-writing papers – I didn't do as well as expected, receiving only second-class honors. However, by the time the results came out I was already in the House of Theology and didn't much care: I had gone from an extremely repressive environment to a far more liberal one.

Walter Keady

The graduate, 1960

Faith Seeking Understanding

Father Mick

Moving from the House of Philosophy to the House of Theology was not supposed to involve any change in the observance of monastic discipline. It was considered to be simply another step on the road to the priesthood and the missionary life. Two years earlier the step would have been just that for me: the then Director of Theologians was an austere man who imposed a severe discipline on his charges. But he had been replaced the previous year by Father Mick, a jolly man called home from his mission in Africa to become the new Director.

Stories about Father Mick's more relaxed attitude had already been transmitted to the House of Philosophy in the mysterious way that news is conveyed when official channels are blocked. So it was with more than a little relief that I carried my few belongings down stairs, across hallways, and up stairs, to my new room on the Theologians' side of the Scholasticate. The

158

change in the social and emotional atmosphere was startling. The Director of Philosophers had created a climate of serious joylessness and stress. Being called to his office was generally the occasion for a panicky examination of recent behavior, since the dread invitation usually meant the Director had become aware of some rule infraction by the person summoned. The Theologians' Director, on the other hand, exuded cheerfulness and good will, and a visit to his office was usually a happy event. More often than not it would begin with the Director leaning confidentially across his desk and saying, "I'd like you to do something for me."

Father Mick used the words of Pope John XXIII when he said, repeatedly, that he wanted to "open a few windows and let in some fresh air" in the House of Theology. One extraordinary change he instituted was that of making a daily newspaper available to us. Outside his office where two corridors converged he had sloping shelves fastened to the walls, on which separate pages of the newspaper could be placed so that several Theologians could peruse the sheets at the same time. Suddenly, after being totally isolated from the outside world, we were learning a little of what was happening there.

The Director also refurbished a couple of rooms for our use during recreation periods, converting one into a community room where we could play cards or watch television or chat, and another into a recreational library with books and music. There I became acquainted for the first time with the novels of Evelyn Waugh and Graham Greene, as well as with art books from the great museums of the world. Some, staff and confreres, were shocked at the art books Father Mick placed in the library, with their occasional displays of 'obscene' works, such as the female nudes of Titian and Ingres. I myself wasn't sure how to deal with those: they certainly caused me sexual arousal. However, I

159

reasoned, if Father Mick put them there it must be lawful to gaze on them. Which I did, though surreptitiously lest a confrere observing my gazing might consider me some kind of deviant.

The vow of obedience required us to ask permission whenever we wished to leave the Scholasticate. The Philosophy Director did not easily grant such requests, consequently he was rarely asked. So when shortly after moving to the House of Theology I received an invitation to my cousin Tim's wedding in Galway I was extremely doubtful that I'd be permitted to attend. Nevertheless, because of the more relaxed environment, I decided to ask. I marshaled my reasons in advance: Tim and I were the same age and I had spent many vacations at his home; we went to boarding school together; his father was my godfather; the family would all be very disappointed if I didn't turn up. And so on.

"Come in, sit down." Father Mick said affably when I knocked on his door. "What can I do for you?"

"I got an invitation to my cousin's wedding."

"Did you now?" Father Mick smiled at me, though his mind seemed elsewhere. "That's wonderful. I love weddings myself; they're such happy occasions."

"I've only been to a few." Weddings were rare events when I was growing up.

"Who's getting married?"

"My cousin Tim. He's –"

" – Where's it going to be?" The Director seemed to be in a hurry, tapping the back of his pencil on the desk.

"In Galway, Father."

"Nice city, Galway; I like it a lot."

"Me, too, Father."

"So you'll need to stay overnight. Would you have a place to stay?"

160

Leaving the Director's office I felt that I hadn't quite left the world behind after all, and that thought lifted some of the depression I had been experiencing for months. Of course attending my cousin's wedding might well deepen that depression: it might be the occasion for uselessly re-thinking my vocation. In the event, I didn't feel in the least disturbed by the happy atmosphere or the pretty women in their finery. I was at the wedding but not a part of it; content to belong to a different world, firm in my commitment to the religious and priestly life I had chosen.

The Study of Theology

After the demanding University courses in philosophy I found the theology classes rather easy, and somewhat boring. In philosophy we were expected to think our way through difficult intellectual problems and to challenge any conclusions of philosophers with which we didn't agree. Not so in theology: here the motto was *fides querens intellectum* – faith seeking understanding. We first believed the truths of faith that we were being taught, and then studied them with a combination of faith and rational thought in order to understand them. This approach, which required memorizing a great quantity of detailed propositions without questioning their validity or even their reasonableness, did not present any problem to me since all my life I had been accustomed to accepting what was called revealed truth, without analyzing the basis for its veracity.

Dogmatic theology – which deals with the theoretical truths of faith concerning God and His works, the nature of the God-man Jesus Christ, and humankind – was a rather dry subject even for us students who were preparing to spend our lives preaching the truths of our religious faith. It was hard to get

161

excited over such topics as the nature of the Blessed Trinity – the dogma that God is really three Divine Persons but still only one God. I hadn't understood it as a child preparing for first Communion and I still didn't understand it after studying its theological rationale. Theological arguments in general were tedious and involved much hair-splitting, as in, for instance, the quibbling over the dogma called the *Filioque,* which had helped cause a schism between the Roman and Greek Churches that was still ongoing after almost a thousand years. That controversy dealt with the role the Second Divine Person, the Son (Who, to add confusion, was also Jesus), played in the procession (whatever that meant) of the Third Divine Person, the Holy Spirit, from the Father and the Son. It was an esoteric argument that had no relevance to anyone's life and that, even if it had any meaning, neither view could ever be proved. Of course if you were a Roman Catholic and you held the Greek teaching – which denied the role of the Son in the procession of the Holy Spirit – you would be considered a heretic. The converse was true if you were a member of the Greek Church.

I never challenged any doctrine taught in theology courses, even when the Professors of different disciplines contradicted one another. Which they sometimes did. For example, the Professor of Dogmatic Theology took us through the proofs for the doctrine of the Immaculate Conception of the Blessed Virgin Mary, declared a dogma of faith by Pope Pius IX in 1854. The pope had used a verse from the Book of Genesis to prove that the doctrine had been revealed by God: *I will put enmity between thee and the woman. She shall crush thy head. Thee* and *thy*, our Dogma Professor said, was the devil, and *the woman* was Mary. *She* was also Mary. So we must conclude from this verse, the Professor stated, that the Blessed Virgin Mary would crush the devil. And in order to crush the devil she herself must have always been without sin; therefore she was conceived immaculate. However, when the Professor of Scripture referred to the identical passage in Genesis he said that more recent exegesis had found the translations from the original text to be incorrect: that *she shall crush thy head* should be translated *it shall crush thy head*, where *it* meant the Messiah. Having been taught that Catholic dogma should not be subjected to intellectual scrutiny, I closed my mind to the obvious contradiction. Neither did any of my classmates challenge the discrepancy. Raising issues on matters of doctrine seemed akin to questioning one's faith, which might lead to loss of belief altogether. And we had been taught that loss of faith was the sin from which there was no return, and for which there was no forgiveness.

Moral theology was a more interesting subject since it had to do with good and evil, virtue and sin. But it, too, was loaded with hairs to be split in order to separate sin from non-sin, and slight sin – venial – from grave sin – mortal. As an example, all Catholics were bound under pain of grave sin to attend mass on Sundays. But how much of the mass must they be present at to avoid a 'mortaller?' The Church's hair-splitting experts, the moral theologians, decided that as long as you were present from the reading of the first Gospel till the end of Communion you'd avoid mortal sin. But if, for instance, you walked out during the distribution of Communion you would be hell-bound. We also learned that while a priest celebrating mass must have, under pain of mortal sin, a male to serve him the wine and water, it would be a grave sin for a female to serve him. Since after the Vatican II Council women were permitted to serve mass, one can only speculate about the ultimate fate of those priests and women who committed mortal sin through their mass delinquency prior to the Council and who died while in that state.

163

To give us practical experience in resolving moral issues, exercises called *Case of Conscience* debates were held monthly, in which Father Paddy, the Professor of Moral Theology, posed the kinds of problems that he felt a priest would be likely to encounter in the confessional. He'd assign, in advance, students to defend and oppose particular solutions. The witty Professor would sit up on the rostrum, usually grinning, before the students and staff members, and call on the chosen ones to debate the problem of the day. The debate might go something like this:

"Father Murphy, a girl comes into your confession box and says, 'Father, I overheard my father tell my mother that he stole the chicken he gave her to cook for the Sunday dinner. Did I commit a sin, Father, by eating my share of that chicken?' Now, Father Murphy, what would you say to the girl?

Murphy, a first-year Theologian, so not yet raised to the rank of Father, sprang to his feet. "I hold that the girl was a knowing receiver of stolen goods and so she committed a sin by eating the purloined chicken."

Father Paddy gave no hint as to how he viewed that strict interpretation of the moral law. "And what do you think, Father Malone?"

Mickey, a third-year man and soon to be ordained, said, "In my opinion she's not guilty of sin if she was hungry and had nothing else to eat."

"Hmm!" Father Paddy's nod showed he was impressed by this distinction. He pointed towards the back of the study hall. "Well, Father Reedy, you've been ordained, and next year you'll be out in the middle of Africa faced with questions like this. What's your answer to the girl who ate the stolen chicken?"

Father Reedy got to his feet. "The way I look at it is this, Father: maybe the girl wasn't intended by her father to overhear

164

what he told her mother. And if she hadn't overheard him she'd have eaten the chicken in total innocence. So in my judgment if she didn't deliberately eavesdrop on her father, then she isn't to blame for overhearing that the chicken was stolen, and so neither should she be blamed for eating the damn bird."

Father Paddy laughed at this piece of casuistry, then launched into a lengthy monologue on the various ways the problem might be solved. He quoted several renowned moral theologians to bolster his own conclusion that the girl had no right to eat the chicken once she knew it had been stolen.

Of all our theological studies, Canon Law caused the most hair-splitting. It also appeared to be the subject least relevant to our priestly ministry. For instance, I asked myself, when would a priest be called upon to make a decision as to whether a Catholic graveyard needed to be re-consecrated because some drunken lout had urinated within its borders? To make the study of Canon Law more difficult for us, the Code – which very succinctly defined all the Church's laws – was written in Latin only, and translations of it were forbidden lest the accuracy of the text be misinterpreted by English or other impure language. A Jesuit by the name of T. Lincoln Bouscaren had written a commentary, which the Vatican permitted, and which our Professor said was as good a paraphrase of the Code as we were likely to find.

While Canon Law was a dry subject, Church History was a biased one. That history is written by the winners is a cliche, and cliches usually become so by having at least some truth. We studied Church history from the Catholic perspective only: all who separated from the jurisdiction of Rome were heretics, apostates, devil-inspired, while the Church was ever faithful to the truth, regardless of consequences. So in our Church history studies we glossed over men like Savonarola who preached reform, or Giordano Bruno who held different theological views

165

from the Church hierarchy. Such men were condemned as heretics and sometimes burned at the stake. We were not given an opportunity to study their viewpoints, nor were we told the true stories of trail-blazing scientists like Copernicus or Gallileo who challenged orthodox interpretations of the Bible. The Reformation, we learned, was the work of evil men: yes, there was something about individual clerics peddling indulgences and Pope Alexander VI was a bit of a lad, but such peccadillos didn't justify Luther's breakaway from the One True Church.

I accepted the Catholic version of Church history without question. And as part of my class work I wrote a paper on Church and State in America in which I contrasted that relationship with the teaching of the Church on the subject. My paper compared the first amendment clause – *Congress shall make no law respecting the establishment of religion or prohibiting the free exercise thereof* – with the teaching of Pope Leo XIII who had declared that *justice forbids and reason itself forbids the State to be godless or to adopt a line of action that would end in godlessness, namely, to treat the various religions alike and to bestow on them promiscuously equal rights and privileges.* I acknowledged that the American Catholic Hierarchy accepted the present Church-State relationship and that this situation was not likely to change in the foreseeable future. Nevertheless, as a disciple of Father Fahey, I concluded that if a situation were to arise where Catholics constituted a great majority of the population and where public profession of the true religion could be made without serious injury to the common good, then it ought to be done. My Professor of Church history thought my position a bit extreme.

No cleric should be considered trained for the priesthood unless he was thoroughly indoctrinated in the Holy Book which, even for Catholics, was the primary source of Revealed Truth.

166

Yet, in the Kimmage Scholasticate the study of Scripture was rather perfunctory and almost entirely confined to the New Testament. This was in keeping with the Catholic approach to biblical studies at this time, which aimed at keeping interpretation of the Bible free from error at all cost; error being any interpretation not in accord with the Church's traditional teaching. Protestants, for more than a century, had been using the modern tools of textual and literary criticism, archeology, history, historical linguistics, and other disciplines to explore the meaning of the Bible. During much of that time the Catholic Church, after being challenged in its guardianship of divine truth by the Reformation, looked on any new kind of biblical interpretation, however rationally or scientifically based, as at best suspect and at worst as the work of evil men attempting to subvert God's chosen instrument of truth and salvation. Popes Leo XIII and Benedict XV issued encyclicals in which they warned against the dangers of interpreting the Bible in any but the literal sense. Benedict complained in his 1920 encyclical about assailants of Holy Scripture who misused principles of reasoning in order to overturn the fundamental truth of the Bible and thus destroy Catholic teaching handed down by the Fathers.

When Protestant biblical studies could no longer be gainsaid, a more recent pope, Pius XII, acknowledged in 1943 that the Bible might be studied using such tools as literary and textual criticism, and that the sacred texts might be studied in their original languages. He also admitted that many biblical questions remained open for future resolution and that the meaning of only a few passages touching faith and morals had been decided already by the Church or by the consensus of the Church Fathers. In particular, his encyclical stated that exegetes should pay particular attention to the discernment of the literary genre being employed by the inspired writer. Nevertheless, despite this new freedom, and probably as a result of centuries of fear that Protestant-inspired free interpretation of the Bible might be inculcated, Catholic theology professors for the most part trod carefully in their scripture classes.

The study of the Liturgy was also treated lightly by our teachers. We were still in the era of the Latin mass with its minute attention to the details of rubrics and its lack of attention to the role of the congregation. The Scholasticate had one Professor who held advanced ideas on what the liturgy should be – he was even rumored to have mentioned the possibility of mass being celebrated in the vernacular. But such notions were not taught to us Scholastics.

We had no course in pastoral care, an extraordinary lacuna in our priestly training. We were, after all, preparing to be pastors, missionaries, destined to head forth after ordination to *partes infideles* and bring the light of Catholic faith to those who dwelt in the darkness of sin and ignorance. So we needed all the practical training we could get to accomplish our objective. Unfortunately, we were being trained to be monks and theologians rather than missionaries, and we would be sent forth to preach the gospel without learning anything in advance about the ethnicity, culture, language, or even beliefs, of the people among whom we would labor.

Homiletics was a case in point. Preaching is the priest's principal way of teaching his flock the truths of religion. A good preacher can have a positive effect on his congregation; a poor one sends them to sleep. Yet, the art and craft of preaching was not taken seriously in the House of Theology: we had no class in homiletics and had just a few elocution classes from an Abbey Theatre actor. This was in keeping with the low standard of preaching in Irish Catholic churches, where sermons in general

168

were less than stimulating. We Theologians learned our craft by preaching to Scholastics in the refectory. We wrote our sermons, practiced in private – usually during recreation, with a confrere listening and rendering a critique – and on the appointed morning declaimed our message over the clatter of cutlery on porridge plates. Those sermons were more often the source of hilarity than of edification: Scholastics who appeared to be paying attention only to their food were quick to notice any preacher gaffes and would burst into laughter. One Theologian who encouraged his breakfast congregation to aim high in their spiritual lives 'and allow for the drop' did not allow for the merriment his admonition produced. Refectory sermons in general were trite, boring, and not well delivered.

Opening A Window

Social Work

Father Mick told us, insistently, in his evening conferences that the world was changing around us and that we must learn to change with it. Most of us had no idea what he was talking about. How could we? We had left the world before even rock and roll had taken hold and, despite the Director's making the daily newspaper available, we were not a part of the world that was changing. So, many were taken aback when the Director came up with what they thought was a bizarre idea, though it was attractive to some of us. He believed that we theologians would benefit from doing some form of social work *outside* the Scholasticate. Not all staff members agreed with his radical notion, Father Mick said: some argued that it was contrary to traditional Scholastic training, while others felt there were dangers to our vocations if we were let mingle with lay people at this stage of formation. So, if we were to engage in social work, and he hoped we would – it would be voluntary – we must be careful not to give anyone reason to think the experience was in any way harmful to us.

What kinds of social work might we engage in? For a start, we could visit the sick in hospitals and nursing homes, or teach Christian Doctrine classes in schools. I, still vestigially inspired by Firinne ideas, proposed that I give a class on the Church's social teaching to secondary school students. He agreed and found a senior girls class in a convent secondary school a few miles from Kimmage willing to listen.

So I prepared my material, and on Wednesday afternoons cycled to the school. Having previously taught – for just a few weeks – at Blackrock College I felt like a veteran in front of the class. The big difference was that this was a class of nubile women. I loved that. They in turn sat with rapt attention while the young cleric expounded Papal teaching on the ideal social order. One young woman seemed never to take her eyes off me. She was blonde and pretty and several times after class ended she came forward to ask questions. I suspected the questions were merely an excuse to prolong our time together. As a consequence, I always departed glowing and returned each week in happy anticipation of talking to her. When, one Wednesday, she was absent I felt desolate, and worried all week lest she not return. The following week she was back and resumed her after-class discussions with me. My demeanor towards her was always correct of course: I never said or did anything to give her any impression that I found her sexually attractive. Nevertheless, we were flirting, though I didn't consider it a matter for confession because our relationship didn't stir up impure thoughts or desires; rather it gave a cosy sensation of comfort that I felt even a celibate might legitimately enjoy.

Around this time I received an invitation from a friend in Firinne to attend a lecture that the organization was sponsoring. With Father Mick's permission, I attended. The event caused me much confusion: I felt out of place as I sat in familiar surroundings in the presence of people with whom I had once been close friends but towards whom I now felt almost a stranger. The lecture, an overview of the Divine Plan for Social Order, recalled what had kept me involved in Firinne, and re-kindled old desires. I had wanted to promote the social teaching of the Church because I considered that its implementation would lead to justice and fairness for all mankind. Now, having taken on the priestly calling, my life would be given over to priestly work which, though wonderful, was not what I had in mind. An idealist, I had wanted to change society. As a priest my life would be devoted to performing the more mundane work of saying mass and administering the sacraments and preaching the gospel, tasks that at this lecture appeared to me less important than being a gadfly for social change. However, I could not go back now: the die was cast and I was going to be a priest and missionary.

The presence at the meeting of a pretty young woman whom I didn't even know caused me even more confusion. Sitting across from her at a discussion after the lecture and unable to prevent my eyes from straying to her bare knees exposed by a short skirt, I felt a terrible desolation. Though I had cut myself off from the company of women, my whole being still craved that intimacy. It took many days of meditation and prayer in monastic isolation to recover from the perturbations caused by that plunge into a world I thought to have shaken off forever. Conscience reminded me that I had made a permanent commitment to God, and that I must accept whatever suffering went with that commitment. Wasn't that what Jesus meant when he said, *unless a man take up his cross and follow me he cannot be my disciple?* I had chosen to follow Jesus, so I must carry His cross.

The Human Side

We Scholastics were dedicated by our religious profession to the quest for holiness, for we were training to be priests, men chosen by God to mediate between Him and His people. But we had the same yearnings, likes, dislikes, phobias, weaknesses, strengths, that might be found in any cross-section of the population; we differed only in our desire to be priests. Since we remained human beings when we took religious vows, we didn't always base our decisions on what the Lord would have us do. A dichotomy often existed between what we thought of as our prayer life and what we might call our real life. In prayer we pledged to God that we'd be guided only by His Will, which we promised to seek always before acting. Nevertheless, even in the hothouse of the Scholasticate, where piety was a way of life and everywhere there were statues and pictures and set prayer times and specific acts of worship and spiritual conferences to remind us what our lives were supposed to be all about, we often managed to live a Janus-faced existence. Just a little below the veneer of inculcated piety lay our all-too-human passions. So it was hardly surprising to find among Scholastics some of the less desirable traits that are found elsewhere in human society.

One unpleasant human trait, whose effects I suffered from early in life without learning how to cope with it, reared its ugly head again in the Scholasticate. Bullying seems to be a universal vice, found among young children and old people and all ages in between. In boarding school I had allowed a boy my own age and class to bully me because I adhered too closely to the gospel admonition about turning the other cheek. Later I realized that that particular counsel did not, and should not, apply to bullies and I spent years regretting my failure to protect myself against my tormentor. So when a fellow Scholastic attempted to bully me, albeit mildly, in the House of Theology I reacted, perhaps over-reacted, immediately. I was acknowledged to be one of the best Gaelic football players in the House. So when the Theologian assigned to select the team for the annual game against the House of Philosophy, decided, because he disliked me, to demote me in training to the second team, I felt demeaned. Remembering my regret for not reacting to past bullying, I decided to take the only option open to me in this instance, and refused to play at all – games were optional in the House of Theology. Consternation ensued among my football-crazy confreres because the Philosophers had a strong team that year and Theologians, being older, would be humiliated if defeated. So they pressured Jack, who reluctantly selected me.

Though that trivial episode did not provide me with any spiritual advancement, it did teach me a lesson that I have carried through life: bullies must always be faced down. And though I didn't feel that anything in the episode shed luster on the spirituality of the parties involved, it did raise an important question for me: was our piety no more than a veneer that even so slight a scraping could remove? The Scholasticate had rules of conduct and practices of civility whose outward observance could easily mask individual Scholastics' true feelings and beliefs. *There's no art to find the mind's construction in the face*, King Duncan said in Shakespeare's Macbeth. A man who decided to become a priest for an unworthy motive – status, comfort, whatever – and was willing and able to present the required outward facade of piety could, without too much difficulty, succeed in his ambition. I, who considered my own motives to be reasonably pure, though perhaps they were not, felt, from observation, that there were Scholastics whose sometime words and behavior indicated they were here for less than true religious

174

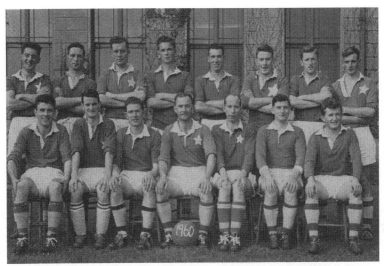

Front, second from right, on Theology football team, 1960

motives. Some did leave before ordination. One would remain a priest and die under a cloud of suspicion about corrupt financial activities. On the other hand, one of the more pious confreres, whom I never suspected of having unworthy motives, was sent to jail many years after ordination for sexually abusing children. Several others, myself included, who were considered model Scholastics with solid vocations, would leave the priesthood.

During those first two years of theological studies I still had no doubts about my vocation. Yes, the issue of celibacy continued to perturb, but I accepted that pain as the inevitable consequence of my decision to make the great sacrifice for the love of God. And though the strain of that anxiety was showing – I still suffered from panic attacks – no one in Kimmage observed it. The Theology Director concluded that I had a solid vocation, since the outward signs were present: I follow the Rule, caused no problems, was outstanding in my studies, gave no hint that I had doubts. What more could he look for?

175

Rule before Reason

All through my second year of theology my mother had been telling me in her letters about my father's drinking problem. She was seriously upset over it, as were my siblings, but they didn't know what to do. I read up on the subject of alcoholism and learned that membership of Alcoholics Anonymous was considered the most effective way to deal with the disease. With that in mind I knocked on the Director's door.

Father Mick scrutinized me. "You look worried."

"It's my father." I was nervous, about to ask for something unusual. "He's an alcoholic and my family doesn't know what to do."

The Director clucked sympathy. "It's a terribly difficult problem. I've come across it many times. And I've seen it in my own family."

"I've been reading up on it. There's an organization called Alcoholics Anonymous that seems to be able to help."

"Yes indeed. They've had a good deal of success with their twelve-point program. The biggest difficulty would be to get your father to join. Usually –"

" – I've been thinking," I jumped in; "if I could spend some time with him I believe I'd be able to persuade him."

The glint in Father Mick's eye told me he understood. "So you want to go to America this summer?"

"My mother is willing to pay my fare."

"I don't see why not."

I could hardly believe the Director had acquiesced so easily. But before I had time to say anything further he added, "you'll need the Provincial's permission to go."

That dampened my elation. "Is he likely to give it?"

Father Mick donned his well-known inscrutable expression. "I can't speak for him of course. But he might. I'll talk to him and arrange for you to see him."

Next morning he stopped me on the way out from breakfast. "If you go over to the Provincial's office immediately after lunch, he'll see you."

Though I was nervous when I knocked on the Great Man's door, the Provincial was affable and put me at ease. "Father Director has told me of your request. It's highly unusual, but he made a good case for your going. So you have my permission." But then, as I was about to say thank you, he added, "however, because the permission is so unusual I'll need to put it before the Superior General. I'll ask him when he comes here next week."

I spent the succeeding days in suspense, and prayed that the Holy Ghost would inspire the Superior General, a physically tiny Irishman from Tipperary, to let me go. The following week the Director stopped me on the way to class. "The Provincial would like to see you after lunch." His expression was enigmatic.

The Provincial looked somber. "I'm afraid I have bad news for you. The Superior General turned down your request. He said we don't do that sort of thing."

Since I couldn't go to New York my mother, who hadn't seen me for three years, decided to come over for the month of August. Again I rented a car and we headed down the West to visit relatives. While I was driving – this time a little better, though I hadn't had any practice in the meantime – she asked me suddenly, apropos of nothing in our conversation, "are you happy in your vocation?"

I was taken aback, and wondered why she asked. "Yes," I said, "I'm quite happy with it."

"No one in the family would be in any way upset should

177

you decide to leave," she said. "It's your life and your decision."

The most important events of our first two years in Theology were our reception of Clerical Tonsure and Minor Orders. With those, we entered the esoteric world of clerics and received the first four in the hierarchy of Orders. Jesus didn't establish that hierarchy, and in the early Church only three Orders were conferred: those of bishop, priest, and deacon. In the third century an extended hierarchy gradually developed to include the Minor Orders of Porter, Lector, Exorcist, and Acolyte, and the Major Order of Subdeacon. In the seventh century a new rite, the Clerical Tonsure, was instituted by which persons, usually boys or young men, were inducted into the ranks of clerics. The rite consisted of a ceremony in which the recipient's hair was shorn, as a sign that he no longer belonged to his family or to the world, but to the Church of God.[1]

In 1961, towards the end of our first year of theology, we received the Clerical Tonsure, now a strictly ceremonial rite, but still the first formal step on the way to the priesthood. We journeyed to the Archbishop's chapel one afternoon to receive it. A certain amount of amusement preceded the event since the principal action in the ceremony consisted of the Archbishop snipping a lock of the recipient's hair. The prelate was known to be unpredictable when using the ceremonial scissors and many newly Tonsured Scholastics had returned to Kimmage sporting

---

[1] In 1972 Pope Paul VI abolished the Tonsure, the Minor Orders, and the Sub-diaconate.

unsightly gaps in their quiffs. However, since in Kimmage any Scholastic might be assigned the function of barber without regard to tonsorial skill, Scholastics' hairstyles were usually less than elegant. On this particular day most of us escaped the Archbishop's scissors without serious blemish to our manes.

After Clerical Tonsure had inducted us into the clerical state, and our Superiors had formally assured the Archbishop that we were worthy to receive Orders, we went again to the episcopal chapel to receive the Minor Orders of Porter, and Lector. The Order of Porter conferred the ex officio power of opening and closing church doors, admitting those worthy to be admitted and excluding the unworthy. We weren't exactly overawed with the reception of such prodigious powers, which no doubt had real meaning in earlier times. One could imagine Quasimodo in Victor Hugo's *The Hunchback of Notre Dame* having the rank of Porter, which would include his bell-ringing function, though not of course the right to kidnap beautiful damsels. The Order of Lector gave recipients the authority to read the Psalms in church, to instruct people in the rudiments of the faith, and to bless bread and new fruits. Though I didn't question the value of the blessing power the Order conferred, I wondered what exactly such a blessing effected. The easy answer was that it called down God's blessing on the bread and fruit, which begged a further question: did eating the blessed fruit or bread make the consumer holier, more pleasing to God?

During our second year in the House of Theology we journeyed again to the episcopal chapel to receive the other two Minor Orders, those of Exorcist and Acolyte. The 1971 novel by William Blatty, *The Exorcist,* and the film based on it, drew popular attention to the Order of Exorcist which, according to Catholic teaching, confers on its recipient the ex officio power to expel devils from any unfortunates the demons should possess.

179

I was never called upon to use that power: Church discipline actually forbids its exercise without the explicit permission of the bishop of the diocese. Nevertheless, in theory any ordained Exorcist could perform such a rite. The Order of Acolyte conferred the rather tame powers of assisting the Sub-Deacon at Solemn High Mass, carrying cruets to the altar and lighting the candles.

I was now officially a Cleric in Minor Orders; next year I would be eligible to receive the Major Orders of Subdeacon, Deacon, and Priest. I had drawn closer to my goal.

Ordination

Learning to say mass

In September, 1962, we commenced our third year of theological studies. The coming year would be the Big One, the year in which we would be ordained priests of the Holy Roman Catholic Church. By that ordination we would be given the power to say mass and to administer the sacraments of baptism and penance and extreme unction, the authority to officiate at the sacrament of matrimony and to preach the gospel.

The first step we took that year towards fulfilling our goal was a very practical one: we began to rehearse saying mass. The power to say mass, in which, according to Catholic teaching, the priest changes bread and wine into the Body and Blood of Jesus Christ, was what distinguished him from the rest of humanity. For Catholics this was an awesome power and was the source of that peculiar reverence they paid the priest. So when I began to practice saying mass I felt I was on the very threshold of my sacred calling. The mass is the center of the Catholic liturgy. It is, according to theologians, not only a commemoration of the Last Supper where Jesus converted bread and wine into His Body and Blood, but also a re-enactment of His Sacrifice on Calvary in which He redeemed mankind. This modulation required much sleight of theological phrasing that I accepted but did not understand.

Although the essence of the mass liturgy consists of pronouncing the words of consecration over the bread and wine and feeding the participants with that sacred nourishment, a plethora of ceremonies and rules had enveloped the rite over the centuries. Those accretions – including the requirement that the ceremonial language used in most Rites must be Latin – turned it into a complex ritual. Every movement, every gesture, every word the priest uttered, from the moment he stepped onto the altar until he left it, was defined and choreographed into a set of rubrics. The priest was not at liberty to modify or leave out even the slightest of them: all were mandated under pain of sin, many under pain of mortal sin. I heard it said that a theologian who once counted the ways in which one might deviate from the rubrics found that a careless priest could commit as many as a hundred and forty different sins while saying mass.

So we practiced the mass rubrics with attention to detail, working in pairs during evening recreation in rooms with altars set up for the purpose, taking turns and critiquing each other. We didn't know it then but we'd have little more than a year after ordination in which to say mass using those rubrics. Beginning in 1964, the Latin mass and many of its rubrics were swept aside as a result of Vatican II and replaced by vernacular versions of the text and with new rubrics.

The Fatal Step

September to March went by much as in the previous two years. We studied and prayed and played football and performed our allotted functions; I put in terms as honey-dipper – cleaning toilets – and librarian. Then in March the time arrived for us to be ordained Sub-Deacons. That Order, the first of what were called the Majors, conferred on its recipient, according to the Roman Ritual, the mundane powers of preparing the bread and wine for mass, of singing the epistle at solemn mass, and of washing linens that had been touched by the consecrated bread and wine. For us recipients, however, the real importance of the Order was the undertaking we would make, the one we worried about most and spoke about least: the obligation to be celibate for life.

One might reasonably ask why this should still be a matter of concern for members of a religious order who had already taken vows of perpetual chastity? Because of Church law, however, there was a substantial difference. A dispensation from the vow of perpetual chastity could be obtained from the Pope for a serious reason and was not all that infrequently granted. However, as was made clear to us at the retreat we made before receiving the Subdiaconate, a dispensation from the obligation of celibacy, undertaken with this Order, was never granted. Never. That was the law and the practice, we were told.

The *manner* in which our commitment to celibacy was asked for and assented to during the Sub-Diaconate ceremony was rather peculiar: undertaken by action rather than by word, as if the obligation were an afterthought. During the rite the bishop asked the recipients, who stood facing him in a single row, to take one step forward as the signal that we accepted the obligation of perpetual celibacy. The step, once taken, could never be retracted.

I retained a vivid recollection of taking the fatal step, and of feeling depressed for days afterwards. My goal was to become a priest, not a celibate. The latter was an obligation imposed on the priest and therefore I accepted it, just as I had accepted the vow of perpetual chastity. But despite my years of prayer, meditation, study, and vow-taking, nature still rebelled at the notion that I should cut myself off from a life of sexual love and requitement, with no possibility of ever being released from the obligation.

A month later we were ordained Deacons. While professional theologians given to hair-splitting disputed whether the Minor orders and the Subdiaconate were part of the sacrament of Holy Orders, all accepted that the Diaconate was a sacrament. I received it in stride: it imposed no further obligation and it brought me to the final step, the priesthood.

Final Preparations

The Orders we had hitherto received had been conferred in private ceremonies. Priestly ordination, however, was a public event. Like a wedding it involved families and relatives and friends. So, as if we were marrying, we had to make preparations for the big event. We were photographed individually for the Congregation's missionary magazine, we selected pious picture cards to distribute in commemoration of the occasion, and we selected invitees and sent them invitations to the ordination ceremony and breakfast. Because of our number – there were twenty-two of us – we were allowed only ten guests apiece for the ordination ceremony and for the subsequent breakfast in the Kimmage refectory,

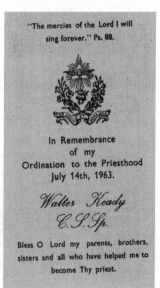

"The mercies of the Lord I will sing forever." Ps. 88.

In Remembrance
of my
Ordination to the Priesthood
July 14th, 1963.

Walter Keady
C.S.Sp.

Bless O Lord my parents, brothers, sisters and all who have helped me to become Thy priest.

a limitation that required careful selection and that made it almost impossible to avoid giving offence to relatives and friends who expected to be invited but were not. Because I had so many relatives traveling from overseas for the occasion I was allowed to invite eleven.

Two weeks before ordination day my father arrived from New York. Mammy had written to say he was coming early to see a bit of the country and visit some relatives. I met him at the airport and was shocked at his appearance: I hadn't seen him for more than six years. He had aged a great deal, looked emaciated, his gait unsteady. And when we shook hands I smelled the whiskey. We took a bus to the city and went to a restaurant for breakfast. I was delighted to see him again and we had much to talk about over the meal. Dad was one of the gentlest and kindest men I have ever known and we always got along very well. When we finished breakfast he excused himself to go to the toilet. After he had been gone for about fifteen minutes I began to worry and went to see if he was all right. He wasn't in the men's room. I hurried into the street and met him coming around a corner; again with a strong smell of whiskey. We took a bus to Tom's in-laws where he was to stay. I returned to Kimmage, distraught at his condition and again felt serious annoyance at the Superior General's *we don't do that sort of thing* when I asked to go to my father' assistance in New York.

I recalled a St. John of God Brother who was a colleague in philosophy classes at the University and who had once mentioned that his Order's work included helping alcoholics. I rang the Brother now and explained my problem. He suggested that I take my father to the alcohol unit at the Order's hospital in Stillorgan. I immediately returned to Ringsend and with much cajoling convinced my father that it was in his best interest to seek help. Once he agreed, I got him into a taxi and took him to

185

the hospital. There, my St. John of God Brother-friend promised to get him into a drying-out program and keep him there until ordination day. He kept his word.

Priested

We spent the week before ordination on retreat, about which I remember nothing except that I was mentally numb: I had committed to the final step and there were no further decisions to make. Remembering the deacon who broke down the night before his ordination, I endeavored to remain calm, and even managed some sleep that final night. In the morning we got on a bus at seven and were driven across the city to the Archbishop's chapel. Though silence was not required during the journey we were eerily quiet, preoccupied with the momentous event before us. In the sacristy we robed in deacons' vestments and walked in procession to the sanctuary.

The ceremony was a blur in my memory afterwards, though I did recall feeling that it was long. A photograph that Seamus took showed forty or so white-clad forms – deacons from other religious houses were also being ordained – lying prostrate before the altar, with the Archbishop and his clerical entourage in the background. Another photograph showed us standing in double file facing the altar; we were lined up for the Great Man to lay hands on our heads and pronounce the words that would made us priests forever.

Which raises a rather curious question. According to Catholic teaching, when a man is ordained a priest by receiving the Sacrament of Holy Orders, he is given the power to change bread and wine into the Body and Blood of Jesus Christ and in

Ordination ceremony, July 14, 1963

doing so to make present again the sacrifice of Jesus on Calvary; he is also given the power to forgive sins in Jesus's name. These are unique powers, so it is critical for both the ordaining bishop and the ordinand to know by what specific act in the long ceremony of ordination they are conferred. Since the sacrament has been administered for close to two thousand years one might expect theologians to have clearly defined that act. Surprisingly, they haven't; and since Vatican II the matter has become even cloudier. The Sacraments, of which there are seven, including Holy Orders, are claimed by the Church to have been instituted by Jesus as symbols through which He makes us holy – like Him. For instance, when He said, *Unless a man be born again of water and the Holy Ghost he cannot enter the kingdom of God*, He was saying, according to the theologians, that baptism by water removes from our souls the stain of original sin and so makes us

187

eligible for heaven. That, it may be argued, is clear enough. But Jesus wasn't at all explicit about some of the other sacraments, including Holy Orders. The Apostles began the tradition of passing the priestly power – administering the sacrament of Holy Orders – by putting their hands on the heads of recipients and praying over them. Twelve hundred years later, when Saint Thomas Aquinas discovered the writings of Aristotle he became enamored of the Greek philosopher's concept of matter and form and applied that concept to the sacraments. He, and the theologians after him, defined the sacraments in terms of their matter and their form. In those terms the matter of baptism is water and the form is the prayer "I baptize thee ..." But, according to the theologians, neither the matter nor the form is clear for Holy Orders. The matter, they say, might be either the laying of the bishop's hands on the head of the ordinand as the Apostles did – in the ceremony the bishop does it twice – or it might be the handing over of the chalice and paten, or perhaps the handing over of the mass vestments. Or all of the above. The form may be any or all of the prayers accompanying those actions. The theologians don't agree on what constitutes the essential matter and form of the Sacrament: according to one theologian-writer they are divided into six different schools of thought on the subject. When one adds the requirement of a right intention – the intention to administer the sacrament – on the part of the bishop in order for it to be valid, a scrupulous ordinand might doubt if he were really ordained. Fortunately for me, I was not aware at ordination time of those theological controversies. Had I been ...?

When we emerged from the chapel to the adoring gaze and congratulations of families and friends, I expected to feel an enormous surge of elation: I had achieved my goal, I was a priest forever. Instead, I felt despondency. Should my mother at that

After Ordination, with family and relatives

moment have asked me if I was happy, and if I were to answer honestly, I'd have had to say no. I expected jubilation but felt only sadness. Fortunately, I didn't have time to dwell on my state of mind: my mother, both brothers, and one sister, had arrived from New York during the week and had picked up my father from St. John of God's that morning. All were present at the ordination ceremony, as were three aunts and three cousins. Aunt Mary was there with her son Tom, the latter a substitute for my Uncle Walter who declined to come to Dublin even for this occasion. There were the inevitable photographs: all the newly ordained, still in mass vestments, were photographed in various poses with families and friends. And eventually we lined up for a group picture with the Archbishop.

Then there were the first blessings. Catholics consider that

Ordinands with the Archbishop

a new priest's blessing has a special value, and the newly ordained priest would find people dropping to their knees before him for the next several months so that he might lay his hands on their heads and invoke the blessing of Father, Son, and Holy Ghost on them. I felt disconcerted at having my parents, siblings, and relatives kneel before me to get my blessing.

Now also for the first time I heard people call me by my new title: I who by my very profession could never be a biological parent was henceforth to be addressed as *Father*. It sounded particularly incongruous when uttered by men old enough to be my father or grandfather. I disliked the title from the beginning and was happy that my family continued to call me by my first name. Whenever thereafter I had to introduce myself I never used the priestly honorific.

Eventually we made our way back to Kimmage for the ordination breakfast. I don't remember anything about the food,

Ordination breakfast

but confreres claimed afterwards that the Scholasticate chef 'outdid himself,' and my friend Noel considered it an honor that I had asked him to serve the meal to my family. Photos that he took at the table show a happy group. Two years later Noel himself was ordained.

After the breakfast most of my newly ordained confreres left for home with their families; each would celebrate his first mass in his parish church next morning. For most it would be a major festive occasion: banners would welcome the new priest home that evening and a reception would be held in his honor; next morning the church would be crowded for his first mass and new priest blessing. For weeks he would be feted in as many houses as he had time to visit and he'd likely return to the Scholasticate somewhat bloated from over-eating.

I, however, was a nomad, belonging to no parish since my family left Ireland. One of my aunts who was a Bon Secours nun arranged for me to say my first mass in her Order's Glasnevin convent chapel. Though it ought to have been a memorable occasion for me, all I recall was meeting some Firinne friends and former Civil Service colleagues after the mass. The remainder of the week was a blur of traveling and meeting people. Tom and Bridie returned to New York, Seamus – who asked that he be called Jim since moving to New York – rented a car, and with our parents we went west to Castlebar. On the following Sunday I said mass in The Neale church where I had served mass so many times as a boy. I found that particular experience very moving, although not many people remembered me – I had left there thirteen years earlier at the age of fifteen. For the next week we toured the beauty spots of Mayo and Galway and visited numerous relatives – my mother was the oldest of fourteen and my father was one of six – and all wanted the new priest to visit them and their families.

On ordination day an older priest said to me, "Welcome to the most exclusive club in the world." I felt the truth of that statement during the weeks that followed: being the center of attention wherever we went, given the place of honor at every table, having festive meals set before me several times a day, being constantly addressed as *Father* – would Father please come to visit us and bless our house. During those weeks I learned the meaning of celebrity. It was all very head-swelling: how could I not revel in my new role after so many years of monastic seclusion and self-abasement. Though an inner voice occasionally penetrated the din of acclaim and decried the whole business as unreal, unnecessary, and most assuredly undeserved.

When we got back to Dublin my father and Jim returned to New York, and my mother arranged a trip to London for the two of us, to visit her brother and sister. It was my first time in an airplane. We stayed with her sister and visited relatives and toured the city. Although it should not have, it came as a shock to find that ordination had not removed, or even lessened, my libido. London was more than a match for Scholasticate self-denial. The years of shelter from temptations, of relentlessly practicing custody of the eyes in a place where there were no visual allurements anyway, the days of silent meditation on the supernatural, all proved of little help when I was faced with London's brash world of beauty and incitement to pleasure. I continued to pray and to remain faithful to my spiritual duties but, though I didn't realize it then, it should have been plain that the training I had received was not in the least adequate for the problems I would face outside the Scholasticate. It wasn't just the blatant sexuality in advertisements and dress, or the seduction of non-stop television, that I found disconcerting. Even more disorienting was the atmosphere of materialism, the obsession of people with shopping and money and possessions. The world I grew up in, of masochistic religiosity and war-time scarcity, had given way over the intervening years to hedonism and the joys of luxury. And that was the world that I, inadequately prepared, would have to face as a missionary priest.

On our return to Dublin, my mother flew home to New York. I returned to Kimmage for a final year of study and priestly work in the Dublin diocese, before commencing my life's work, in some foreign land as yet unknown to me.

A Priest Forever

Performing priestly functions

I was a priest now, with all the powers and responsibilities the Catholic Church attached to that office. And with all the status that Irish culture added: a little less than God, perhaps on a par with the angels, and with expectations that my virtue would match my newly acquired eminence.

Though my confrere priests and I were still students, having a final year of theological studies to complete, we had more freedom to come and go than before. And we availed of it, leaving the Scholasticate for any excuse, and with barely a nod to the Director. Those whose families lived in the vicinity of Dublin paid frequent visits home. I found a second home with the O'Tooles, Tom's in-laws, who were a wonderful and most hospitable family. I visited them often and enjoyed my first real taste of television in their home, watching programs like *The Fugitive, Have Gun Will Travel*, and *The Flintstones*.

Our principal and most important reason for leaving the Scholasticate was to say morning mass in one or other of the city's parish churches or in the private chapels of Dublin's many

194

Orders of Nuns and Brothers. We especially enjoyed the convents because after celebrating mass the nuns treated us to sumptuous breakfasts. Everything was laid on for Father: the meticulously set table with white linen and polished cutlery, the half-grapefruit, the heavy cream for the porridge, the rashers and eggs, the toast and marmalade, the aromatic coffee. That reverence of nuns for the priestly state was a tradition that would be abandoned after Vatican II, with demands for equality, including their own ordination to the priesthood.

We new priests also engaged in weekend ministry, saying Sunday masses in various churches in the city and throughout the archdiocese, substituting for priests who were sick or on holidays. Which gave rise to another Kimmage custom, the Saturday evening supper for fourth-year theologians. Priests were obliged to fast from midnight till after the last mass they celebrated on the following day. On many Sundays we Kimmage priests said midday masses, so we had a more than twelve hour fast. To lessen the hardship, we were permitted a special late supper on Saturday evening with a better quality food than the normal Scholasticate supper fare. It seems like a trivial concession, but to us it was a significant privilege; there was a festive air about it and the usual mealtime silence was ignored.

On occasion we were assigned a Sunday mass in an outlying town that required going there the night before and sleeping at the parish priest's house. Among such was one ministry we all disliked: it involved a bus ride to a town in Wicklow where on arrival we got a frosty greeting from a very grumpy and sad-looking parish priest who totally ignored us thereafter. I pitied the man and prayed that I'd never be reduced to such an unhappy state.

We weren't permitted to preach at any of those Sunday masses, nor were we allowed to hear confessions during our fourth year of studies: both acts required the Archbishop's permission, which he did not grant. Since preaching and hearing confessions were essential priestly works it seemed a failure in our training system not to have the opportunity to perform those functions at that stage.

Theological Studies

Our fourth year theological studies involved completing the cycle of classes we had been taking for the past three years, in dogma, moral, canon law, history, and scripture, classes we shared with all other members of the House of Theology. In our final year we took two additional classes, which we did not share with our junior confreres. The first and most extensive of these was the course dealing with sex. That subject was reserved to fourth-year students, presumably because we were considered to be more mature, having been ordained priests and by the grace of ordination better able to withstand the temptations inherent in studying that seductive subject. The tract, called *De Sexu*, was known to generations of Kimmage Scholastics as the dirt tract. As described in our clinical Latin textbook, the sins against Holy Purity constituted a sordid list; indeed the manual portrayed sex as such a joyless endeavor that had the mythical Man from Mars read it before experiencing sex, he might well have wondered why anyone would want to engage in such a squalid experience. Fortunately, our professor, Father Paddy, took a fairly light-hearted approach to the theologically dismal subject. He used humor to lighten the inevitable tension, and occasionally referred to such then-current sex-pot luminaries as Raquel Welch and Gina Lollabrigida when giving examples of feminine voluptuosity. His approach was a happy contrast to that of his

196

predecessor. Father Edward had his students wear surplices and hold lighted candles in class to ward off any temptation that the subject matter might present to his priestly students.

Of course, we had all learned about sexual sin long before the dirt tract. Now, however, we studied, in minute detail, the circumstance in which sexual activity was lawful or unlawful, the definition and nature of sexual deviations, and the reasons why Mother Church considered unlawful enjoyment of sex to be so heinous. In a world of common sense and of law guided by rational thinking, sexual acts would be considered bad when and only when they were harmful to others. In such a world, rape, incest, and sex with minors, would be universally considered criminal. Adultery might be considered naughty but not necessarily illegal. And fornication might not be considered either naughty or illegal. But in Catholic theology, as developed over the centuries, the goodness and evil of sexual acts were not based on common sense or on the harm done to others – though the latter was given as added consideration when determining the evil of some acts. For the Church the guiding principal was what was perceived to be the Will of God, as extrapolated from a small number of biblical statements, principally those of St. Paul and Moses' sixth and ninth commandments. The Will of God, in the Church's interpretation, was perceived to be stern and all-forbidding. It might seem that the God who created the sexual function came to detest it later: why else would He ring even its lawful performance with such restrictions? Of course it might be asked if the extrapolations were really the Will of God or merely the warp of sex-hating theologians?

The second new course given to fourth year Theologians was Catechetics, which dealt with the teaching of Christian Doctrine. Our professor was Father Maurice, a learned scholar who was totally unconnected to either his students or the real world, and who made an already dry subject positively Saharan. His dreamy, almost ethereal, manner of lecturing touched our very bored funny-bones and seriously hindered us from learning the subject matter of the class. On one occasion, at the time when the American boxer, Cassius Clay, was in the ascendance and declaring himself to be *the greatest*, Father Maurice dreamily told his class that "Saint John Baptist de la Salle was the greatest ..." At which point the learned Doctor paused long to find the appropriate noun, even as his students burst into laughter. Such lack of respect for the Professor made me suspect that we were shaking off the monastic shackles that had bound us for so long, now that we had achieved our goal of ordination and would soon be on our way to missionary destinations.

Winding Down

The bloom, it would seem, was also fading from my own spiritual fervor. How else explain why I, who from the Novitiate on was almost fanatical in observing the Rule, now thought it oppressive whenever that same Rule interfered with my enjoyment of life. On one particular occasion I was actually angry at having to obey. The fourth year men were given a week's vacation away from the Scholasticate over the Christmas holidays, with the stipulation that we be available to say Sunday mass wherever in Dublin we were needed; and Sunday happened to fall in the middle of the vacation. The day after Christmas I borrowed a car from a generous cousin in Dublin and drove west to be with Aunt Mary and family. Saturday came all too soon and I had to return to Dublin to say seven o'clock mass in a convent on Sunday morning. I rebelled inwardly at the inconvenience, though outwardly I obeyed. After driving back to the city on

Saturday evening – a more than four-hour trip – I behaved irresponsibly towards my vows of poverty and obedience by going to the cinema to see a movie before returning to Kimmage late at night. It might seem a trivial fault, and it was, but in retrospect it appeared to be indicative of a changed attitude on my part to the religious life.

Shortly after Christmas I received a phone call from a Firinne friend who had married the previous year. James had just become a proud father, and would I be willing to baptize his little boy? He had got the required permission from his parish priest and had arranged for the baptism to take place the following Sunday afternoon in his parish church. I immediately studied the baptismal liturgy – we didn't cover it in our courses – and was ready when James called on Sunday afternoon. I was proud to usher my first new Christian into the Good Shepherds's fold.

In April, as the Scholastic year was coming to a close and the time drew near for us to go to our assigned missions, we were told we might state our preferences regarding missionary destinations, though with no guarantee that our preferences would be honored. Most of the Congregation's missions were in Africa. However, in order to foster vocations to the missionary life, the Congregation also owned and staffed three secondary schools in Ireland and another in Trinidad. The previous year, too, the Irish Province of the Congregation had opened a new mission field in the hinterland of Brazil and had sent a first contingent of six priests there. For most of my life I had been hearing stories of the African Missions and the work of missionaries to 'save the souls of black babies,' and while I was prepared to go to Africa to help in that work I was not particularly enthusiastic about it. I was even less interested in spending my life as a teacher in one of the Congregation's Irish schools. Brazil, however, struck an intriguing chord: it was a new mission and it seemed a bit exotic, perhaps because of my almost total ignorance of the country's people and culture and history. So I stated my preference for Brazil. Early in June we were given our assignments by the Provincial Superior and I, along with four other confreres, was appointed to Brazil. The Provincial ordered us to report to our mission Superior in that country by the middle of October.

Classes were now ended so we could devote time to preparing for the big adventure. One of the first items on the list was a vaccination against smallpox, administered by a nun-nurse in the Scholasticate infirmary. I suffered such a severe reaction to the vaccine as to feel, when the fever reached its peak, that I would like to die. Curiously, neither the fear of hell nor the enticement of heaven in any way influenced this feeling. I recovered of course and resumed my desire to go on living.

I planned to spend my final month in Ireland visiting and saying goodbye to relatives and friends, then to fly to New York for a two-month holiday with my family. But first there were a multitude of preparations. I bought, with money made available by the mission bursar, an old steamer trunk, into which I put those belongings that I wanted shipped directly to Brazil – mostly books, a pair of hiking boots and a silver chalice presented to me by my family at ordination. The steamer trunk was to be taken by one of my Brazil-bound confreres who would travel by ship from Liverpool to Santos.

Sister B

Sister B was one of my many nun-cousins, an older woman and a first cousin of my father. She contacted me shortly after my ordination and we met several times. Though she was a strong and forceful personality we hit it off well and had many discussions about our common ancestry: her mother and the Grandpa I had lived with as a child were siblings. After receiving my assignment to Brazil I mentioned to her that I would be visiting relatives in the west prior to leaving. She suggested that I also visit her family home in Cork; her mother would be delighted to see me, she said. When I lamented that lack of a car would not allow me to undertake such a trip, Sister B immediately volunteered to get me one. She brought me to a car dealer in Dublin with whom she was on friendly terms and whom she told that she needed a car for the summer; she also told him that I had volunteered to be her chauffeur. The dealer said he would be delighted to loan her a car for six weeks without charge. To satisfy her conscience that the car really was for her use, Sister B asked me to drive her to a convent where she had been Reverend Mother several years before. I was happy to do so, and one morning drove her over the Dublin mountains to her former convent in Wicklow. She didn't invite me into the convent and I wondered why. However, she had brought me a picnic basket, so I was content to wait for her in the car. When she finished her visit we drove back to Dublin. The car was mine for the next six weeks to visit relatives and friends. Many years after Sister B died I discovered that the convent she visited that day had attained notoriety as one of the industrial schools where orphaned children were housed and abused for many years. Sister B was in charge of that convent for about ten of those years. I had great difficulty associating my kind and considerate nun-cousin with the sadistic treatment those children were subjected to. The evidence, though strong and damning, also made clear, from testimony given to the commission of inquiry, that Sister B had inherited a very bad situation when she was appointed Reverend Mother and that she did make considerable improvements to the institution, particularly by improving the health care and education of the children. Nevertheless ....

Final Preparations

Since there was no Brazilian consulate in Dublin, my confreres and I who were bound for Brazil had to go to that country's consulate in Liverpool in order to get entry visas. On a summer evening in June we took a boat from Dublin to the Mersey-side city. It so happened that I had another nun-cousin in that city. I had never met Sister K, who was a niece of Sister B, but she invited me and my confreres to visit her convent when we came to Liverpool. Sister K was a beautiful young woman with whom I could have fallen in love if we were not both religious celibates. As it was we expressed mutual regret at parting and arranged to meet again when I visited her family home in Cork a few weeks later: she'd be home for a visit at that time before setting out for a missionary tour in Nigeria.

On return to Kimmage, I packed my clothes and headed West in Sister B's borrowed car. After a week visiting my mother's relatives and another week with Aunt Mary and family, I drove to Cork to visit Sister B's and Sister K's family. Sister K was already home, very Audrey Hepburn-ish in her nun's outfit, and again a challenge to my priestly vows. I noticed that she smiled at me a lot and apparently enjoyed my company, too. We were, after all, at a time of life when we ought to be sexually active, and this was as close to such activity as our vows permitted. So we made the most of our brief time together. Which ended all too soon when we returned to our respective institutions, she to get ready for Nigeria, I to make final preparations to depart for America and Brazil.

American Interlude

A Celibate in Manhattan

On August fifteen, nineteen sixty-four, I left Ireland and flew to New York on a Boeing 707. It was a happy day and a sad day. I was going to New York for the first time, and I was going to spend two months with my family – who wouldn't be happy at that thought. But I was also leaving my homeland forever. Brazil would become my new home: I could have no expectation of ever returning to Ireland, except for an occasional visit. So departing did hurt: I was leaving behind friends and relatives, all the people associated with my life. There was also that intangible attachment to my place of origin: it might sound mawkish, but I loved the old country. Many times, before I went to the Novitiate, I had said, on hearing that another friend had emigrated, "I would never leave Ireland; I love it too much."

My mother, two brothers, and a sister met me at Idlewild – my father was working away from home at that time – and welcomed me with hearty handshakes. Three American cousins, attractive young women, who also came with my family to meet me, welcomed me with uninhibited embraces and kisses. Which I found most embarrassing – I hadn't been hugged and kissed since I was a baby – but they seemed to regard it as a perfectly normal way of greeting a new cousin.

Tom drove us to our parents' apartment in Queens in his enormous American car. The sights and sounds of New York amazed me: the skyscraper skyline of Manhattan visible in the distance, the overhead trains, the massive bridges and overpasses, the varied tones of cacophonous sounds. Above all, I was astonished at the many-lane highways with their endlessly flowing traffic. By comparison Dublin seemed a quiet little town.

Apart from the years I spent in institutions, I had lived all my life in frugal houses and had no experience of flats – or apartments, as Americans call them. So I was enchanted with the fifth-floor dwelling in which my parents, Jim, and Bridie, lived. It was roomy and cheerful and had better furniture than any we had when I was growing up. I was happy that my family seemed prosperous after their many years of poverty.

I got my first taste of seriously hot weather: New York in August was steamy. And people dressed accordingly: my puritanical Irish eyes thought the women were dressed inadequately and in poor taste, while my reprobate self enjoyed the bare legs and arms and cleavage so generously on display everywhere. For the first time since going to the Novitiate I ventured forth in public dressed in short-sleeved shirt and trousers, with no insignia to identify me as a man of the cloth. Initially, I felt almost naked and guilty, but soon overcame my reticence and wore clerical dress only when walking to say mass in the local church each morning, and when paying formal visits with my mother to American relatives; of which there were quite a few in the New York area.

My mother was proud of her son the priest but was appalled at my shabby clothes: I was wearing the one black suit

204

I possessed, which she had bought me the year before my ordination and which I had worn most days for the past year. So she took me to a Manhattan store that specialized in outfitting clergy and bought me a gorgeous silk suit. Then she scheduled weekend visits to various relatives to show me off. Those visits were both enjoyable and disconcerting. I was suffering the natural frustration of a twenty-nine year old male let loose in a society that commercialized sex but whose vow of celibacy placed it out of bounds. One hot Sunday afternoon we visited cousins in New Jersey, an Irish-American couple with a grown family. Their youngest son was visiting home that day with his fiancée, a beautiful young woman whom the elder cousins told us, sotto voce, was Jewish. They had a backyard above-ground pool and the son invited me to join him for a dip, giving me one of his bathing suits. He and his fiancée, who were having a lot of fun splashing around and throwing a ball, invited me to join in. The young woman engaged in physical contact in a way no woman had ever done to me before, having none of the reservations of Catholic women about flirting with priests. I was sexually excited and reciprocated her flirtation. It took me several days to recover priestly equilibrium from that event.

Those first weeks in New York were exhilarating: not good for the priestly soul but intoxicating for the man behind the clerical facade. What to my family were everyday events, like being caught up in the evening subway crush or walking among the skyscrapers of Manhattan or browsing in bookstores of a dimension I had never seen before, were new and exciting experiences for me. Being feted by relatives and family friends, while no longer a new experience, made me feel once again that I was a person of importance. It was a sentiment hardly laudable for a priest who had renounced the world and its vanities, but I found it a pleasant antidote to my years of monastic humility,

205

with its inculcated belief that I was nothing without God. My recovery from eight years of Scholastic taming began in the experiences of those weeks .

Anne, a pretty young cousin, invited me to accompany her to the World Fair which was being held that summer in nearby Flushing Meadows. We had an exciting day wandering through the many international pavilions, and by evening when it was time to go our separate ways I was once again infatuated. I discovered afterwards that my mother had asked her to take me to the Fair and had given her money for expenses. Years later my mother told me that Anne had admitted that she also fell in love with me that day. Later still I discovered that my future wife was working at the Fair: we might even have seen each other!

Despite the distractions and temptations of New York I never once thought of abandoning my priestly vocation. I was willing to be titillated by, and suffer the anguish of, unrequited love, but I never considered breaking my vows. My faith was strong, I was a priest forever, I had committed myself to God for life, and I was going to be faithful to that commitment. I said mass each morning, recited the divine office, and completed the daily spiritual exercises that my Congregation imposed. In weekly confession I begged forgiveness for my sins and promised God I would do better.

Touring in the South

Jim, who was employed by American Airlines, got free passes for himself, Mammy, and me, to fly anywhere in the United States for thirty days. My mother was thrilled: she loved to fly and to visit relatives. At the beginning of September the three of us flew to Dallas. I had thought New York heat was excessive, but it seemed moderate compared to the blast of furnace air that struck us on stepping onto the tarmac in Dallas. We rented a car and drove to Texarkana to visit Sister Ethelreda, my mother's nun-sister, who worked in a Catholic hospital there. That two-hundred-mile drive, in a non-air-conditioned car, was a foretaste of the heat I would soon experience in Brazil.

The South during the summer of 1964 was also steaming in the aftermath of President Kennedy's assassination, and was in the throes of the Civil Rights agitation. Having come from Ireland, where blatant bigotry existed mainly between Protestants and Catholics in the North, to which I hadn't been exposed, I wasn't able to understand the irrational prejudice that existed against black people in America. That discrimination was brought home to me in a very particular way when we stopped at a wayside ice-cream shop and saw separate entry doors marked *white* and *colored*. Imagining myself a black person in that milieu, I felt rage at such treatment. A few day later I encountered the bigotry in a more personal way when we visited well-to-do cousins in an elegant suburb of Shreveport; the conversation there was blatantly racist when the cousins discussed their black fellow men and women. In contrast, when we visited two Irish cousins of my father, Sisters Lourdes and Louis, who ran a school for black children, we found ourselves in a section of Shreveport where the houses were ramshackle, the streets unpaved and without sidewalks, and the children poorly dressed. And nuns who were loving and caring towards their underprivileged charges.

Jim left us to return to work. My mother and I drove to Natchez, where Tom's uncle-in-law was a pastor. We drove through a part of that city where black men, looking sullen and lethargic, were congregated on the streets. The Monsignor told us they were expecting race riots at any time. The Civil Rights Act

With Sister Louis in Shreveport

had just been signed, and riots had already occurred in several cities across the country.

I was surprised at the opulent living style of the Catholic clergy in Natchez. The Rectory was elegant in structure and furnishings; the Monsignor treated us to dinner in a fine restaurant; that evening we sat in a beautifully furnished living room and watched the Miss America pageant on television. I was shocked that priests would watch, with obvious pleasure, what seemed to me such a blatant worldly and sexually titillating program.

We visited more cousins and aunts in Lake Charles and Beaumont – my mother seemed to have relatives everywhere in the South. By now I was forming an opinion of the United States,

208

and I didn't like what seemed its unrestrained materialism. People everywhere presented themselves as obsessed with acquiring money and material things. Discussions of wealth and houses and cars and furnishings and clothes dominated most conversations. It was all contrary to my chosen vow of poverty, and I concluded that I could never live in this country.

Fund-raising

However, despite my lack of interest in things material, I remembered that I had been admonished by my Kimmage Superiors to collect funds in America to help the Congregation's fledgling mission in Brazil. I mentioned this fact to Sister Ethelreda, my nun-aunt in Texarkana. She immediately thought of a wealthy Catholic she knew – a millionaire, she said in a tone of awe – who was a patient in her hospital and whose prognosis was for a very short stay in this life. She promised to blarney the old man by talking about her nephew's future missionary work before introducing us. When she eventually brought me in to meet him he was sitting up in bed staring into space. The watery eyes behind the rimless glasses and the blotchy skin of his bald head did indeed give an impression of one not long for this world.

"I hear," he said, in a quavering voice, "that you're going off to Brazil to spread the gospel of the Lord."

"I am indeed." My tone exuding unction: I had hitherto been remiss in

Sister Ethelreda

209

seeking funds, so a substantial donation from this man would help offset my delinquency.

The aunt discreetly left the room.

"I'm a very religious man myself." The old fellow stopped to cough. "And I wholeheartedly approve of what you're doing."

"It's important work."

"The vineyard of the Lord! That's where you're going to harvest souls."

"It is indeed."

"The harvest is great but the laborers are few."

"There were many millions of people in Brazil."

"Blessed are the feet of them ..." He stopped again to cough."

"Indeed!" Stifling my impatience: I didn't need a sermon, just a check.

"Most laudable." He spat into a tissue.

"Someone has to do it." Was the fellow going to die before he got to write a check?

"And I'm not able any more." His attempted grin was ghastly.

"*They also serve who only stand and wait.*" Not Biblical, I thought, but appropriate.

"What was that?" The old fellow stared vacantly at me. "I suppose. Anyway, I'd like to give you something to help God's work in your mission field." He reached laboriously for the checkbook on his bedside table.

"Everything helps." I was almost salivating.

"This is for the Lord's vineyard." He uncapped a fountain pen with difficulty and wrote slowly.

Though carefully avoiding any show of interest, I counted three zeroes. A thousand dollars would be most helpful to my work in Brazil.

"God bless your work for the Lord." The old man tore off the check and handed it to me.

"May the good Lord reward you." I pocketed it without a glance.

The aunt was waiting outside the sick man's room. "How did you get on?" Excitement in her whisper.

"Great! He gave me a check."

"I knew he would; he's a generous man. How much?"

I took the check from my pocket and looked at it.

"What's the matter?" the aunt cried, seeing my look of dismay.

"It's for ten dollars and no cents." I showed her the miserable piece of paper.

From Dallas my mother and I flew to California. She had visited Hollywood in the late nineteen twenties and had fond memories of her visit there, which included, she said, meeting the actress Clara Bow. We spent a few days in Los Angeles, where a man I met after my morning mass gave us a tour of the city and environs. We visited Disneyland in Anaheim before flying north to San Francisco. I had arranged to meet one of my father's cousins at the airport, a wealthy businessman whom I had hopes of milking for mission funds. But the wealthy are wily when it comes to parting with money, and this man was even less forthcoming than the dying millionaire in Texarkana. When he said goodbye he wished me luck in my missionary endeavors but offered no pecuniary support. We also met his son, a Benedictine monk studying for the priesthood, who had driven his father to the airport in the new Thunderbird the old man had bought him for his vacation use. American Scholastics had obviously different notions about the vow of poverty than we had in Kimmage.

My mother and I toured San Francisco for a couple of

days, and visited some wineries in Napa Valley before flying home to New York. On return we found that my father had a drinking relapse, so I enlisted the help of a local Alcoholics Anonymous group. With the help of a member, I found a "drying out" center in upstate New York and persuaded my father to go there. The member drove us up the Taconic State Parkway through the glorious fall foliage whose spectacular beauty enthralled me. My father remained at the center until it was almost time for me to leave for Brazil. On his return to the city he seemed full of hope, and promised to remain free of alcohol.

My American vacation came to an end. On October 14 I said goodbye to my family and flew to Miami. From there I took another plane to São Paulo, with stops along the way at Panama City and Lima. I woke in the morning to see the Andean peaks reaching up and looking most intimidating in their stark ruggedness. The flight from Lima crossed the South American continent, including the massive jungle of Matto Grosso. That afternoon I arrived in São Paulo and was met at Congonhas airport by Father Banaghan, a Kimmage confrere who had been in Brazil for the past year.

Introduction to Brazil

Initial Shock

I realized it only after my arrival in Brazil. It was ludicrous: I had committed to spend my life doing priestly ministry here in this big and populous country, but I knew nothing about its people, its language, its history, or its culture. Why hadn't the Scholasticate prepared me? And why didn't I wake up to my ignorance when I learned I was being sent here?

I couldn't even hazard a guess regarding the Scholasticate's failure. The Congregation's stated objective was to preach the gospel of Jesus Christ to those most in need of it. So why didn't it adequately prepare its future missionaries for the work they were ordained to do? Suitable preparation would surely include learning the language and understanding the history and culture of the people among whom we would minister. But Kilshane and Kimmage had trained us to be monks rather than missionaries. Was it the Congregation's theory that good monks would ipso facto make good missionaries? That if we were holy we'd be automatically prepared to teach and preach and cope with the unexpected in a culture we didn't understand? If so, the theory was woefully deficient, akin, I thought, to preparing a football team through body-building exercises alone.

As regards my own failure to realize my lack of preparedness before I arrived in the country, the answer, I believed – while not excusing my own blameworthiness – lay with the environment in which I had been raised. The fourth commandment, as interpreted by priests and teachers, demanded blind obedience: children were to obey their parents and teachers, Catholics were to obey their priests and Church teachings. In that environment it was considered more virtuous to follow the herd and obey than to be a maverick and question. I had always been an obedient boy and was much praised for it, so I had no incentive to rebel. And from the moment I decided to become a priest my path was charted by the Congregation. The objective of the vow of obedience was that I should follow orders. I had to make only one decision, to become a priest in the Congregation. All other determinations – to take vows, to be ordained – were simply presented for my acceptance, as consequences of that first choice. Thus, I didn't have to think for myself – until I arrived in Brazil.

What now? Strangely, I never asked that question, even after arriving in Brazil. I wasn't aware that I should ask it. I was excited to have come to this vast country and to be facing a future that, though unknowable yet, promised to be exotic, or at least different from anything I had so far experienced. So I allowed myself to be directed by my new Superior into a groove of missionary work and to get carried along in that groove. Beyond that I didn't think. Unfortunately, my Brazilian Superior who, after thirty years in Nigeria, knew something of the people he ministered to in that country, knew nothing at all of Brazilian culture or language.

Brazil, as I learned after my arrival, was huge: territorially the fifth biggest country in the world. It boasted a river – the

Amazon – with the world's largest volume of water, the most extensive rain forests in the world, and was the only Latin American country in which Portuguese was the national language. Politically, the country was a Federative Republic, composed of twenty-six States and a Federal District that contained the capital city, Brazilia, which was only then under construction. Seventy percent of Brazil's more than one hundred and thirty million people were poor, most of them desperately poor. The country was governed by a military dictatorship which had overthrown the democratic government just a few months earlier. That military coup didn't scare me; I had only vaguely heard about it before I arrived and had no idea what, if anything, it would mean for me and my fellow missionaries.

My four Kimmage confreres traveled by ship from Liverpool to Santos because it was cheaper than flying, especially with all the luggage they were bringing. They arrived before me and I met them in São Paulo at a house owned by priests of the German Province of the Holy Ghost Congregation.

"I hope," I joked to confrere Paddy, after we had swapped stories about our adventures since we parted in Kimmage, "you didn't forget my steamer trunk."

The confreres looked at each other. For a while no one spoke. "Well," Paddy said eventually, "I've been meaning to tell you about that."

"You forgot to take it off the ship," I yelped in mock horror, expecting a bit of leg-pulling.

"It fell into the sea at Liverpool," Steve blurted.

From the look on their faces I knew Steve wasn't joking. "You're codding me," I said anyway.

"I'm very sorry," Paddy said. "It was one of those bloody freak accidents. They were transferring our luggage from the boat we took to Liverpool onto the steamer that took us to Santos and

215

the fellow handling your trunk let it fall into the water."

"We dried it out as best we could," Jimmy said, "but the books were all destroyed."

"What about my chalice?" Panic in my voice: the chalice, that precious ordination gift from my parents, was the one item in the trunk I really valued.

"It's damaged, but I'd say it can be fixed," John said.

"The trunk was insured along with the rest of our stuff," Paddy added. "I already put in a claim to the insurance company, so you'll get some money out of it."

My practice of Poverty during the past eight years stood me in good stead now: once I got over the initial shock I felt no sense of loss. Later on, the insurance money was to become a problem.

Our Congregation Superior in Brazil was Father John. He came up from his parish in Florida Paulista – a town about four hundred miles west, in the hinterland of São Paulo State – to meet us. Though we hadn't hitherto met Padre João – as his parishioners called him – we had heard of his reputation for making snap judgments of people, and standing by those judgments. So we were on our best behavior in order to make a good initial impression, since he'd be assigning us to our parishes. His own parish, he told us, as well as two others in the same area that were manned by Irish Holy Ghost confreres, was in the diocese of Marilia. The Irish Province also staffed two parishes in the State of Goiás.

One of Padre João's first snap judgments after meeting us was to choose me as assistant pastor in his own parish. It was an important posting, he told me: I would be virtually the *vigario* – parish priest – since he himself would be in America and Ireland most of the time raising funds for our mission. He reassigned the confrere who for the past year had been his assistant, because, he informed me, he considered him too 'flighty.' He didn't explain the epithet and I didn't probe. Nevertheless, I was nervous about my new appointment: my instincts told me that Padre João was somewhat capricious and might be difficult to get along with. However, since there were other parishes manned by confreres in the diocese I wouldn't lack for congenial company.

We spent our first few days in São Paulo going to various government agencies, in order to acquire the permanent visas that would allow us to work in Brazil. Padre Miguel introduced us to cafezinho, one of the national drinks, a potent coffee available in bars on every street and served in a demitasse. It took me a while to get used to its bitter flavor, but once I acquired a taste for it all other coffees seemed inadequate. I also developed an appetite for the German breakfast, courtesy of our German hosts' hospitality. On our only Sunday in São Paulo we all went to a soccer game where we witnessed the fevered partisanship of the Brazilian male futebal fan – and it was male: there were almost no women in the stadium. We were fortunate to see Brazil's most famous player, Pelé, play with his Santos team; he was at the height of his playing prowess at that time.

Learning the language

For the first week, we newcomers were in Brazil but not yet of it. Because we didn't speak the language we talked only to each other and to the German Fathers, who spoke English quite well. Our only contact with Brazilians was in the government offices we visited to get our visas. In those places we just stood and gaped, leaving the negotiations to Padres João and Miguel, whose Irish accents stood out as they endeavored to explain our needs in halting Portuguese. Listening to their efforts I promised myself that I'd learn to speak the language of the country well.

A week after arriving we boarded a bus for the city of Anapolis, more than a thousand miles away, where Padre João had arranged that we take a crash course in Portuguese. The ride took us through a type of land that was very different from the fields of Mayo, for which I found myself yearning now. The longing of the exile for his native country has been recorded down through the ages, and on this tedious journey through unfamiliar terrain I experienced it first-hand. We drove through dusty scrubby land, parched from continuous drought, and only sparsely inhabited by humans. We discovered for ourselves what one of the German Fathers had told us, that Brazil was occupied more by insects than by people: along the way we saw a multitude of giant red humps in the scrub-lands – some as big as two-storey houses – that were ant-hills built out of red clay. And when we pulled in to rest-stops at night we saw hordes of flying creatures swarming around the outside lamps. Altogether, I found the journey depressing: I was thousands of miles from home, wondering what I was doing in this alien land where so much seemed unconnected to my life experience. And, since I couldn't speak the language, I felt very much separated from the people among whom I had come to minister.

Anapolis was an oasis in the semi-desert center of Brazil, and this was especially true of the Franciscan Monastery that hosted our Portuguese language course. The Friars' welcome gave me an immediate feeling of security in what seemed a rather primitive and inhospitable country – an initial feeling that time and the Brazilian people would prove entirely wrong. The monastery, an outpost of the Franciscan Friars of the Atonement whose headquarters was in Graymoor, New York, was equipped with the many types of ecclesiastical comforts that I had noted during my holidays in the United States. In our Novitiate and Scholasticate we were told that poverty of spirit – *Blessed are the poor in spirit* – was more important for Religious than mere material poverty. At the same time we were taught that material poverty – doing without non-essentials – was an indispensable aspect of spiritual poverty. However, the Americans, it seemed to me, practiced spiritual poverty without depriving themselves of material comforts. Furnishings were all first class in this Franciscan monastery: couches and chairs were luxurious, and my bed was the most comfortable I had ever slept in. The food was excellent, too, and it was American cuisine rather than Brazilian. I tasted pizza for the first time the Sunday after our arrival. The cook had the night off and one of the Friars, Father Rocky, recently arrived from the United States and a self-proclaimed expert pizza maker, treated us to what the Americans present said was an outstanding example of its kind. However, on first tasting this Italian-American delicacy I was less than bowled over by the new addition to my limited palatine repertoire.

But it wasn't the pizza that gave me diarrhea during my first week in Anapolis. Most likely it was the water I swallowed while brushing my teeth: we had been strongly advised by our hosts not to drink the water. So severe was the bout that after a few days without eating, and feeling weak, I was carted off to the local hospital. The diagnosis was dehydration so I was kept overnight, with an intravenous tube in my arm. My nurse was a pretty young woman whose terribly sad expression I couldn't but notice. I mentioned that fact to the night nurse, an older woman, who told me that her young colleague had the Chagas disease, for which there was no cure: she would die from it in a couple of years. The insect that carried the disease, called o barbeiro, the barber, was commonly found in the mud huts of the very poor.

We began to learn Portuguese. Our teachers were young

women students from the local escola normal – teacher training college – who used a version of the total-immersion-in-the-language technique. We spent our days listening to them pronounce common phrases in Portuguese and repeating those phrases. Our teachers corrected us ad nauseam until we pronounced each phrase with a semblance of accuracy. I found Portuguese fairly easy to learn since, in words and grammar, it resembled Latin. The difficulty lay in the, mostly nasal, sounds that were foreign to my English-habituated vocal cords; though familiarity with Irish language sounds helped somewhat. After a couple of weeks of relentless practice we could speak passably well and even make up sentences. But for the most part we were not yet able to understand our teachers – who spoke no English – when they talked in the rapid tones of everyday speech. As students of a second language often do, we committed some comical blunders. Breakfast in the Franciscan community was a casual meal; when we arrived in the dining room each morning we'd go to the kitchen and place our orders with the Brazilian cook. Father Rocky, the pizza maker, decided to try out his new language skills one morning and, to the cook's great amusement, ordered two fried grandmothers for breakfast.

We were just two weeks into the Portuguese course when the Franciscan Superior asked me to say one of the Sunday masses in their nearby parish church. Naturally, I'd have to preach in Portuguese, the Superior added, without even a suspicion of a smile. I accepted the challenge and, after spending many hours writing a sermon, presented it to one of our teachers for review and correction. Several drafts later she pronounced it fit to be read on Sunday. Since after Vatican II all masses were to be said in the vernacular I also had to learn the Portuguese-language version of the mass. The parish congregation didn't show any wild enthusiasm for my preaching, but at least it was reasonably intelligible, according to my teacher-mentor who was present.

Christmas in the Hinterland

On Christmas Eve I went to the nearby city of Goiânia to assist Father Enda, a confrere who had come to Brazil the previous year and was pastor of a parish on the outskirts of that city. He asked me to go that afternoon to an outlying chapel at the far end of his parish where there was no resident priest, to hear confessions and say mass on Christmas morning. Getting there required a three-hour trip in a no-frills bus on unpaved roads that gave a jolting ride through the scrubby countryside. I arrived at a village that resembled the cowboy towns I had seen in old Western films, with its unpaved street of ramshackle buildings, in front of which horses and mules were tied to hitching rails. The chapel, which I located by walking down the center of the street – there were no sidewalks – was a small spare whitewashed building with double doors that were locked. After much asking in my imperfect Portuguese, I encountered a man who knew where the caretaker lived; he pointed to a rundown-looking shack. The caretaker, an old man with the sad air of one who expected nothing of life, was both annoyed and apologetic.

"They didn't send me word that you were coming or I'd have met you at the bus."

"I didn't know myself until today that I was coming."

"We haven't seen a Padre here for almost a year. Although the people here are *muito Catholico* – very Catholic."

"That's a pity."

"We have a terrible shortage of priests in Brazil, Padre. Most of those who come to visit us in this town are from far

221

away. Where are you from yourself?"

"I'm from Ireland."

The old man looked confused. "I haven't heard of that place. What part of Brazil is it?"

I explained that Ireland was a different country. Near England, I said. The old man's expression lightened. "The English I've heard about. Are you English?" His tone turned suspicious.

"No. We Irish don't like the English."

"That's good. I'm told the English aren't nice people." Then he added, "there are some very bad people here, too. Someone stabbed a man to death last night in a bar down the street."

That was a shock; the place might really be like the wild west of the cowboy films. "I wish I'd been here," I said, though I didn't mean it. "I might have saved the soul of the murdered man."

He ignored that statement. "I'll take you to the house where the priest stays whenever one comes – not that they come very often. Although the people here are *muito Catholico*." He sounded aggrieved. "The landlady is a nice woman," he added.

By now it was dark – night falls quickly here after sunset – and we walked to the landlady's house in the light of occasional street lamps. Her's, too, was a simple wooden structure, though it looked neat and was well lighted. A tall angular woman, gray-haired, of uncertain age, came to the door when the caretaker clapped his hands and called in to her.

"I wasn't expecting a padre." She ignored me and looked at my guide with a hurt expression. "Nobody told me he was coming."

"I didn't know myself." The old man seemed a bit timid in

222

her presence. "You'll take care of him anyway?"

"Of course I will." She seemed insulted that the matter could even be in doubt. Then she let her eyes roam over me, as if to ensure I was really a priest; apparently I passed the test. "I'll give you supper, Padre, and get your room ready."

The caretaker left after telling me he'd come by in the morning to wake me. The landlady sat me down at a small table in what looked like a one-room cabin, and a few minutes later put a plate of rice and beans before me. Then she disappeared. I was hungry so I pitched in. I had heard that rice and beans were the staple food of the poor but had never been served them. The rice was tasteless and the beans were bitter but my hunger didn't wait on tasty food. The landlady returned just as I finished.

"I'll show you to your room now," she said, her manner still brusque but not unfriendly. "The padres who come here have always found it comfortable."

She led me to a small whitewashed lean-to attached to her house; its only furniture was a cot in the corner. A bare light bulb shone from the ceiling and there was a tiny window high up over the bed. I, who had always been timid in the face of physical danger, didn't feel any fear after she closed the door and left me to spend the night in this austere room with a door that couldn't be locked, in a wild-west town where a man was stabbed to death the night before. On the contrary, I felt a sort of thrill at being a real he-man missionary at last, out in the wilds by myself without my confreres. But my feelings didn't include the spiritual zeal of a Francis Xavier reveling in the possibility of martyrdom at the hands of infidels. I felt quite safe because I was in the midst of a people that called itself *muito Catholico*.

After spending a couple of hours writing a sermon for the morrow while sitting on the cot I slept the night through without waking. In the morning the caretaker clapped outside the door to tell me it was time for confessions and mass. I suggested that I'd like to shower and shave first: the heat and humidity in Brazil made it imperative to shower daily. Showering was out of the question, the old man said; they didn't have any facilities. But there was a spigot on the wall outside the door that I could use for shaving. I managed to remove the facial stubble with cold water and without a mirror, and then went to the chapel.

The congregation was small, made up mostly of poorly dressed women and children. I heard confessions for a short time: there weren't many who wanted to be shrived, even though Father Enda had said there hadn't been a priest there for many months. Still, it was a moving experience for me; I was on my own, no one spoke my language, and I could speak theirs only passably. But I understood a good deal of what they said in confession so I was privy to people's feelings about religion in a way I hadn't experienced since arriving in the country. Some of the women were vocal about their piety. I'm very Catholic, padre; I say the rosary every day; I teach my children how to pray; I wish we could have mass more often. I don't speak badly about others; you'll come more often, padre, won't you? And they talked freely about their spouses' shortcomings, revealing a patriarchal society in which they felt downtrodden and not respected. I said mass and read my prepared sermon on the meaning of Christmas, looking out at my small congregation as often as I dared, while keeping my finger on the place from which I was reading.

The men were notable by their absence, so the stereotype of the Brazilian Catholic community that I had been hearing since arriving in the country – the women went to mass and the men did not – was all too apparent here. But I believed they all had immortal souls that needed to be led towards heaven, and felt glad that I had become a missionary to help in that leading. However,

I sensed the disdain of the men as I walked down the street after mass, conspicuous in my white soutane. A few nodded wary greetings, many others ignored me in a way that I felt was almost hostile. Some turned their backs when they saw me coming. Overall, I intuited that my presence here was tolerated by them rather than welcomed: I was an intruder, not a savior. So I was glad to catch the only bus of the day back to Goiânia.

Graduation

After Christmas we took a short break from the monotony of repeating Portuguese phrases, and a few of us took off by bus to see the new capital, Brazilia, which was about a hundred miles away, and was still under construction. Oscar Niemeyer's architecture already had a city-of-the-future appearance, though only a small portion of it had yet been completed. Designed to look like a huge airplane when seen from the air, the tail – the parliament building complex – had been built, as had the presidential palace. The frame of the cathedral, which looked like a giant crown, was in place though the body of the church hadn't yet been built. Newly laid-out streets over-passed and under-passed one another without the need for traffic signals.

We visited an American rectory that had just been completed. Priests from the diocese of Camden, New Jersey, volunteered to spend three year stints there, ministering to the workers who had come from all over Brazil to help construct the new Capital. The rectory was a magnificent structure, architecturally worthy of the new city. One of its unusual features was a beautifully designed stream that ran through the gorgeous living room. I thought the rectory was a crass display of conspicuous wealth in the center of the community the priests were serving. It was located in the midst of shacks, in a shanty town outside the city proper, that housed poor laborers and their families. Even poverty of spirit was missing here.

Back in Anapolis, I was awakened one morning in the still-dark hours by the sounds of singing. At first I thought some careless person had turned on a radio, as harmonious voices rang out in a rendition of the beautiful *Cielito Lindo*. Then I realized that the music was coming from somewhere outside. From my window I spied three men strolling along the well-lit street singing, one of them strumming a guitar. It was a trivial incident, though I thought it unusual and charming, indicative of the gentleness I was to find among Brazilians: the singers, who very likely had a little too much to drink, were on their way home at an ungodly hour, and instead of being rowdy they channeled their high spirits into lovely music.

In mid-January we graduated from our Portuguese course. There was no test: that would come when we reached our assigned parishes and attempted to communicate with our new parishioners. One confrere went to a parish near Goiania, the rest of us returned to Sao Paulo in order to reach our various destinations. We took a bus to Rio first, a twenty-two hour ride that became a thirty-two hour endurance test when the bus broke down and we had to wait for a replacement, which also broke down. Another bus from Rio took us to Sao Paulo, from where I boarded a train at night for a twelve-hour ride to Florida Paulista. The train was a surprise: clean, comfortable, and with a white-tablecloth dining car that had food to match.

When I arrived at the Florida Paulista station Padre João wasn't there to meet me, so I hailed the only horse-cab at the station and asked the driver to take me to the *Casa Paroquial*.

226

Parish Life

Initiation

I was feeling grumpy and depressed as the horse pulled the lazy *carro* through what turned out to be Florida Paulista's main street. It was just after eight in the morning and there were no people to be seen anywhere. This was my new home town, but it didn't offer me any welcome. Dammit, I felt! Where was Padre João and why wasn't he at the station to meet me? And if priests were so scarce here that the bishop of Marilia had to reach across thousands of miles to find an Irish priest willing to come to his diocese, why didn't he delegate someone to meet and welcome the new priest on arrival? Even the cab driver wasn't disposed to talk, and I didn't feel my knowledge of Portuguese was good enough yet to engage him in conversation. My first sight of the *Casa Paroquial* did nothing to lift my spirits: it was a drab-looking shack, like the houses I saw in the black section of Shreveport. And the church in front of it had an unfinished look. I paid the cab driver, grabbed my suitcase and, after knocking, walked through the open front door of the house into a small shabby room.

"*Bom dia, Padre!*" said the dark-skinned roly-poly woman

227

from a doorway at one end of the room. "*Seja bemvindo* – you're welcome." She continued in rapid Portuguese, of which I captured just enough to grasp that she was the housekeeper and she welcomed me and said that Padre João had gone to minister to a dying woman which was why he wasn't able to meet me at the station. But he should be back shortly. Her name was Dona Zelie and she showed me around the house, which took about thirty seconds. The little room I had entered was the living room, furnished with a sorry-looking couch and a couple of hard chairs; off this room on one side was a tiny dining area with a table and four chairs, off which were the bathroom and the kitchen, small though not tiny. On the other side of the living room were two small bedrooms.

"Padre João sleeps in the back room," Dona Zelie said, "so you'll have the front room."

I dumped my suitcase on the floor of my dank and dark bedroom. Against the wall, a narrow bed took up half the room; a mosquito net that hung from the ceiling surrounded it. In the corner between bed and window were make-shift doors that suggested a closet. Wooden shutters, which the housekeeper opened inwards, covered the small window. She raised the lower half to let in hot humid air. I spotted a green lizard racing sideways along an upper wall and pointed it out to Dona Zelie.

"That's good," she said. "He eats the mosquitoes."

Padre João soon returned, looking fresh and vigorous after performing his priestly duty. Dona Zelie served us breakfast – boiled eggs, rolls that were fresh, and coffee that was black and bitter. Afterwards, Padre João took me on a tour. Just beyond the front door stood a door-less garage that housed a jeep, a green hardtop affair.

"The parish bought it for me last year; it's rugged enough

to handle any kind of terrain. And it needs to be. Wait till you see the roads!" He seemed proud of what looked to me like a tin can on wheels; I was still feeling grumpy.

We looked at the church from the outside. "It holds five hundred people." Padre João grinned ruefully. "Not that it's filled very often. And it's still unfinished: the tower isn't complete yet."

"What's the purpose of the tower?" It looked to me like an unnecessary piece of architecture, standing apart from the church.

"None. It's a useless appendage. But Brazilians don't consider their church properly finished until it has a tower. And a city isn't considered a city until it has a church tower with a clock face on all four sides." Padre Joao sounded both amused and frustrated.

"So when are you going to finish it?"

"As soon as we raise the money, which might take another couple of years or more. But that's another story." He didn't elaborate.

The inside of the church was spare, though it did have pews; its high windows were plain glass. The new high altar, at the front of the chancel as Vatican II mandated, looked like a big table; the original marble altar nestled against the back wall looking neglected, its gold-leaf tabernacle doors gleaming in the soft light. Padre João pointed to a marble side altar on the right, beneath which was a statue of the dead Christ.

"That's Sir Mort," he said, laconically.

I looked at him without comprehension. "Sir Mort?"

He grinned – I soon discovered there was often a hint of triumph in his grin, signaling that he was putting one over on his victim. "It's a statue of *Senhor Morto* – the Dead Lord – and it's terrifically important to the *Brasileiros*."

At the risk of being the straight man I felt obliged to ask: "what's important about it?"

"You'll find out in due course." Again, he didn't elaborate and I didn't enquire. There was a hard edge to his humor that didn't encourage badinage.

He took me on a tour of the city in the jeep. In front of the church was a large octagonal garden-in-the-making, which he called the *praça*, from which all the principle streets of the city emanated like wheel spokes. Only the main street, which had open-front shops, was paved; all others were of red packed clay.

"The main street," Padre João said, "leads out to a highway called the *rodoviario*, one of the main transportation arteries in the State: a two-lane paved road that runs from São Paulo City to the Parana river, a distance of more than four hundred miles."

"I think I've heard of the Parana river."

He looked at me as though marveling at my ignorance. "It's one of the biggest rivers in South America and the ninth longest in the world. It separates the State of São Paulo from the State of Mato Grosso which is mostly jungle and is more than twice the size of France." He leaned over and slapped my knee. "And that's your geography lesson for today, Padre."

The houses in the city were for the most part simple wooden structures like the Casa Paroquial, with here and there, in utter contrast, a beautifully architected home.

"This one belongs to the *Delegado*." Padre João pointed to an elegant modern-style structure set back from the road, with a manicured garden in front.

"Who's he?"

"The chief of police; he's the second most important man in Florida Paulista."

"I notice," I said, "that next to his mansion there are simple wooden houses on either side. The rich wouldn't live next door

230

to the poor like that in Ireland or America ."

"They claim," Padre Joâo's tone expressed disbelief, "that there's no racism or class-ism in Brazil. I don't believe that's true; it's just that Brazilians are a bit more subtle about their prejudices."

That raised a question I was curious about. "What's the ethnic make-up here? Is there a mixture of races like we saw in São Paulo?"

He paused before answering. "Probably not as diverse as in the big cities, but quite a mixture all the same. They're mostly Italian and Portuguese around here; also lots of Blacks and Japanese; and some German. And many many of mixed race."

"Do they have miscegenation here? They told me in America that marriage there between blacks and whites is rare. It's even outlawed in some States."

Padre Joao waved back to a man who saluted as we passed. "Inter-marriage between all colors is common in Brazil. And socially acceptable, they tell me, except among the very wealthy. I've performed several black and white weddings here in the past year." He turned as we approached the *praça* again. "Still, though no one admits it, it's obvious from their conversation that a lot of people with white skins look down on blacks. But there's no segregation, like in the U.S." He slowed and pointed to an old very thin black man lounging on a seat in the *praça*. "See that old fellow? He was born a slave, would you believe?"

"Really?"

"Did you know that Brazil only abolished slavery in 1888?"

"They didn't teach us that in Kimmage."

As we turned into the Casa Paroquial Padre Joâo pointed to an elegant house just across from the church. "That's the *Prefeito*'s house."

231

"I take it he is someone important?"

"He's the Mayor, the most important man in Florida Paulista." Padre João grimaced as we swung into the garage. "Domingos is a very cute politician. He never goes to mass, but we have to be nice to him because he controls all the patronage."

"What's the patronage?"

"Jobs." We got out of the jeep. "This is Brazil, Walter. All the good jobs in Florida Paulista are either municipal or State jobs, and Domingos controls the giving of them all."

"But why do we have to be nice to him if he doesn't even bother coming to mass?" I decided – this was entirely new for me – that I wasn't going to accept answers I didn't understand. "I mean he doesn't control *our* jobs."

Padre João guffawed. "All Domingos has to do is send out the word, and hardly a single man will turn up in Church again. Even worse, they won't help us with the *campanhas*."

"What's a *campanha*?"

As we walked into the house Padre João put a fatherly hand on my shoulder. "There are campaigns or *campanhas*, as they call them, for everything here, Walter; everything from getting kids to make first communion to praying for rain. What I was talking about regarding Domingos is a campaign to collect money. We need moolah to keep the parish going, you know."

That was something I ought to have been aware of, but had never seriously thought about, apart from those tentative endeavors to raise money in America for the missions.

"We get the Brazilian equivalent of about four dollars in the collection plate at the Sunday masses," Padre João continued. "And we say mass most days for a one dollar stipend. So without the *campanhas* we couldn't survive. And that's why we have to be nice to Domingos."

232

Dona Zelie served us *almoço* – lunch – the main meal of the day. The rice and black beans were just a little more palatable than those I had for supper on Christmas Eve. The housekeeper cleaned up when we finished and then left. "She only works half days," Padre Joâo explained. "She's the mother of fourteen children, so she has her hands full." Then he added, "I pay her ten cruzeiros a month, which is about the average wage for a part-time housekeeper in Florida Paulista."

I had learned to convert Brazilian currency, so I did a quick calculation and figured she was getting about four dollars a month. My Firinne study of the papal encyclicals on social justice and the moral requirement of a living wage came back to me. We, priests of God, were being unjust to our housekeeper, defrauding her of a living wage, committing a sin that theologians said cried to heaven for vengeance. Of course I could do nothing about it while Padre Joâo was in charge. When he went away, however ....

Over the next few days Padre Joâo filled me in on the routines of the parish. He himself said morning mass at seven in the main church, which was attended by about a dozen women. I would say the evening mass at seven, with a similar size congregation. My morning assignment would be to say mass in one of the *fazendas* – cattle ranches or coffee plantations, of which there were many – for the workers. On Saturday afternoons, Sunday mornings, and Sunday afternoons, I was to say masses in three of the twelve outlying *capellas* – chapels – in the rural parts of the parish, such that each capella would have a mass once a month. On those occasions I'd also hear confessions and perform baptisms. There were thirty primary schools in the parish and one of my duties would be to visit each in turn to ensure that the *professores* were teaching Christian Doctrine and preparing the children for First Communion. Baptisms were

233

performed in the main church on Saturday and Sunday mornings, a task he, Padre João, would undertake. Unfortunately, the previous pastor, a Brazilian, allowed people to bring children for baptism at any time during the week. Padre João was trying to break them of that habit because it disrupted the other work of the parish.

He had a side project that he was excited about: writing a book on missionary life in Brazil, which he was going to get published in Ireland when he went there to raise money. He had already drafted some of the book, which he was going to call *'Padre Joâo and Co.'* His grin demanded my approbation. "Of course you'll all be in it," he added.

Before he left for Ireland he was going to organize a *campagna de amendoem* – a peanut campaign – to raise money for the church tower. The peanut harvesting season was approaching and he must take advantage of it. The Brazileiro, Padre João declaimed – he called male Brazilians the Brazileiro

Distributing Communion in Florida Paulista

– didn't like to part with his money, but he was usually willing to give up some of his crop. So, with Santos, the sacristan, to show him the way, he was going to visit all the peanut farmers in the parish and get them to pledge as many sacks of peanuts as they were willing to donate. Then when they harvested and sold their peanuts they'd give the value of the pledged sacks to the church tower fund. Next morning he took off in the jeep with Santos to commence the campaign.

Shortly after he left, while I was in my room trying to compose my Sunday sermon, Dona Zelie knocked at the door.

"There's a *caboclo* – a backwoods man– at the door, Padre, and he wants to talk to you." She rolled her eyes to indicate, I presumed, that the man was a bit strange. An oldish fellow in torn clothing stood with his back to the door.

"*Bom dia,*" I said.

He turned, displaying missing front teeth, and spoke rapidly; I had no idea what he was saying. Fortunately, Dona Zelie was standing behind me and translated into her somewhat more intelligible Portuguese. "He said," she said, "'Padre, I made a promise to *Nossa Senhora Aparecida* – Our Lady of Aparecida

235

– and I want to fulfil it.'"

"Good! Very good indeed!" I nodded and told the caboclo in my best Portuguese. "It's most important to keep your promise to Nossa Senhora." I had heard about the Brazilians' penchant for making religious promises.

"So, Padre, I want your permission to set off fireworks in the church." When Dona Zelie translated that, she looked astonished.

"You what?"

"I promised Nossa Senhora Aparecida that if she made my wife well after having our baby I'd let off fireworks in the church in her honor."

"What was that about the baby?" I asked Dona Zelie, having got the gist of the remainder.

"He said I could?" The caboclo looked hopefully at the housekeeper.

"*De jeito nenhum!*" – no way – she howled.

"Absolutely not," I added, glowering at the man. "If you let off fireworks in the church you're liable to set the place on fire."

"But I promised Nossa Senhora Aparecida."

I paused a moment to reflect before replying. "You tell Nossa Senhora Aparecida that the padre said you can fulfil your promise to her by going to mass."

"Really?" He looked at Dona Zelie for confirmation.

"Of course," she asserted.

"There's mass here in the church every evening at seven," I told him.

He hesitated. "Nossa Senhora Aparecida won't be mad at me?"

"She'll be very pleased." I said. "She wants you to go to mass."

"Very good!" he said. I watched until he was well away from the church.

Padre João returned in the evening, exhilarated and optimistic. "We've been pledged enough peanuts today to complete the tower. It's amazing the effect of focusing on the tower has on the Brazileiro." He looked at me to determine my interest.

"How is that?"

"The eyes glaze over when you ask him to pledge peanuts for the church, but as soon as you mention that it will go to complete the bloody tower his face lights up and he's all enthusiasm. And of course a pledge is a *promessa* – promise – to Nossa Senhora Aparecida, so we're guaranteed he'll keep it." Padre João seemed awfully pleased with himself.

Padre João Departs

A few weeks later, during breakfast on a Monday morning, he sprang the news: "I'm leaving for the States and Ireland tomorrow to raise money for our mission." His raised brows suggested he expected me to collapse at the news.

"Okay." I said, with a nonchalance I didn't feel.

"You'll be able to manage here on your own, won't you?"

"Of course!" I had been mentally preparing myself for this. I drove him to the train next morning, and then I was on my own to run the parish.

An hour later, while still somewhat in a daze over Padre João's lightning departure, and wondering how I'd get along with my little knowledge of Portuguese and even less knowledge of parish work, a man came to the door and clapped his hands; unshaven, dressed in rags, hair sticking up when he removed his shapeless hat.

Being & Becoming

"*Bom dia*," I said and waited for him to state his business..

"*Batizado!*" he barked. He stared at me and said no more.

I understood what he wanted. I also remembered Padre João's stated intention to perform baptisms on Saturday and Sunday mornings only. "You'll have to come back on Saturday or Sunday," I explained. "We only do baptisms on those mornings."

He unleashed a rapid flow of words that I failed to understand, though his body language – folded arms and stern face – suggested he didn't accept my decision. Dona Zelie overheard the conversation and hurried to my rescue.

"He said he came all the way from the *roça* – back country – with his wife and children, and it will be months before he can come again, so you have to do the baptism now."

What was I to do? Suppose the child died before he came again? I had learned that the infant mortality rate in Brazil was very high. Would an innocent soul have to spend an eternity in Limbo because of our 'Saturday and Sunday only' rule? With poor grace I told the man to wait in the church.

Santos

"*Coitado!* – poor fellow – " Dona Zelie said.

Those were not my sentiments, but I had obviously much to learn about Brazilian culture. And I badly needed the help and friendship and advice of Santos, who walked in the door shortly after I performed the caboclo's baptismal

238

ceremony. Officially, Santos was the sacristan, for which duty Padre João paid him some minimal wage. In fact, Santos ran the parish. A young fellow, still in his twenties and married with two children, he was popular with the parishioners and totally reliable. He took the lead in anything church-related that he saw needed to be done. So if I didn't know what to do or how to handle a situation, I consulted Santos. The parish comprised about thirty thousand Catholics: about eight thousand in the city and twenty-two thousand scattered over the rural municipality that measured approximately fifty kilometers by thirty. I found the prospect of being its only priest exhilarating. After a lifetime of being told what to do I was now in charge. And though I had very little idea how it functioned, Santos knew everything there was to know about the parish and its works and activities and personalities, and was happy to share his knowledge.

The heart of the parish, he said, were the *irmandades* – the Sodalities: the men's – called *Marianos*, the married women's – *Apostolados*, and the unmarried women's – *Fihas de Maria*. The members of those Sodalities were the backbone of the church here; they were the regular mass-goers and the people who helped out with parish affairs. He himself was the head of the Marianos. Dona Rose, the doctor's wife, headed the Apostolados. I had met Dona Rose, a beautiful woman with delicate features and a shy smile who played the harmonium before and during Sunday mass. Niuza, a pretty young teacher, was president of the Filhas de Maria; she was to play a crucial role in my life.

I remembered the promise I had made to myself to give our housekeeper a living wage as soon as the opportunity presented itself. Now was the time, so on the next monthly payday I gave Dona Zelie forty cruzeiros, four times what Padre Joao was paying her. This made her, she said gratefully, the best-paid housekeeper in Florida Paulista.

239

A Different Concept of Religion

Weekend of a Padre

Padre João had indeed spread the word that weekend mornings were the only times when baptisms would be performed in the church, so on Saturday morning families were assembling in the church by nine o'clock. I went to the sacristy to fill out the paperwork: the names of parents and godparents and baby had to be entered in the register, from identity cards which all Brazilians had to have.

A mother who looked rather old – and very poor, to judge from the way she was dressed – presented her card, which told me she was twenty-six. She said the baby in her arms was her tenth child. It crossed my mind that there was something wrong with the idea of this poor woman having ten children by age twenty-six. And though I thought no more of it at the time, the memory of that woman and her ten children would have serious consequences for my life.

From my desk in the sacristy I glanced up at the woman next in line. She was young and pretty and carried an infant. I asked for her identity card, she handed it to me, I began writing,

240

Baptism - 2 hrs

the baby started crying – a piercing shriek close to my ear. I looked up instinctively and saw the pretty woman whip out a voluptuous pink-nippled breast. The baby stopped crying and started sucking and I looked down at my paperwork, hoping none of the waiting mothers had noticed my embarrassment. I had never seen a woman's breast before except in art book paintings. However, I'd soon become accustomed to the sight: Brazilian women habitually nursed their babies in public.

There were fifteen babies for baptism that morning. After I finished the paperwork we adjourned to the baptismal font at the back of the church. I arranged them in a circle around the font and went through the liturgical rite, while babies cried and mothers rocked and suckled them, and godfathers shuffled with the tedium and fathers looked sheepish and I felt stressed. It was a tiresome ceremony and almost two hours long: there were twenty-five parts to the rite of baptism, many of which had to be repeated for each infant, including breathing on each, twice placing my hands on each, putting salt in each infant's mouth and commanding the devil to depart, making the sign of the cross on the front and back of each infant, making the sign of the cross on each forehead, putting my saliva on each infant's nose and ears, anointing the breast of each infant with the oil of catechumens. A prayer accompanied each of those actions, and I had to ask the godparents to renounce Satan on behalf of the infants and to make profession of faith on their behalf. By the time the ceremony was over and I got back to the Casa Paroquial for lunch I was mentally and emotionally exhausted and irritable.

But I could not rest yet. After lunch Santos, Niuza, and I went off in the jeep to one of the parish's dozen capellas for mass and more baptisms. We brought everything we needed for the ceremonies in a suitcase. Though it was a journey of only about twenty-five kilometers, it was a slow ride over pot-holed dirt

241

With Marianos and Sister Patricia at a capella

roads. We drove by fazendas covered with coffee bushes and by acres of grassland with Brahma cattle grazing around the blackened stumps of trees where the forest had been recently cleared. The capella, seeming in the middle of nowhere and with a capacity of about twenty people, was much too small for the congregation of more than a hundred who were waiting. While I heard confessions inside the tiny chapel Santos held a meeting of the local Marianos outside and Niuza met with the Filhas de Maria under a tree.

The heat in the capella was stifling. I sat on a chair and the penitents entered and knelt to recount their sins and receive absolution. They were mostly women and children; half a dozen men braved the contempt of their fellow men by kneeling before the padre. As I strained to understand the tales of the penitents – their Portuguese was rapid and, for the most part, not well pronounced – the sweat dripped off my forehead and formed a pool on the floor. One sleeve-end of my white soutane turned

242

greenish when the metal band of my watch oxidized. Santos and Niuza arranged an altar by the door. The congregation stood around outside while I said mass and read my homily. After mass Santos and Niuza did the paperwork and I baptized several babies. We returned to Florida Paulista around six, and I spent an hour in the confessional before seven o'clock mass.

Confession, I had been taught in schools and pulpits and Scholasticate, was the sacrament of reconciliation with God. It provided the opportunity for the sinner, who had become His enemy by sin, to become friends again with the Almighty. So for the minister of the sacrament, to whom had been given the awesome power to forgive sin in God's Own Name, the confessional ought to be a place of immense satisfaction. However, I found it a most boring experience. The banality of evil was a cliche; sin, as defined by the Church, sounded even more banal when whispered in my ear. Disrespect for others, lies, failure to attend Sunday mass, sexual thoughts, improper sexual acts, backbiting; those were the petty everyday activities that the Church considered offenses to God and that were repeated over and over, week after week, in the confessional, and by the same pious people. I rarely heard the big sins: murder, robbery, extortion, enrichment at the expense of fellow-men, and the like. Perhaps the people who committed those sins didn't come to confession.

And if the confessions of adults were banal, those of children were more so. When I'd walk out of the sacristy to the confessional on Saturday evening I'd find a line of giggling, jostling, whispering, seven to ten year olds of both sexes, lined up along the wall. I'd enter the box and pull back the grill. A small voice would begin rattling off her so-called sins, completing her story in a single breath:

243

Being & Becoming

Bless me Father for I have sinned. Xingei ... I cursed my mother, I cursed my father, I cursed my sisters, I cursed my brothers, I cursed my uncles, I cursed my aunts, I cursed my grandmother, I cursed my grandfather, I cursed the whole world. That's all.

What could I say? I had been taught in the Scholasticate to give each penitent a little homily about amending their ways, before assigning a penance and pronouncing absolution. But after hearing almost identical tales of normal child misbehavior spewed out in the same breathless tone, and repeated every week, I ran out of things to say. Worse still, I couldn't believe there was value in my saying anything, or even in their confessions.

Men's confessions, when there were any – other than those of the sodality members that were the usual boring tales of weakness – were more interesting. Men tended to camouflage major sins in meaningless words. *I was disrespectful,* for example, might elicit, with a judicious question, that the penitent showed disrespect to his girlfriend when he got her pregnant. Or he might have come to confession because he was getting married and his fiancée wanted the marriage to take place with a mass, so he had to receive communion. It might have been ten years since his last confession but he admitted only that he missed mass a few times. However, on questioning, it would likely turn out that he hadn't been to mass since the last time he confessed, and that he had committed a multitude of other grave sins. I remember one penitent whispering that he was fifty-five years of age and had not been to confession since he got married thirty years before. So I said, "go ahead and tell your sins."

"I have no sins, Padre."

"I beg your pardon!" This to me was a new tack, even for a Brazilian male: they always acknowledged some sin, if only to

244

keep the padre happy.

"I only came because I made Nossa Senhora Aparecida a promise that I would."

"All right. So tell me your sins."

"Padre, I never killed any man, I never robbed any man, I never took another man's wife. I have no sin." Then the non-penitent got up and left.

I often pondered that man's non-confession. I had been indoctrinated to believe that sin lurked around every bend, that there were a thousand possibilities of offending God every day. After all, didn't the gospel say *if we say that we have no sin we deceive ourselves and the truth is not in us?* And didn't Proverbs say that *a just man falleth seven times*? Yet this man reduced all sin to three big ones and said he hadn't committed any of them. No doubt he was understating the ways one might offend the Almight, but perhaps also the theology that had evolved over the millennia was overstating them?

Sunday morning I said mass at seven and delivered the sermon I had written on Friday and that Niuza had vetted. After breakfast there were more baptisms. Then it was time for lunch, after which I was off to the roça again with Niuza and Santos to repeat the Saturday afternoon performance at another capella. We were back in Florida Paulista again at about six. After saying the seven o'clock mass and making myself a hasty supper I got into the jeep once more and visited Steve, a confrere who had a parish about twenty miles away. Steve and I, in casual dress without any priestly insignia, ended a tiring weekend by going to a late movie in the local cinema.

Being & Becoming

Married Padres?

I had a lot to learn about Brazilian customs and thinking and culture. The caboclo who wanted to set off fireworks in the church awoke me to that fact. It was inconceivable that an Irishman would go to his parish priest and make that kind of request. And there were other customs that I found strange, but which Brazilians took for granted. Like the men's habit of hugging and back-slapping each other; even if they met several times a day they must each time perform the ritual. A few of them knew me well enough now to give me what they called *um abraço* – a hug – and a hearty back-slap.

The women, on the other hand, were most reserved in their dealings with the padre. Which didn't necessarily mean that they might not find him sexually attractive, as I discovered shortly after Padre João took off. A pretty seventeen-year old began attending evening mass with her mother: Brazilian girls matured early and a seventeen-year old would often have the aspect of an Irish woman of twenty five. I had come to know the mother, Dona Maria, a regular at daily mass and a very scrupulous woman who spent much time in church. Since only about a dozen women came to the evening mass I couldn't help noticing her daughter when she joined her mother at the altar rails. The pair came into the sacristy one evening after mass while I was removing my vestments.

"Padre, this is my daughter, Regina. She has decided to come to mass with me every day." The mother beamed, while the daughter gave me a radiant smile.

"That's wonderful."

"A lot of girls her age don't go to mass any more, you know, but my Regina is very devout."

"Oh, Mother!" Regina rolled her eyes in embarrassment.

"And did you notice that she goes to communion every day as well?"

"I did." But I didn't mention a habit her daughter had that I found disconcerting. It was normal practice for communicants to close their eyes when they put out their tongues to receive the Sacred Host; Regina, however, kept her eyes open and fixed on me when she put out her tongue.

One Saturday evening shortly after, a female voice in the confessional said, "Padre, I'm in love."

"That's hardly a sin," I said. "Being in love is a good thing."

"But, Padre, I'm in love with someone I shouldn't be in love with."

"Oh." An illicit love, I guessed. I hadn't heard this before in the confessional. "He's married, I suppose?"

"No, Padre. But he's not free to marry."

For just a moment I was confused, then light dawned: I thought the voice sounded familiar. "For your penance say three Hail Marys," I said, and gave her absolution in a hurry. It was flattering of course, but I was a priest and must show absolutely no interest in women, least of all in seventeen-year olds.

The young-lady-in-love, however, didn't subscribe to that view. A few days later her father, the Director of the *Cartorio* – the government records office – dropped by the Casa Paroquial and invited me to join him and his family for dinner at his home the following week. Since the man, who was an important person in the town, never came to church I immediately suspected that the invitation was coming from Regina. But I also knew from my little Brazilian experience that to turn down the invitation would be a grave insult to her father. So I accepted and went to dinner on the appointed day. Dona Maria was a marvelous cook and we had a scrumptious meal. Afterwards, we all sat in their elegant parlor and sipped wine and chatted. They were curious about Ireland and I answered many questions. Then, apropos of nothing, the father remarked,

"I understand the pope will soon allow padres to marry."

I curled my toes and tried to control my expression: no doubt the daughter had put her father up to saying it. "There's some talk about it," I acknowledged. And indeed it had been the subject of much recent speculation in the newspapers. "But I have serious doubts that it will ever happen."

"But supposing it does happen," the father pursued, "would you consider getting married?" Regina was the man's only child so I must suppose she had him wound around her little finger. I felt her eyes on me now, though she didn't say anything.

"I really haven't given it any thought." Which was a lie of course: I was very conscious of the possibility. "But I suppose I'd have to consider it." I tried to change the subject. "You obviously have been following the reports of the Vatican Council?"

"I read about them in the *Estado de São Paulo*. That's where I came across the article about the padres being allowed to marry. It's of great interest to us Catholics, you know. Many think that celibacy for priests is nonsense, if you'll pardon my saying so."

Which statement was like a landmine for the padre to step on. "There will likely be many changes as a result of the Council," I offered.

Regina continued to make eyes at me from the communion rails and, mirabile dictu, I now spotted her father at the back of the church on Sunday mornings.

Walter Keady

Religious Practice

In Ireland I had learned and accepted that the practice of religion, which we were told was required to enter heaven, necessarily included attendance at mass and reception of the sacraments. In Florida Paulista, I gradually learned that at least half my parishioners thought otherwise. Males came to church for the first time when they were brought to be baptized. Many did not come again until led there by their brides to be married. And practically all were brought by loved ones on their way to burial. In between, most male visits to God's house were few and sporadic. With one annual exception, Good Friday, when they came to honor *Senhor Morto.*

I was surprised and overwhelmed on my first Good Friday in Florida Paulista by the size of the crowd and its seriousness. People began to arrive at the church before midday: men, with their women and children following, streamed in from the countryside. At twelve o'clock the Marianos removed the statue of Senhor Morto from its glass case under the side altar and with great reverence placed it on a catafalque in front of the high altar. There it remained for veneration by the people for three hours, the time-span that represented Christ's agony on the cross. At three, the hour at which Jesus was said to have died, Senhor Morto was placed on a litter and carried by the Marianos in procession through the streets of the city. By now the crowd was vast: people had come from all over the parish to take part in the procession, which meandered through the streets for a couple of hours, with hymn-singing led by the sodality members. When the Marianos finally returned Senhor Morto to the church they placed it again on the catafalque in front of the high altar.

Since saying mass was not permitted on Good Friday according to Catholic liturgy, and the huge crowd, which Santos estimated at about fifteen thousand, was waiting for some kind of ceremony, I stood on the top step at the front of the church, facing them – they covered the entire praça and the surrounding streets – and did my best to preach an extemporaneous sermon. Since I had no amplifier, I was quite sure that most of them didn't hear a word I said. Not, I suspected, that they cared much: they were waiting for the high point of the day when they'd enter the church in single file and kiss the feet of Senhor Morto. That ceremony began immediately I finished speaking, and it was after eleven that night when the final stragglers kissed the holy feet, blessed themselves multiple times and departed, and Santos closed the church.

The Easter Liturgy on Saturday evening, the high point of the Church year, was anti-climactic, and lightly attended.

The feast of Corpus Christi didn't attract as big a crowd as Senhor Morto, but it was nevertheless a major festival for the Catholics of Florida Paulista. I was apprised of its importance by Niuza. "For the Corpus Christi procession," she told me a few days earlier, "we'll lay down a carpet for the padre to tread on when you're carrying the Blessed Sacrament in procession through the streets."

"We'll need either a very long carpet or a very short procession."

Her smile – which caused the butterflies to flutter in my interior: she was a very attractive young woman – told me I didn't understand. "The carpet will be made of colored sawdust; we'll lay it down the morning of the parade."

"I see." Which I didn't. "And who are the *we* who are going to lay it down?"

"The Filhas de Maria and our helpers." She smiled again. "We'll bring along brothers and *namorados* – boyfriends; we make them all do their bit."

And they did. At about eleven on the morning of the Feast Niuza was at my door. "Come and see our progress, Padre."

It was astounding: many-hued sawdust turned into intricate shapes and images, including one of the Monstrance and one of the Lamb of God. Hundreds of yards of carpet were completed already. "Could you make a Celtic Cross?" I asked.

"If you show us what it looks like."

I found a picture and gave it to her. A few hours later she brought me out again to inspect a beautiful Celtic Cross designed with colored sawdust and integrated into the carpet.

The Marianos led the late afternoon procession in their purple uniforms and banners, Behind them I carried the Blessed Sacrament in the monstrance, followed by the Apostolados in black, the Filhas de Maria in white, and a large crowd from the city and the roça. Many more lined the sidewalk and knelt as we passed. The Sodality members led the singing of hymns. Afterwards, all agreed that it was *uma procissão formidavel* – a wonderful procession.

Religious diversity

Singing and processions seemed to be the heart of religious expression in Brazil, not mass and confession and communion, as in Ireland. Another facet of Brazilian spirituality new to me was its admixture of Catholic and African worship. When slaves were brought to Brazil from Africa they took with them their religious beliefs. However, since the slave owners forbade them to practice what the Church considered to be heathen worship, the slaves incorporated their African religions into the trappings of Catholicism, the religion they were forced to practice. They gave their gods the names of Catholic saints and mixed in their worship of them with the rituals of Catholicism. When they gained their freedom in 1888 they began to practice openly their mixture of African religions and Catholicism, under the names *of Candomblé, Umbanda*, and, more generally, *Macumba.* The African elements included sacrificing fowl, making offerings of flowers and candles, and dancing, while the Catholic elements included the worship of the cross and of such saints as Jesus, Our Lady, St. George and St. Sebastian. *Spiritualism*, a feature of Macumba, involved making contact with the dead through mediums who went into trance-like states in order to communicate with their holy spirits.

Macumba was practiced in Florida Paulista, and many Catholics practiced both forms of religion. Of course they didn't tell the Padre of their dual practice, so I only heard tidbits about it here and there. "They come to mass on Sunday morning," Santos told me, "and on Sunday evening they go to Macumba sessions."

"What goes on at those sessions?"

"I don't know much about them," he admitted. "Apparently they dance a lot. I'm told that some of them spin around and around in a trance until they pass out."

At about three o'clock one Monday morning I was awakened by loud knocking on the door. I was alone in the house, so the knocking somewhat unnerved me in my semi-somnolent state. Without opening the door I asked who was there.

"Padre, come quick, my wife is very sick." A man's voice, a caboclo, I suspected, from his speech.

I steeled myself to go and asked,"where do you live?"

"In the roça."

"Where in the roça?" It could be many miles away.

The man named a place that was at least twenty miles from

252

the city. "I have a jeep, Padre; I'll bring you."

"Why didn't you come to get me before this?" Something didn't seem quite right to me.

"She just got sick in the head tonight, Padre. So now you must came and bless her."

"Is she physically all right?" Sick in the head might be a Macumba trance gone wrong.

"She's very sick in the head, Padre. You must come right away."

"Is she able to walk?" I needed to go only if she was in danger of dying.

"Oh yes, Padre. But she needs a blessing to make her head all right."

That did it. "Come back in the morning and I'll go to see her." She was very likely sick from too much spinning at a Macumba session.

I returned to my room. The man banged the door a couple of times and then took off. He didn't return in the morning and no one died in the parish that week.

"She most likely got sick from Macumba dancing," Santos agreed when I told him. "It's a common occurrence, they tell me."

Macumba was not to be confused with other non-Catholic religious groups, of which there were many in Brazil and several in Florida Paulista. American Evangelical missionaries were active in the country and they had made some inroads here. Catholics called them by the disparaging name of *Crentes* – Believers. Sodality members told me, often angrily, that the evangelizers were very aggressive. But since neither they nor their converts ever came to the Casa Paroquial, I had no way of knowing how many Catholics joined their churches.

253

The Dark Side

Religion and Politics

Brazilian politicians, I discovered, differed radically from their Irish counterparts in their relations with the Church. Irish politicians didn't interfere in Church matters; rather it was the Church that interfered in State matters. In the old country the bishops and priests kept the politicians firmly under their clerical thumbs, and the latter displayed publicly their obedience to the former. The influence of the bishops in the drafting of the Irish Constitution demonstrated that; and the Mother and Child Scheme in the fifties showed who would triumph in any clash between Church and State. In Brazil, however, or at least in Florida Paulista, politicians were quite willing and able to interfere in Church matters. That willingness came home to me in the matter of the Feast of St. Christopher.

Before Padre João left, he put a bee in someone's bonnet, without informing me – I only heard of it from Santos – that Florida Paulista should have a special celebration for the feast of St. Christopher on July 25. So I was left with the task of organizing it, though I had no idea what to do: all I knew about St.

254

Christopher was that he was the patron saint of travelers, and that people carried his medal for safety when going on journeys. There seemed to be no particular connection between the Saint and Florida Paulista.

However, I soon found out that I didn't have to plan any festivities: the *Prefeito* himself decided to take on the job. A burly man with a black mustache and an imposing presence, Domingos exuded power, and everyone in Florida Paulista recognized that fact. Although he wasn't a religious man and hardly ever came to mass, when he heard of the proposal to celebrate the feast of St. Christopher he immediately saw its possibilities for political glory. So he took the matter in hand and, without consulting me, invited the Sodality members to a meeting at which he would, he told their leaders beforehand, outline his proposals for celebrating the feast. Santos, although he was beholden to Domingos for the menial municipal job that put rice and beans on his family table, informed me of the upcoming meeting. He also explained Domingos's reason for not inviting me.

"Since you're new to the parish, Padre, and you're young, he didn't feel you'd be able to pull off the kind of celebration he'd like to put on."

I felt very hurt at being bypassed. What right did Domingos have to ignore me, my ego asked? I decided to stand up to the Prefeito. The Sodalities were Church organizations and no one had a right to convene them without my say-so. Furthermore, since I was the religious leader of the municipality it was I, with the assistance of the Sodalities, who should determine the nature of the St. Christopher celebration, not a politician who rarely came to mass. Thoroughly annoyed, I told Santos to inform the Sodality members they were not to attend the meeting with Domingos. Santos told them and they respected my wishes. The Prefeito was crushed, he told me himself, when he came charging

255

in to the Casa Paroquial next day.

"I'm destroyed, Padre." Arms flailing in protest at the awful humiliation that I had inflicted on him. "Totally devastated."

"The festival of St. Christopher is primarily a religious event," I pointed out. "So the *vigario* is responsible for organizing it."

He looked at me in shocked surprise, not accustomed to being thwarted. Then he relaxed and raised placating hands. "You're right of course, Padre; you're absolutely right. But I was only trying to help. You see, this could be a huge event for Florida Paulista; it could create an enormous amount of *movimento*."

Ah! He had uttered the magic word. *Movimento* in Brazil-speak connoted a multitude of activities. Domingos was using it to conjure up religious fervor for the Church, as well as fun and

Domingos and successor Prefeito,1965. Padre João in background

excitement for the people and business for the merchant community. By now I had heard the term used often enough to have an inkling of what he had in mind, and to know that my parishioners would say I was committing an unforgivable sin if I were to block such *movimento*. Anyway, now that I had Domingos's attention, I was willing to do business with him.

"Perhaps we should work together on the festival?"

Domingos extended an immediate hand. "Padre, together we're going to create such movimento that will make this a historic event in the life of Florida Paulista."

"I'll ask the Sodality members to work with you."

Domingos had power and money at his disposal, and with my blessing and the support of the Sodality members he planned the kind of festival *we* could not have done without him. He had a magnificent platform built at the entrance to the city, which was to be the center of the festivity. He organized a procession of vehicles that on the day of the feast threaded its way through the city streets to the festival center, led by cars with dignitaries of Church and State. Those dignitaries then assembled on the festival platform, with Dom Hugo, the bishop of the diocese, in the seat of honor. Padre João, who returned from Ireland just in time for the celebrations – his timing was always masterful – sat next to the bishop, and I, demoted to assistant by his return, sat next to him. State and municipal politicians and dignitaries, including Domingos himself, occupied other seats of honor. The huge gathering on the road in front of the platform was the result of massive advertizing with posters and radio broadcasts.

Domingos, a State Congress man, and several municipal dignitaries made speeches. Dom Hugo gave the final address with a flowery oration, after which he celebrated mass, the central act of the festivity. Then all returned to the Praça for a *quermesse* – a cross between a bazaar and a party – at which varieties of food and drink were sold, music and other entertainments were provided, and people socialized and celebrated the great day.

Afterwards, everyone allowed that the celebration had been a huge success, much *movimento* had been achieved, and Senhor Domingos was a wonderful man indeed. Beaming with success and to show that he bore no ill-will towards me for my initial challenge to his authority, the Prefeito invited both padres to dinner at his home the following Sunday, at which we relived, and congratulated one another on, a most successful event, one that had created such marvelous movimento for Florida Paulista. Padre João beamed with pleasure at the success of his great idea.

Wealth and Poverty

I had come to love Brazilians, as manifested in the people of Florida Paulista. They were kind, easy-going, polite, generous, sociable, garrulous; they had so many qualities that I admired and respected that I felt content to spend the rest of my life in the country. Yet, there was a dark side to the Brazilian way of life that greatly disturbed me: a terrible unfairness in the distribution of wealth in that great and potentially rich country. Potentially only because, despite its wealth of natural resources, most Brazilians were poor, many were very poor, and there was no national plan to improve their condition.

Why had the country remained so poor? State and Federal legislators were for the most part rich and had no incentive to share their wealth with their poverty-stricken constituents. The latter comprised, according to national statistics, at least seventy percent of the population. That poverty was visible all around Florida Paulista. During my second year a drought caused the crops to fail. As a result, rice and beans, the staple food of the

258

vast majority, were scarce and expensive and many went hungry. I myself lived simply, having barely enough money to pay Dona Zelie and Santos and my grocery bills, and buy gas for the jeep. Though I didn't go hungry: I had a roll and an egg for breakfast, rice and beans and sometimes chicken for lunch, and another roll and egg for supper. As a result of the drought many poor people came to the door of the Casa Paroquial asking for food left over from my lunch. I was happy to share what little I had.

The poverty of the many was in sharp contrast with the wealth of the few. On the vast coffee and cattle fazendas that I visited to say mass for the workers I saw the opulent homes of absentee owners. While housing their poorly paid badly fed workers in primitive shacks, they spent most of the year in city homes in Rio or Sao Paulo. Many of the workers were employed on a seasonal basis only, so they were on the road with their families looking for work and food and shelter for much of the year. Many of them had migrated from the North-East of the country, where drought was endemic, in the hope of a better life.

There was also a class of small farmers who made a simple living on farms they acquired when the forests were burned and the land was made available by the government. Some squatted on unoccupied land and in time they, reasonably but naively, regarded it as theirs. A *fazendeiro* – rancher – in the Florida Paulista municipality, who owned a large tract of land on which he raised cattle, discovered that many of those small farmers had no legal titles to their land. He hired experts to buy legal titles to those properties and then informed some eight hundred small farmers that their lands were now his, and that they were to vacate them immediately. Many did leave, fearing the power of the fazendeiro, but some objected. The fazendeiro hired a gunman to make an example and one small farmer was shot dead. The rest left without further protest. The hired gunman was sent to jail but the fazendeiro remained free to enjoy his additional land.

In a country where machismo might be called the primary religion of men, women were regarded as second class citizens. While the developed world in the mid-sixties was slowly waking up to its ill-treatment of women Florida Paulista, and indeed most of Brazil, was still very much asleep in that respect. Fathers kept their daughters strictly in check lest prowling males should endeavor to take advantage of them, while at the same time they encouraged their sons to take advantage of other men's daughters. It was not uncommon for fathers to take their sixteen year old sons to the red light district – every city had one – to be initiated to sex.

Although I myself was not yet sensitized to the equal rights of women in society – the Ireland I grew up in was not exactly a precursor of progressive thinking in that respect – I could not help noticing how poorly many Brazilian men treated their wives. Many times I saw men walking into the city from the roça on Saturday, striding along many yards ahead of, and apparently oblivious to, their wives who were carrying babies and trying to control small children. Once, while driving to a school in the roça on a particularly hot day, I met a man riding a mule and holding a parasol aloft to ward off the sun's scorching rays; a woman, presumably his wife, was following on foot, several paces to the rear, without a parasol and carrying a small child.

Doutor Antonio

Among the rich of Florida Paulista was Doutor Antonio, the husband of pious Dona Rose, the church organist and president of the Apostolados. Although he rarely came to mass, the doctor was a delightful man to talk to and I liked him a lot. He

260

owned and ran a small hospital in the city and had a fazenda in the roça. One Monday morning I met him on the street.

"Bon dia, Padre! how is the health?"

"Good, Doctor. I've recovered well." I had been unable to eat properly for more than a month because of severe diarrhea. Doutor Antonio had met me while I was ailing, took one look at my pale face, and brought me, protesting, to his hospital where an examination revealed that I was dehydrated and that my blood pressure was extremely low. With tests the doctor diagnosed my ailment – a common parasite – gave me medication, and in a few days I was on the road to recovery.

"Would you like to come to Mato Grosso with me?"

"I'd love to." I lived within forty miles of one of the world's great jungles and never had an opportunity to visit it.

"I'm buying a cattle fazenda in there so I'm taking a trip to check it out the day after tomorrow. Rose and the children are coming, so it will be wonderful to have you with us."

We set out early Wednesday morning in the Doctor's van and drove along the State road to the Parana river. An hour later we crossed a three-kilometer bridge into the State of Mato Grosso. From there on we traveled on hard-packed dirt roads as we drove through the deep jungle with only occasional clearings. The Doctor's fazenda foreman who came along to help evaluate the property, did most of the driving, though Antonio and I spelled him at intervals. Once in a clearing we met men on horseback driving a herd of Brahma cattle. The men, with revolvers at their waists and lassos on their saddle horns, resembled the cowboys I had seen in Western films. By evening we arrived at a village that also looked like the cowboy towns of film-land, with its muddy street, haphazardly-constructed houses and commercial builings, horse-back riders wearing broad-rimmed hats, hitching rails outside buildings. Half-way down the street we passed a jeep coming in the opposite direction . "Oh my God!" the Doctor shouted, turning to stare after the jeep. "Turn around and follow that jeep," he ordered his foreman. We followed it until, after a short distance, it stopped, and a man got out and went into a building that had the word 'Medico' written across the front..

"What's going on?" I asked.

"That fellow was my former assistant at the hospital in Florida Paulista. Did you recognize him, Rose?"

"I did. But how –?"

" – A few months ago," the doctor explained, "I gave the fellow money to go to São Paulo and bring back medicines that I need at the hospital. He didn't return and I never saw the money or medicines again."

"We need to keep going if we're to get to the fazenda before dark," the foreman advised.

The doctor agreed. "I'll look into it on the way back."

The fazendeiro was absent when we arrived. "He's gone to look at some land in the Pantanal, but he'll be back tomorrow," his wife told us. "In the meantime our home is yours."

Their home was large and sumptuous and the hospitality was generous. I had my own elegant bedroom, and I stayed awake for hours listening to jungle sounds. Next morning when we were finishing breakfast the fazendeiro landed his private plane in a clearing near the house. After lunch he took the doctor and foreman up to view the fazenda and its herd of three thousand cattle from the air. "It would take a week to look at it all on horseback," he explained.

We spent another hospitable evening at the fazenda, in which we were lavishly wined and fed, and entertained with stories of life in Mato Grosso where, our host averred, the law of the forty-four prevailed – (meaning the forty-four revolver) He told of fazendeiros who still kept slaves and lived like kings, and of outlaws and robbers from all over Brazil who were wanted but who could never be found here in the jungles of Mato Grosso.

In the morning we set out for home. When passing through the village the doctor enquired at the medical building and discovered that his former assistant was posing as a physician there. There was no way the doctor could recover his money, but at least he had the satisfaction of preventing the fellow, who had no medical training whatever, from harming people.

A few weeks later I met Antonio again. "I've been swindled," he said. "The three thousand head of cattle the fazendeiro showed us from the plane, and which I paid him for, belong to a neighboring fazenda. And after he took my money the fellow disappeared into the Pantanal." This latter was the most inaccessible part of Mato Grosso,

"Is there any way to get your money back?" I asked.

"I've sued him in court but I have no hope of getting anything since no one knows where he is. As he said himself, people go to Mato Grosso to disappear."

One night – it got dark between five-thirty and six-thirty, depending on the season – shortly after our return from Mato Grosso, Doutor Antonio sent a messenger asking me to come to the hospital: a patient was dying and requested Extreme Unction. I grabbed the holy oils and Ritual and ran to the hospital, which was only a few hundred yards away. The place was empty and quiet. The Doctor, tight-lipped and silent, brought me to the patient's room. A young woman – she didn't look more than eighteen – lay unconscious, an oxygen mask on her face. She looked the picture of young health. I gave her absolution and anointed her with the holy oils while reciting the prayers from the Ritual. As soon as I finished, the doctor removed the oxygen mask and the young woman ceased to breathe.

"She's dead," he said. "I only kept her breathing until you anointed her."

I walked slowly home, hoping that, as a result of administrating Extreme Unction – the first time I had conferred the sacrament – the young woman's soul was now in heaven. When I arrived at my house I discovered that I had anointed the dying woman with the oil of catechumens, oil episcopally blessed for anointing baptismal recipients. I remembered that theologians considered anointing with the wrong oils made the efficacy of the sacrament doubtful. Dear God above! What had I done? Had I denied this young woman heaven through my carelessness in using the wrong oil? I agonized over that error for days until I accepted that it was an honest mistake and that surely a merciful God would allow for it.

Much later, after reflecting on what might have caused the young woman's death, remembering how well she looked, and the fact that no one was with her, I concluded that she was probably the victim of a botched abortion.

Perturbations

Padre João

Despite Padre João's elusiveness, away from Florida Paulista much more than he was there, and despite his autocratic attitude, he and I had established a good rapport as friends and co-workers. We were intellectual equals, enjoyed conversing together, liked classical music, and – what was most important for the relationship – he liked me. The latter fact was a cause for some ribbing from my confreres, who told me that I was obviously Padre João's white-haired boy. When four new confreres arrived from Ireland the following year and the bishop offered new parishes to the Irish missionaries, Padre João told me that I could have one if I wished, though he would prefer if I stayed in Florida Paulista.

What could I do but stay? Besides, I did like him, even though he was dragging his heels with regard to many progressive ideas that Vatican II had opened up. He had spent the first thirty years of his priestly life in Nigeria building up a conservative Irish-style Catholic school system, and he was determined to turn the public schools of Florida Paulista into similar institutions, where children would learn to believe and behave like traditional

265

Irish Catholics. In his first year in Florida Paulista, before my arrival, he had convinced the teachers, who were all Catholics, of the need to teach their pupils the basics of their religion. Before he left on his first fund-raising foray he instructed me to visit the schools regularly in order to maintain that religious instruction *movimento*. So I visited the schools and talked to the teachers and found that they were preparing their first grade students for first confession and communion, as he had requested. To help them in their task he had written a simple catechism with questions and answers very similar to those I myself was taught in The Neale National school. Remembering my own reaction to those incomprehensible questions and answers about the nature of God and sin, and based on my experience of hearing children's confessions since I arrived in Florida Paulista, I felt strongly that his catechism was not the better way to instill religion into the young. Since I wasn't sure what was the better way I decided to discuss the matter with him when he returned. Which I tried to do a few months later when he came back.

Padre João was delighted with himself when he returned, having concluding another triumphant financial campaign. He enquired ever so briefly about the parish – "how are things going in Florida Paulista?" – before launching into a description of his fund-raising adventures, replete with pseudo-modest stories of his outstanding successes. He had managed, he implied, to wrest money from extremely unlikely sources through extraordinary rhetorical legerdemain: like the thousand dollar check he got from the millionaire Muslim he met in a hotel and regaled with stories of the starving children in his parish. "There may not be starving children in Florida Paulista," he justified to me, "but there are hungry ones; and anyway there are lots of starving children all over Brazil." I listened to his tales of financial conquest for over an hour before I succeeded in raising the subject of his catechism.

"I've been reading up on some new ideas emanating from the Vatican Council," I opened, "and I was wondering if the old catechism methods are the best way to prepare the children for first communion."

"Are you talking about the catechism I wrote?" His tone switched instantly from affable to feisty.

I hesitated. "Well, its –"

" – I wrote that catechism," he interrupted huffily, "on the basis of my thirty years experience of teaching children Christian Doctrine in Nigeria."

I was going to have difficulty articulating my objections to his catechism, but I tried anyway. "I know that your catechism is great: it has the same questions and answers I learned at school myself. But I was –"

" – And look what they did for you!" Triumph in Padre João's voice.

I gave up: I should have known better than to try changing the man's view of the road to salvation. Then I had to endure a homily about the virtues of the old-fashioned catechism that had helped to keep our forefathers in the faith and would likewise light a fire under the young Brazilians of today.

Arrival of the Nuns

Padre João then sprang the major triumph of his recent trip. "While I was in Ireland I visited the Holy Rosary Convent in Killeshandra and persuaded the Mother Superior to send three of her Sisters to Florida Paulista."

"That's wonderful." Though I had no idea what the nuns would do here.

A week later Padre João's enthusiasm for the nuns waned

after he received a letter from Killeshandra . "They're sending Sister Patricia in charge of two other Sisters," he told me in a tone that suggested doom, if not the end of the world.

"Oh!" I had no idea what the gloom was about.

"I worked with Patricia in Nigeria." His tone dripped disgust. "She's a very difficult person to get along with."

Over time, from tidbits of stories and information he let drop, and that were sometimes tinged with venom, I pieced together his objections to Sister Patricia: she was a missionary nun of independent spirit who knew what she wanted to accomplish and went about doing it in her own way. Worst of all, she was unwilling to kowtow to the superior status of male missionary priests. I looked forward to meeting her. Not so Padre João, who arranged to be gone on another fund-raising trip when the nuns would arrive. Before leaving, however, he persuaded the city authorities to build them a house next to the municipal hospital; the Sisters were qualified nurses and would help to train hospital staff.

The Sisters duly arrived by train from São Paulo. Remembering my own unheralded arrival, I arranged a welcoming committee of Sodality members, municipal authorities, and fellow Irish missionaries from neighboring cities, to greet them. A band played as the train came to a stop. Domingos's successor as prefeito was there to meet them on behalf of the city. One of my confreres who liked to be first in all things jumped aboard the train to be first to welcome the newcomers. Unfortunately for him they exited before he could reach them, right by the train door at which I happened to be waiting.

I soon fell victim to Sister Patricia's no-nonsense-from-the-clergy attitude. One evening shortly after their arrival, Sister

Kathleen came into the sacristy while I was un-vesting after evening mass. She asked me about something and apparently I did not respond with the required respect: most likely I made a flippant remark, as I often did with friends. Sister Kathleen apparently was not amused and Sister Patricia descended on me at the Casa Paroquial next morning with demands for an apology. Which I gave, making a mental note to be henceforth very correct in my dealings with the Sisters.

Despite that early contretemps, we developed an excellent

The Sisters with confreres

working relationship, and became good friends. At Christmas, which came in the middle of the hot season, the Sisters decided we should have a community dinner to which we'd invite the neighboring Irish confreres. We agreed to hold it on the day after Christmas since we'd all be too busy on the festival day to get together. Sister Patricia wanted a turkey dinner with all the traditional Irish trimmings, no simple request-demand in Florida Paulista where turkeys were hard to find. I scoured the *roça* for a week and, after many enquiries, found one just a few days before Christmas. I gave it to Dona Zelie to cook. Since there were so many of us, and the Casa Paroquial was tiny, we set a table in the hall attached to the church. Dona Zelie cooked the turkey, the Sisters cooked the trimmings, and we all sat down to a festive meal. Alas, the turkey had turned rancid, so we had to settle for a dinner of trimmings. Nevertheless, 'a good time was had by all.'

Death of my father

I had little contact with my family in New York. Though we had a phone in the Casa Paroquial, the service was both unreliable and, for long distance calls, prohibitively expensive. I wrote to my mother fairly regularly but received only occasional letters in return; she was a sometimes correspondent, and neither my father nor my siblings ever wrote. One morning, about a year after my arrival in Florida Paulista, I received a phone call from a telephone operator in São Paulo saying she was putting through a call from New York for a Walter Keady. Then the line went dead. I heard no more, and was left wondering what had prompted the call from my family, assuming it was from them. A week later I received a telegram saying our father had died in Ireland

270

the previous week.

I ought to have been grief-stricken: I had always been very fond of my father. But to my surprise and horror I felt almost no pain. Such lack of natural sorrow at the passing of my parent was cause for anguish in itself, but I did not feel even that. I meditated on such a lack of sensibility and reached the startling conclusion that I had become so detached from family and friends over the years that I now felt invulnerable. I had confreres and colleagues and parishioners here in Brazil, I had family and friends thousands of miles away, but I had no one whose loss would seriously hurt me. I was shielded from the trauma of mourning because I no longer had loved ones to lose. Perhaps, I thought, I had developed that invulnerability as self-protection after losing Marjorie. At any rate, my immunity-to-feeling was terrifying. Had religious training inured me to human emotion and forced me to give up human caring to focus on Divine Love? Was I now so out of emotional balance that I would go through life without feeling anything for anyone? Without a sentiment of human love? Without ever again experiencing what it was to love, or feeling an acute sense of loss at the death of a loved one?

Nature, however, if not God, has a penchant for restoring balances. Without my conscious knowledge, the process of redressing began, unheralded, soon after my father's death, with the episode of the twenty-six year old woman who came to have her tenth child baptized. On that particular morning the seed was sown for my mind to challenge Church teaching. On later reflection about the episode – reflection was a new activity for me where Church doctrine was concerned – I found it absurd that my Church should require a woman who was already mired in poverty to go on having babies. Thereafter, when women – and of course it was always, and only, women – told me in confession that they were practicing birth control I did not – as the Church's

271

moral code required that I should – admonish them to stop the practice.

I didn't realize yet that I had taken my first step in rejecting Catholic teaching. Up to that point I had sought only to understand the teaching and to follow it. All my schooling in Catholic doctrine had been directed to absorbing what teachers and preachers assured me was the truth, the whole truth, and nothing but the truth. Trained to obedience and to respect authority, I had not hitherto even thought to question what that authority taught me. Such abdication of my critical thinking faculties, was my condition until the beginning of 1966 in Florida Paulista. At that time I had no premonition that my new attitude towards Church teaching on birth control would lead to ending my career as a Catholic priest. The Vatican Council had just completed its work and the winds of doctrinal change were in the air. I, and most of my priestly brethren, along with many eminent theologians, believed that the Church's teaching on birth control would soon change. So I remained an otherwise obedient priest as I went about my parish duties and awaited that change.

Social Action

As a dedicated missionary I was constantly looking for ways to improve the spiritual – read *Catholic religious* – life of my parishioners. Padre João believed that the Sodalities were the mainstays of the parish. However, in his absence I attended their monthly meetings and found them disappointing. All had as their primary focus the spiritual welfare of their own members: they had no interest in promoting that welfare among those in the parish who did not belong to a Sodality. So after telling them that they were to be as leaven for the entire parish, I set about trying to make them so.

I began with the married women's sodality, the aptly named Apostolado. Marriage counseling had come into vogue in the Catholic world as a result of Vatican Council pronouncements on what it called that Holy State (incongruously, all the Council Fathers, being celibates, had renounced that Holy State for themselves). So I created a Marriage Counseling Group from among the members of the Apostolado with the objective of their providing spiritual advice on Christian marriage to other married couples in the parish.

I myself was ex officio head of the Group, which had its first meeting in a Sodality member's home. The women attended with husbands in tow and, as they sipped coffee, all looked expectantly at their priest to give them direction, the padre being also ex officio omniscient. However, common sense seeped into my celibate brain and, after some perfunctory pious remarks on the sanctity of marriage, I informed the Group that since they, not I, were the experts on marriage it was their duty to give advice to those couples who needed it. This casting of responsibility on their lay shoulders caused a certain amount of consternation at first: in the Apostolado they were accustomed to accepting spiritual advice from the padre but never giving it to others. However, they soon got used to the new idea, and they planned visitations to the homes of couples they felt were in need. In this way a small gust of the fresh air that Pope John XXIII envisioned the Council would bring to the world began to blow through the windows of Florida Paulista.

The other Sodalities seemed too set in their ways to carry out the kinds of modern apostolate called for by the Vatican Council. The Marianos were an organization of men, both married and unmarried; with their purple uniforms and banners they specialized in marching in religious processions, so much so that Padre Joâo irreverently called them *The Boys of Wexford*, after an Irish marching song. The Filhas de Maria were composed of unmarried women, a euphemism for young ladies waiting to be married, which most seemed in a hurry to be. One of its members, an extremely pretty eighteen-year old, came to me in tears one day to ask my advice: a young man had asked her to marry him but she didn't love him; on the other hand, she said, if she turned him down she might never again get an offer of marriage and she'd be left 'on the shelf.'

I racked my brains but failed to find any useful parish work that members of those two Sodalities could perform. Then I recalled the Legion of Mary, an Irish-founded Catholic organization composed of men and women, married and unmarried, of which I had been a chaplain during my final year in Kimmage. According to its handbook, the Legion's objective was the glory of God through the holiness of its members, a holiness that was to be developed not just through prayer but also through active co-operation in the work of the Church. Every Legionary was required to carry out a weekly apostolic work, such as visiting families or visiting the sick.

I recalled that the self-styled militant members of Firinne tended to sneer at Legionaries as Catholic wimps who were fearful of getting involved in big issues like promoting Catholicism in politics and fighting against the Satanic forces of Freemasonry and Zionism. That recollection took me to the very unsettling conclusion that I liked social work of the kind I engaged in with Firinne more than the priestly activities of saying mass and administering the sacraments that I was now engaged in. Social work was more meaningful to me because it involved trying to improve the lives of my fellow human beings in practical ways, either through attempting reform of the political system—

274

though I no longer subscribed to Firinne's political philosophy – or by trying to change the inequities of capitalism that caused such unequal distribution of the world's goods. Unfortunately, the social action that was needed in Brazil – redistributing the country's wealth and raising up those who were mired in poverty – was fraught with the kind of political dangers that Firinne's crusaders did not encounter: I had heard that a Brazilian priest in a not very distant parish was engaged in such social work, but that priest was under constant surveillance by agents of the military dictatorship and was liable to be arrested at any time for what the government regarded as subversive activity.

So since I didn't have the courage to engage in actions that might get me imprisoned, I founded a Branch of the Legion of Mary and recruited members from the Sodalities and elsewhere. Recognizing that a strongly motivated person was needed to lead the new organization, I chose Niuza as presiding officer. She was already President of the Filhas de Maria, was an active helper in my treks to the capellas on weekends, and she vetted my Sunday sermons for correct Portuguese. She was also a very attractive young woman and I had grown more fond of her than a celibate priest should.

The Legion proved popular with the new members. They held meetings every week at which, as the Legion handbook required, they intermingled prayer with reports of their activities and discussion of future projects. They sought out families to visit who needed their help – both spiritually and materially – and reported their activities at the weekly meetings. Working with them made me feel I was doing a worthwhile activity. The members were enthusiastic; like me they had found work that they felt good about, and they soon bonded into a coherent organization.

Doubt and Resolution

Love and Celibacy

The Legionaries, following a recommendation in the handbook, decided to hold a social function to honor the birthday of the Blessed Virgin Mary, the Legion Patron. The function they chose was an outing to a local lake where they could picnic and swim. As their chaplain, I was expected to take part. Although I swam very poorly I donned a bathing suit and splashed in the water with the members. My eyes strayed often to the swimsuit-

Niuza

clad forms of the young women; in particular, I sought out the company of Niuza – prettiest of them all in my eyes – and once more regretted my vow of celibacy. That day, more than any since my arrival in Florida Paulista, I felt the burden of being cut off from the companionship of women. Most disturbing was not being able to share in the easy inter-sex banter that took place among the Legionaries.

276

In the days and weeks following the outing I found Niuza more and more in my thoughts. I looked forward to being in her company on the weekend trips to the capellas, and paid more visits to her school than to others. I found excuses to pay evening visits to her home in hopes that she'd be there, which she usually was. Her mother, a daily mass-goer, welcomed the padre, not suspecting my motive. One such evening, while drinking coffee at her house I glanced at Niuza sitting opposite and found her gazing intensely at me. In one of those defining moments in life I realized I was in love with her and she with me. I returned to the Casa Paroquial in a state of euphoric shock. The last time I had fallen deeply in love I was a free agent. Now I was a priest who had made a commitment to life-long celibacy; the tender emotion had no place in my life.

Or had it? But that question, which arose unbidden, I had no right to even ask. Yet my mind continued to ask it, at night, alone in the Casa Paroquial. Should I discuss the matter with a confrere and ask for advice? With whom? I couldn't ask Padre João: he was away on another fund-raising mission. Not that it mattered: I could never raise the subject with him because I knew his answer would be a simple withering *get over it, Walter, for God's sake; you're a priest and a missionary; pray to our Lady, and God will give you the strength to overcome the temptation that Satan has placed in your path. And that every priest faces at least once in his priestly life.*

But I wasn't every priest. And Niuza was not a satanic temptation. I couldn't feel bad about being in love with her. Neither could I discuss the matter with any of my other confreres: what could they say differently from Padre Joâo? And since the only words I'd want to hear from them would be the kind of encouragement that they, as priests, couldn't give, it would be unfair to put them on the spot. I must answer the question myself and take responsibility for my answer.

At this time, too, I found myself challenged by another problem. The Legion of Mary and its social work, about which I was enthused, brought to the fore the feeling of discontent regarding my priestly work that had been festering within me for some time. I celebrated mass so often – more than a dozen times every week – that it had become an almost mechanical routine. Hearing confessions was a chore that I often felt was pointless: the parishioners with serious spiritual problems rarely came, leaving me to deal with the peccadillos of Sodality members and their well-trained children who confessed every week. Preaching at mass was somewhat platitudinous since those who came to mass were the 'good people' who had heard all I had to say many times before. And I had grown to detest the baptism ceremony: squalling babies, indifferent parents and godparents, an often unintelligible-to-its-audience ritual, all combined to obfuscate any spiritual meaning the ceremony might have.

But while the clouds of unrest were darkening my priestly vocation, I was not facing up to the consequences they held for my future. I had already rejected the Church's teaching on birth control, I was now in love with Niuza, my priestly duties no longer had meaning for me. Yet I hadn't given serious thought to alternatives. I was being driven to the future without any idea as to what I should do when I got there. My life before ordination had been focused on the Big Day. It was followed by the excitement of coming to Brazil. And now I had been here for two years. I had sought a way of life and had achieved my goal, only to find that I didn't really want it after all. So where did I go from here? One afternoon as I sat in the church meditating on my life and attempting to pray, I found myself asking the awful question: is this what I still want to be doing ten years from now? The emotional answer came back, loud and clear. It is not.

On occasional visits to São Paulo city – since it was a twelve-hour train journey each way, trips were infrequent – I browsed in bookshops and was acquiring a small library of Portuguese and English books, mostly spiritual. Among them was a volume, titled *Tradition and Traditions* by a French theologian named Yves Congar, on the place of Tradition in Catholic theology. I spent many afternoons walking the center aisle of the church reading that book and meditating. I was seeking an escape from my commitment to life-long celibacy, an escape that would allow me to avoid the damnation of my soul. The task was exacerbated by the fact that I had a terribly logical mind, a quality that I believe was partially innate but that had been finely honed through my studies in philosophy and logic and theology. In my present state of mind I could only accept conclusions that, to me, were logically consistent and didn't admit of reasonable doubt.

I discovered from reading Congar how tenuous was the certainty of dogmas I had been told in theology courses were *de fide definita* – matters of faith which all Catholics must believe. Doctrines had arisen from "traditions" that had grown up over the centuries, culled from the opinions of learned men, until at some stage they had hardened into certainties-that-are-divinely-revealed. Some of those opinions-turned-certainties-become-dogmas, such as those relating to the nature of God, could never be proved or disproved, while others had been disproved by science later, such as the doctrine, held in the time of Gallileo, that the earth is the center of the universe and that the sun revolves around it. I concluded from reading Tradition and Traditions, and reasoning about it, that the Church was fallible! And that therefore the Pope was fallible.

That was the breakthrough I had been looking for. The fallible Church made mistakes in her doctrines. And obligatory

279

clerical celibacy was not even considered to be a doctrine: it was simply a practice of the Western Church, a discipline not enjoined on the Eastern Church. Therefore, it was reasonable to argue that the requirement of celibacy came not from God but from the rulers of the Church who, because they were subject to error, might or might not reflect the Will of God. At the back of my mind also was a principle I learned from Canon law to the effect that any rule or law that limited one's freedom was to be interpreted in the narrowest possible manner. And what law was more restrictive of freedom than clerical celibacy? So if celibacy imposed an undue burden – which it certainly did – and if there was a suspicion that the law which imposed it was in error – that it was not God's Will – then I would be justified in contravening it. I believed I had found a way out, but I was not about to act on it precipitately. I'd let it stand the test of time, my time of course.

Milaré

Monsignor Milaré, Vicar General of the diocese, came by one morning for a visit. A bluff gregarious man about my own age, he was known to be friendly with lots of women, an accomplishment I only pretended not to envy. During our chat on this particular day, after Dona Zelie brought us coffee, the Monsignor turned the conversation to some recently published documents of the Vatican Council.

"They're talking about allowing us priests to marry." He cocked a quizzical eyebrow at me. "Did you know that?"

"I don't believe it will happen," I replied.

"But you'll take advantage of it when they allow it, won't you?"

I looked warily at the Monsignor: did he know something

Padre soccer team; Milaré next to me, right front; Padre João standing

about my feelings for Niuza? He couldn't, of course, because no one, not even Niuza, knew about them. "I haven't given it a thought," I lied. "Do you think the Pope will allow it?"

"Who knows." The Monsignor sipped his coffee. "But there's been a lot of discussion of celibacy at the Council."

"I read in the *Estado de São Paulo* that Bishop Koop (of our neighboring Lins diocese) raised the question of having a married clergy here in Latin America." I had been able to keep up with the Council deliberations through the *Estado*.

"Ah! So you *are* interested!" The Monsignor chuckled.

"The paper said Bishop Koop is concerned about the lack of priests here in Brazil and he thought that –"

" – Pope Paul has discouraged any discussion of married

clergy," the Monsignor interrupted. "He told the bishops not to discuss the matter in Council. He said he respected their freedom to discuss whatever they liked. However, those who wanted to discuss a married clergy were to put their thoughts in writing and send them to him." He grinned. "So what do you think of that, Padre?"

I smiled and raised my eyebrows, not yet ready to publicly air my views on papal fallibility. Besides, the Monsignor might be an episcopal spy, going around testing the allegiance of Dom Hugo's clergy. I needn't have worried on that score: a few years later the Monsignor would himself leave the priesthood and the Church, and go into the business of promoting birth control to the poor women of Brazil.

Decision Time

If you believe you are in love with Niuza and if you believe that she is in love with you, then it behooves you to either act on those beliefs or to forget about her. Fish or cut bait, Walter! I arrived at that conclusion one afternoon as I paced the church with Congar's book. Having already determined that the rule of celibacy did not come from God, rejecting it no longer posed a moral problem for me. However, I could not flout celibacy and remain a priest; the Church did not yet allow priests to marry. So in order to marry Niuza – which was what I wanted to do, assuming of course that she'd marry me – I'd have to give up the priesthood.

That made me face the biggest hurdle: was I ready to renounce the priesthood? Could I give it up and remain a friend of Jesus? He had called me to His service, I had accepted His invitation. Now I wanted to back out. How could I rationalize that? I recalled my years of rejecting the lure of the priesthood because I didn't want to live without the company of woman. Yet I finally overcame that argument because I believed more strongly that God was calling me. So, was I justified in reneging on my commitment to Him?

A revolution in my thinking was now taking place. During all my hitherto rational life I had accepted without challenge what I had been told regarding the purpose of my life and the means of achieving it; which had led me into the priesthood. The key words were *accepted without challenge*: I had used my intelligence to absorb and implement what was presented to me, but not to challenge its veracity. I had been taught to think, but not to engage in independent thinking about Church doctrine. However, I could not resolve my present dilemma using that paradigm: I must work through the dilemma by thinking for myself. So I spent weeks thinking and praying, pacing the afternoon church, marshaling the arguments.

For leaving, there was the conviction – which had been creeping up on me even before I fell in love with Niuza – that my priestly ministry was not accomplishing anything useful for my fellow men, that I would be better off doing some kind of social work. Did God want me to spend my life doing something I no longer believed in? I recalled the unhappy priest I met in my Dublin ministry; I didn't want to end up like him. Which was likely to happen if I stayed in the priesthood.

For staying, there was my lifetime dedication to God in the priesthood. However, I debated whether I should keep a promise I had made with far less understanding of its consequences than I now had. Hadn't I told my parishioners that God would not hold them to promises they made that were impossible to fulfil – like the man who promised to set off fireworks in the church? A promise is always contingent on the consequences of its fulfilment: if the consequences are bad or dangerous or impossible then the promise should not be kept.

After much agonizing, intellectualizing, and praying, I convinced myself that God did not expect me to remain in the priesthood at the expense of a life of misery. But that intellectual conviction did not allow me to ride happily into the sunset. I discovered that intellectual conviction is not necessarily accompanied by emotional acceptance: while my rational, logical, mind was satisfied that I was justified in leaving the priesthood, my non-rational, emotional, self feared that I might be making a wrong decision. So for weeks I remained in a funk. Eventually, I forced myself to ask Niuza if she would come to the Casa Paroquial some day after school as I had something I wished to discuss. Though I was still unsure what to do if she validated my belief in her love. She arrived at my door on a Wednesday afternoon. Dona Zelie had left for the day.

"Come in," I invited.

She hesitated. "It might not be appropriate," she murmured.

That demure response told me what I wanted to know. "Let's go to the church then." She concurred and we walked the short distance to the sacristy. Once inside I took her hand; she offered her lips. From then on we were lovers, though we never engaged in anything more than kissing.

Early in October Padre João returned from his latest fund-raising trip to Ireland and regaled me with more stories of his success. He also informed me that another four young confreres would be arriving shortly. And "with the new men arriving I've arranged for us to take over several new parishes. Including a big one north west of here, in a city called Mirandopolis."

"That's interesting." I suspected what was coming. Padre

284

Joao was looking at me as if sizing me up.

"I suppose you'd like Mirandopolis, wouldn't you? You're certainly entitled to it."

I gathered from his tone that again he didn't want me to leave Florida Paulista. After all, I was the de facto parish priest here since he was away most of the time. There was also a suspicion among the confreres that he might be grooming me to replace himself in time as Superior of the Holy Ghost Brazilian mission. And then there was the momentous decision I had just made, to leave the priesthood altogether – though I didn't know yet when or how I'd accomplish that deed. "You'd like me to stay here," I parried.

He didn't hesitate. "I would." His gaze a plaintive plea. "But if you really want to go to Mirandopolis, the parish is yours."

"I'll stay."

So when the new men arrived he assigned them their

Mingling with the new arrivals, 1967

285

parishes and gave Mirandopolis to a confrere who had been ministering in Goiás for the past two years.

It was difficult for Niuza and me to find a suitable place to discuss our future. Even though Padre João was away most of the time, the nuns had arrived and were in and out of the Casa Paroquial a lot. So I suggested we meet away from Florida Paulista. She'd be on vacation from school in January, she said, at which time she'd be visiting relatives in Sao Bernardo do Campo, a suburb of São Paulo. So we agreed to meet in the big city at that time.

Padre João encouraged me to take a vacation after Christmas. "Take advantage of my being here to get away for a few days. It'll do you good."

We met in front of the Cathedral in the Praça da Sé in the early afternoon of a hot summer day in January. Since it didn't seem appropriate to carry on our discussion inside the Cathedral, we found a movie house. During the film I turned to her and uttered the fateful words, "eu te amo." She reciprocated and held my hand. Afterwards we went to a restaurant and talked about the future. We agreed that we'd like to marry, but, as she also was aware, there were serious obstacles to be overcome if a celibate priest was to lawfully wed within the Church.

Monsignor Milaré's optimism notwithstanding, there was little likelihood that Pope Paul VI would abolish the rule of celibacy. And, although the clerical grapevine had been carrying stories that Pope John XXIII had granted dispensations to individual priests, there was no information as to whether his successor was doing likewise. Since at that time neither of us considered the possibility of marrying without the Church's blessing, the road ahead was murky; I would have to leave the priesthood and apply for a dispensation, which might or might not be granted. So we agreed on the need for patience, and meanwhile committed to keeping our engagement a secret from everyone, including her family.

Padre João went off on his travels again shortly after, so I wouldn't be able to start the process of leaving the priesthood until he returned. Niuza and I got together whenever we safely could, always without much intimacy. Once, while being driven by a confrere to a gathering, we held hands in the back seat of the jeep. It might be asked how I reconciled my behavior with the obligation of life-long celibacy that I assumed at ordination. For, although I no longer believed that celibacy was commanded by God for priests, I was still bound by my vow until formally released by the Pope. The short answer was that I could not. Since I first acknowledged that I was in love with Niuza I had been saying mass and administering the sacraments of penance and baptism, all of which required me to be in 'the state of grace' – free from mortal sin. I had been confessing my sins as usual to a confrere at my monthly confession.[2] But now, confessing to a confrere presented a problem. I knew of course that priests were bound never to reveal anything they heard in the sacred tribunal. However, I didn't want any confrere to know my plans. So I told them nothing in confession that would give a clue to my intentions. How could I justify that? Was I not committing sin by kissing Niuza? And putting myself in an occasion of sin by consorting with her? Shouldn't I confess that? The answer is that I had learned my theological casuistry only too well. Kissing was seriously sinful only if I deliberately took sexual pleasure in it; I

---

[2]We all confessed to each other; I heard my confreres' confession, too, including that of Padre João, and so, incidentally, I knew about *their* difficulties in practicing chastity.

convinced myself that I did not, so the occasion of sin was remote. Consequently, I never mentioned in confession anything concerning my romantic relationship. I worried that parishioners, particularly the pious women, would notice that a special friendship had sprung up between Niuza and me. But if they noticed anything they said nothing to me about it. Or, more importantly, to Padre João when he was there.

The months slipped by; Padre João was still away; Niuza and I continued to meet clandestinely whenever the occasion allowed. In July two confreres and two nuns decided to take a vacation trip to Brazilia, and they invited me to join them. We set out on a Monday morning, five of us packed into a Volkswagen. It was a thousand mile journey over mostly dirt roads but we were young and undaunted and we stopped overnight on the way. When we reach the State of Goiás, the two confreres, both of whom had served in parishes there, decided to stop at a ranch to visit some old friends. We were warmly greeted by the family, including their two nubile daughters. After a meal the daughters took us on a tour of the ranch. I noticed as we walked around, that my confreres were holding hands with the daughters. Which made me wonder if they were also on their way to leaving the priesthood. One of them did leave several years later, the other remained.

Leaving the Priesthood

The Big Step

On our return a letter from Padre João awaited me: he'd be back in a week and then we'd move house! Without telling me, he had negotiated with the city to replace our dingy Casa Paroquial with a nearby elegant house that had come on the market. When he returned we moved – there was not much to move – and settled into the new house. Then he told me that he had to go to São Paulo in a couple of days to meet the Superior General of the Congregation, Archbishop Marcel Lefebvre, who was coming to visit our mission and would be our guest in the new Casa Paroquial.

In the meantime I had made a final commitment to Niuza that I would leave the priesthood as soon as possible. So I decided to tell Padre João of my decision the morning he left for São Paulo: that would give him time to mull over his options, and also keep him from pressuring me to change my mind.

"I'm planning to leave the priesthood," I told him after breakfast as he was packing an overnight bag for his trip.

"You're what?" He stopped packing and looked at me in confusion. I had been wondering if any parishioner had apprised him of my friendship with Niuza: apparently no one had.

"I'm leaving the priesthood to get married."

He stared at me. "You can't do that." And continued packing.

"I can, and I am."

He looked at his watch: I had timed my announcement well. "Look, Walter, I can't talk about this now; I have a train to catch. But don't do anything until I get back and then we'll discuss the matter."

"I'm not going anywhere before you get back," I assured him. "But my mind is made up." He finished packing and I drove him to the station in silence.

Two days later he returned with Archbishop Lefebvre. I knew nothing about the Archbishop at the time except that he was the Superior General of the Congregation. He was a refined and elegant-looking man with courtly manners, who spoke English with a strong French accent – when he addressed the assembled

Archbishop Lefebvre

confreres in the new Casa Paroquial on the evening of his arrival he spoke a great deal about the importance of what sounded like 'grass'; eventually I realized that he was speaking of the importance of 'grace' in our priestly lives. At the Vatican Council deliberations he was known as an advocate of many extremely conservative positions: he had excoriated the declaration on religious liberty, saying the Catholic Church alone had a right to such freedom; he had rejected the Council's declaration

290

that the Jews were not guilty of decide; and he had rejected its directive that the mass be said in the vernacular of the country.

Padre João had told the Superior General of my decision to leave the priesthood, so on the evening of his arrival in Florida Paulista he invited me to his room and chided me for my decision. "The priesthood is like marriage," he said, "once you enter it you cannot leave." A few years later he himself would quarrel with the Vatican over the Latin mass, found his own seminary of right-wing young men whom he would ordain in defiance of Rome, disobey the Pope, incur excommunication, and unlawfully consecrate bishops.

After the Archbishop left, I had to face Padre João. He was outraged; I was disgracing the Church, the Congregation, and myself, he said. And I was putting the lassie's soul – referring to Niuza – in danger of hell's fire. I said nothing, understanding his anger: he had such a high regard for me and I was letting him down. When he finished berating me and I had made clear that I would not change my mind, he modulated into damage-control mode. He discussed the matter with the bishop, Dom Hugo, and the latter decided that I must leave not only Florida Paulista but also Brazil before he would agree to forward my petition for a dispensation to Rome. Furthermore, the confreres were not to be told of my perfidy. Padre João would inform them that I was going to the United States to take some university courses. The parishioners likewise would be kept ignorant of the reason for my leaving, and my departure was to be low-key.

Padre João assembled the confreres for a lunch at which he announced my departure for the United States to undertake a course of study. The confreres wished me well, though it was obvious to me that, while they went along with the pretense, at least some of them knew the truth. I had much sympathy for Padre João at this time: he had a right to feel hurt and betrayed. But his

291

later actions greatly diminished my sympathy. Many years later, after he had retired to Ireland, he wrote an autobiography and, in the section on Brazil he did not so much as acknowledge my presence. Perhaps the hurt caused his memory of me to be blocked.

I had very little money, just about enough for my airfare from São Paulo to New York, and Padre Joâo refused to give me any, though he was well-heeled after his recent fund-raising trip. When my trunk had fallen into the sea at Liverpool three years earlier it had been insured. The insurance money was duly paid to the confrere to whom I entrusted the trunk. However, that confrere – call him A – loaned the money to another confrere – B – who failed to return the loan. So at the time of my leaving I still had not received my insurance payment, money that would be very useful to me at that point. B was present at the farewell lunch, but when I asked him to return the money he said he didn't have it. However, he said, a young Holy Ghost missionary would shortly be coming from Kimmage to help him in his parish and he'd be passing through New York on the way. B would tell him to contact me there and pay me what B owed me, from the money the new confrere would collect for the missions when passing through New York. I accepted that compromise.

I arranged to take an evening bus from Florida Paulista, which would arrive in São Paulo the following morning, and to fly to New York from there. Before leaving I managed a few private moments with Niuza; we said our goodbyes and committed to writing each other. I promised that when I was settled in a job in America I'd return and we'd be married. She alerted a few of our friends and they met at the bus stop to see me off. When the bus was pulling away and I saw Niuza and those friends standing at the curb I broke down, one of the few occasions in my adult life that I allowed the tears to flow. That childhood disease, boys-do-not-cry, still afflicted me and would continue to do so.

Home to New York

I had written my mother to tell her I was coming, but without giving the reason. She assumed that after three years on the missions I was taking a well-earned vacation. She welcomed me warmly, my siblings did so in their usual casual way. Since, in the official terminology of the Vatican, I was still a priest in good standing I said mass in the local parish church next morning. On my return to the apartment my mother made me breakfast. We were alone. She was standing by the refrigerator when I broke the news of my departure from the priesthood. She displayed neither shock nor surprise.

"It's your life and your decision to make." That was all: she didn't ask for my reasons, and she never questioned me on the subject again. Casually, without explanation, she informed my siblings and her friends. All were unfazed by the announcement: my siblings weren't particularly religious and, I suspected, they had always thought my becoming a priest an aberration.

That was not the case with some relatives in Ireland. Shortly after my arrival in New York I wrote to inform Aunt Mary. I wasn't prepared for her reaction: she – a former nun who had received a dispensation from her own vows to leave the convent and marry – wrote back to say that I was doing a terrible thing and that she could not accept my decision. Furthermore, she said, having discussed the matter with Uncle Walter, who was horrified as well, she decided to cut all ties with me; she would not write to me again and I would not be welcome in their home should I come to Ireland. She also passed word of my scandalous

293

action to other relatives in Ireland. My mother got a letter from a cousin of my father's who commiserated with her on the terrible scandal and added, "I'm sure you wish you were dead." My mother, chortling, read me the letter.

I wrote to Niuza, assuring her that I was well. She wrote back to tell me that because of the 'scandal' our relationship had caused in Florida Paulista she was going to live with her relatives in São Bernardo do Campo, and had already got a teaching post there. We continued to write each other every week while I sorted out my situation, which was precarious. On the positive side I was with my family and had a place to stay for the time being. On the other hand I was in the United States on a visitor's visa, with which I would be unable to get a job. And I was still a priest, bound by my priestly obligations. However, I decided that since I was soon to leave the priesthood I would cease to say the divine office or celebrate mass.

Two major tasks confronted me: to acquire a dispensation from celibacy, and to obtain permanent residency in the United States. I had no intention of returning to Ireland where I would very likely be unwelcome and where finding a job would be well-nigh impossible: Ireland was still a poor country where jobs were few and emigration levels were high. I had no idea what kind of employment I would be able to get in the United States: a degree in philosophy and four years of theology did not easily translate into marketable skills. Tom had friends who worked on Wall Street and thought they might be able to get me a job there once I acquired a Green Card, but nothing came of those efforts. Jim helped me with the immigration application and suggested that I should become a computer programmer like himself. I felt that my background would best qualify me for some kind of counseling work, but I had no formal qualifications.

Padre Joâo, in a generous moment before I left Brazil, told me he would write to a Holy Ghost confrere at Duquesne University in Pittsburgh – a Congregation University – and request that I be allowed to take some courses there to qualify me for a job. He supplied me with details for contacting the confrere at Duquesne. So I arranged to meet the confrere in Pittsburgh, flew down, was met at the airport by another Holy Ghost priest who informed me that the confrere I had arranged to meet was out of town, so I'd have to make another appointment, and another trip. I returned to New York, and after a few days made another appointment, flew to Pittsburgh again, was met by the same Holy Ghost confrere as before, who told me that I was in luck this time: the confrere I came to meet was available. I met him at the Congregation house, he invited me to stay for dinner, and over the course of the meal I broached the subject of my visit.

"I understand Padre João has written to you about me?"

"Yes. I received his letter." The confrere's tone was pleasant, friendly. I felt my hopes rising.

"He told me you would be willing to help me take some courses."

The confrere's manner changed from friendly to official. "I understand that you have no money to pay for any courses?"

"That's true."

"Then there's nothing I can do to help you."

On returning home I wrote Padre João a courtesy letter telling him of my experience. He replied several months later.

I had time on my hands to enjoy the sights of New York again but little money with which to do it. I was grateful to my mother, who had recently regained her nursing license, for maintaining me, and to my sister Bridie for the weekly pocket money she gave me. I was pleasantly surprised when the young priest whom confrere B promised would contact me in New York on his way to Brazil did so. He had collected money for the missions and handed over the insurance money that confrere B owed me. I was now able to buy some non-clerical clothes and had money to sustain me during the six months I had to wait before I received immigration clearance to work.

Father Mick, my former Director of Theologians, was passing through New York and called on me. I was happy to see him. Father Mick was an exceptional human being and priest; in Kimmage, the good of the individual and common sense always took precedence over rules. We spent a pleasant evening together chatting about Kimmage, the missions, and the confreres. Father Mick didn't ask me why I was leaving and made no attempt to dissuade me; his only reference to the subject was to offer a listening ear should I ever wish to talk to him.

Shortly after, one of my Brazilian confreres, Father Maurice, arrived in New York and came to visit. An affable man, Moss, we got along well, having also been confreres in Kimmage for many years. Moss had an aunt in Connecticut whom he wished to visit and needed help in getting there. So I borrowed Tom's car and drove him to Hartford. We stayed overnight at the aunt's home and in the morning she invited Moss to say mass in her house. He asked me to concelebrate, which I did, though feeling a bit uneasy about doing so. It was the last time I celebrated mass. A few years later, Moss also left the priesthood.

Seeking a dispensation

Getting a release from my priestly obligations turned into a more-than-three-year saga. I was given no information by any Congregation Superior as to the proper way to apply for the dispensation, so I took a two-path approach, writing to the

296

Chancery of the Brooklyn diocese in which I resided, and to the Superior General of the Congregation.

In October of 1967, the Brooklyn Chancery summoned me to a Tribunal to judge my case and send its recommendation to Rome. I presented myself at the appointed time and was shown into a room that resembled the courtrooms I had seen in film and television dramas. The room was empty except for two men in clerical garb. One of them asked me to sit on the witness stand, and asked a series of formal questions: my name, address, background, priestly studies, date of ordination, subsequent posts, reasons for wanting to leave the priesthood, etc. The other cleric sat at a table and took notes. The proceeding was very formal, and afterwards I was dismissed with the statement that my request would be forwarded to Rome in due course.

In my letter to Archbishop Lefebvre I asked him to forward my petition for a dispensation to Rome. Shortly afterwards I received a reply from the Secretary General telling me that the Congregation did not forward such petitions to Rome; I would have to write a personal letter to the Pope and send it to the Cardinal Pro-Prefect of the Congregation for the Doctrine of the Faith. He included information about the kind of personal data it should contain. I composed the letter and sent it as directed.

In December I received a reply to the letter I had sent to Padre João in September after the Duquesne fiasco.

> *Dear Walter,*
>
> *Thanks for your letter. I was wondering about the situation, having heard nothing. Finally, I wrote to the American Provincial. From his reply I deduced you had antagonized him – gave the runaround, criticized the Church, etc. He wasn't pleased with me for sending you. The lads here know your story and are very disappointed*

and critical. But that would be expected.

*As you've sent on the petition to Rome, it is chiaou (*sic*)to CSSp and the priesthood obviously. I presume you mean petition to marry, because obviously you have first to be 'reduced to the lay state.' I think that's the term. Means release from the obligations to say office, and the right to perform any 'priestly' acts – mass, etc.: also release from prohibition to ---- (*illegible*), and from all religious obligations of rule. I understand 'laicisation' is easy to come by and you have probably got it by now if you followed the correct procedure. Some ex-members of the Irish Province got it in the past. It is the only alternative while the Catholic priesthood remains celibate officially. Anyway, saying mass, etc., after a bloke decides to chuck everything is somewhat hypocritical and I have no doubt you'd be a lot happier laicised.*

I understand permission to marry is quite separate and subsequent to the other – and much more complicated. But never having dealt with a case, I am dependent on hearsay.

*I heard from Ireland that Doheny (*Father Mick*) has seen you and regarded you as a 'hopeless case.' Depends on what he was hoping for!*

Your mother. I feel terribly sorry for her and was on the point of writing several times, but couldn't. A big cross for her.

> *With kind regards,*
> *J. Jordan.*

I received regular letters from Father Mickey, a confrere in Brazil who had been a close friend from Kilshane and

Kimmage days. Mickey kept me apprised of gossip among Brazilian confreres. He told me that they were all aware before I left of the reason for my leaving, but Padre João had warned them not to talk about it or pretend to know. They were not at all upset and wished me well. Though one of them had accused me – he didn't say who – of stealing the insurance money I got from the confrere en route to Brazil. Mickey also told me of a rumor that Padre João and Dom Hugo had decided to forward to Rome their objections to my dispensation. This latter clarified, and made ominous, Padre João's statement in his letter – *I understand permission to marry is quite separate and subsequent to the other – and much more complicated.* It also helped to explain the long-drawn-out dispensation saga that ensued.

Independent Thinking

Weakening faith

The reading and meditating that allowed me in good conscience to abdicate my priestly life had the unintended side-effect of raising doubts about other aspects of religion. While I awaited permission to look for work I spent much time walking the streets of Manhattan and browsing the religion sections of its many bookstores. The insurance money allowed me to buy books, and with lots of time on hand I read them and meditated more deeply on the religion I was reared in and to which I had hitherto given the greater part of my life. The result was a steady weakening of my faith in the Church that I had once thought I could never challenge. That weakening did not come about overnight: my faith in the Church had been solidified by a lifetime of indoctrination in its beliefs, participation in its rituals, and acceptance of the Catholic perspective on life. Only an earthquake-like upheaval in belief could separate me from those rituals and that perspective. However, though I wasn't aware of it for some time, the cataclysmic upheaval that caused me to leave the priesthood was now separating me from the Church as well.

300

Surprisingly, and this became clear only long afterwards, the Vietnam war had a profound effect on my thinking and, indirectly, on my leaving the Church. On arrival in the United States I was inundated with reports on, and discussions of, the war. My new-found ability to think independently, which was forced on me to justify leaving the priesthood, now let loose within me an extravagance of independent thinking on all subjects, so that I tended now to challenge the veracity of everything presented to me. It required only a little independent thinking for me to conclude that the war on Vietnam was unjustified, an opinion that, though already adopted by a few public figures like Eugene McCarthy and Robert Kennedy, was still very unpopular in America. Even my brother Jim became angry with me when I shared my opinion with him.

Jesus and Sex

After judging that the Vietnam war was immoral I examined another war, one I had been fighting with myself all my adult life: the war of the flesh against the virtue of chastity. I focused my newfound independent thinking on Catholic doctrine about sex, and it soon seemed ludicrous to me that the loving God portrayed by the Gospels would as severely punish an unchaste thought as He would a brutal murder. Yet that was what the Church taught.[3] As a way of arguing against this teaching I imagined a dialog between Jesus and a moral theologian (MT). The latter attempts to justify the existence of the myriad types of sexual sins that fellow theologians have deduced over the centuries.

---

[3] And, it may be argued, still teaches: cf Catechism of the Catholic Church, 2351ff.

Being & Becoming

Jesus: What's your problem?

MT: Sexual sins, Lord.

Jesus: Sex sins are the least of my worries these days; much more troublesome to me are the wars and greed and prejudices that are rampant throughout the world. However, go ahead, tell me about your sexual concerns.

MT: I'd like to verify that all the sexual sins listed in our theology books are really acts that are condemned by You.

Jesus: What sins? I don't remember ever condemning any sex acts. Except maybe when I told the woman who was taken in adultery to sin no more. And that was just a sort of slap on the wrist to keep the Pharisees happy.

MT: Let me start by invoking St. Paul: he says that fornicators will not inherit Your Kingdom.

Jesus: The only thing I said about fornication was that a fellow could divorce his wife if she committed fornication. I didn't even say he had to divorce her, merely that fornication was a valid ground. I intended, of course, that a wife could divorce her husband for the same reason: sauce for the goose, etc.

MT: But, Lord, Your Church has based practically its whole code of sexual morality on what Paul said. We conclude that all human sexual activity is intended by You to be primarily for the purpose of creating new human life, and that all sexual activity must therefore be open to the procreation of life. So to engage in human sexual activity one must be in a position to create and nurture human life.

Jesus: Where does that leave people who are too old to have kids? You think old people don't want sex? Or what about young people who aren't yet ready to marry and have kids but whose hormones are raging? Or people who don't

302

want kids, or who don't want them right now but who do want sex right now? Or what about those who should never have kids because they'd make lousy parents? And what about those who are infertile?

MT: *We do make exceptions, Lord, for the satisfying of lust, and for the old and infertile. As long as they don't practice birth control, the married may have sex.*

Jesus: *But not the others I mentioned?*

MT: *No, Lord. We deduce from what Paul said that sex is allowable only within marriage. The principal being that if you want to have fun in bed you must be prepared to pay for it with marriage and children.*

Jesus: *Did Paul make that up, too? Don't blame me for it.*

MT: *Actually, most of it came out of the early Church, as a reaction to Roman and Greek hedonism.*

Jesus: *Well, let me tell you, those hedonist fellows were closer to my way of thinking than you prigs. I get the impression that all you Catholic moralists hate the human body. You certainly didn't get that notion from me – remember how I enjoyed having my head anointed? You probably got your inhibitions from Greek Spartans and Roman Stoics.*

MT: *We got them from the early Fathers, too. Hermits flagellating themselves in the desert, that sort of thing. And the Gnostics who thought the body was deeply alien to the soul. And the Manichaeans who thought the body was a lost cause.*

Jesus: *Let me tell you, the human body is my masterpiece.*

MT: *We reverence it, Lord, as the temple of the Holy Ghost.*

Jesus: *So why do you insist that it must always be covered up?*

MT: *We do teach that just looking at other people's bodies, especially at what we call the "less decent" parts – female breasts – or the "indecent" parts – the genitalia of either sex – is mortally sinful.*

Jesus: *Where did you get the idea that I would send people to hell for looking at a naked human body?*

MT: *Our argument is that such looks are bound to arouse lust. And to deliberately arouse the lust beast is mortally sinful.*

Jesus: *I suppose you'll tell me next that if God had wanted you to go naked you'd have been born that way. Anyway, what about doctors? They're always examining naked people.*

MT: *Doctors are free from sin if they look at or touch naked bodies in the course of their duties – on condition that they don't take sexual pleasure in such looking or touching.*

Jesus: *How do you expect a normal red-blooded human being not to enjoy looking at a beautiful human body, male or female? I made them so you'd enjoy looking at them.*

MT: *But, Lord, didn't Pope Gregory the Great say that taking pleasure even in marital intercourse is unlawful. And You made the popes infallible, didn't you?*

Jesus: *I did no such thing. Pius IX did that. Anyway, didn't I reduce my commandments to one – love one another. So sin arises only from a failure to love.*

MT: *So You want us to throw the whole tract on sex out the window, Lord?*

Jesus: *As long as sex is consensual between adults and is a part of showing love for each other and is not harming anyone else, I consider it holy – which means I like it.*

This belief led me to give up going to confession and Communion, for those acts were forever associated in my mind with the restrictions of Holy Purity. From there it was an easy step to be unconcerned about missing Sunday mass. I was gradually ceasing to be a practicing member of the Church.

This doesn't follow

Walter Keady

IBM

In January of 1968 I received a call from the United States Immigration and Naturalization Service to come for an interview. The officer told me that although it would be several months before my Green Card was issued I might now look for a job. Going home on the train I perused the New York Times and spotted a half page ad by IBM seeking Programmer Trainees in a place called Poughkeepsie; any college degree would be accepted, it said; interviews would be held that evening in the Time-Life Building. I knew nothing about computers or programming except what Jim had told me – that it was an interesting job and paid well. I still didn't know what I wanted to do with my life, so any job that supported me in the meantime would serve. I went to the IBM interview, took a programming aptitude test with about fifty other applicants, was interviewed by a pleasant man who invited me to Poughkeepsie for further consideration. In Poughkeepsie, after a day of interviews, IBM offered me a job as a programmer trainee, which would entail six months of programming school, with pay. I accepted the offer, which came with a generous salary, and was told to report for work on March 18.

I needed a car, so with a loan from my mother I bought a 1958 Cadillac, a huge machine with tail-fins of such proportions that when looking in the rear-view mirror I had an impression of being closely followed by another car. On March 18 I reported for work in the company of about twenty other new hires. We spent half a day listening to talks on IBM and its policies, and were then dismissed for the rest of the week so we could find housing for ourselves. After renting a one-bedroom apartment I began training as a computer programmer the following Monday. I felt that the atmosphere in IBM was kindlier and more considerate

305

than that of my former religious Congregation.

Back row, third from left, with programming class at IBM, 1968

Walter Keady

Leaving the Church

The Dispensation Saga

In the meantime, I was concerned about the progress of my application for a dispensation. I heard nothing from the Brooklyn Diocese, and my letter to the Pope wasn't acknowledged. So in February of 1968, after receiving IBM's job offer, I sent another, rather impatient, letter to the Secretary General of the Holy Ghost Congregation,.

Dear Father Farrelly,
As you so kindly took the trouble to reply to my previous communication I'm writing you in the hope that you can clarify things a little for me. Approximately four months ago, acting on your advice and instructions, I sent in my petition to the Holy See. Since then I have heard nothing. My letter was not even acknowledged.
Principally for the sake of my family and others concerned I'm deeply interested in settling this matter in the proper way, i.e. by getting a dispensation. But such action requires co-operation; my goodwill is not sufficient. If the Roman authorities decide to ignore my petition and hope

307

that by so doing the matter will solve itself, at least it
would be an act of charity on their part to let me know that
that is their intention. Then I would be free to solve the
problem according to the dictates of my own conscience.
Perhaps, Father, you would be so kind as to find out what
exactly is the position re my petition and let me knew as
soon as possible.
Sincerely,
Walter Keady

All this time I had been writing to Niuza and she to me. I missed her very much and, now that I had a job, was impatient to get the dispensation so we could marry. But time went by and I still didn't hear from Rome or get a reply from Father Farrelly. Then in June I received a letter from the Brooklyn Chancery.

Dear Mr. Keady,
This is to inform you that your case was forwarded to
Rome on June 25, 1968. I mailed it personally by
registered air mail, for purposes of speed and security in
transmission. The delay since your interrogation here (8
months) has been due to problems in having the acts typed
and in my own problems in fitting in the work on your case
between other obligations which have been more
burdensome than usual.
Cordially yours,
Joseph Konrad

On July 5 I received a letter from the Secretary General.

Dear Walter,

I visited the Congregation for the Doctrine of the Faith shortly after the receipt of your letter. The only information I could get was that your case is filed there and is receiving attention. It is not the practice of that Congregation to acknowledge such letters, but action is always taken on them, however slow, and the final decision is eventually communicated to the petitioner. Cases of young priests take more time, because of the hope of a change of heart and the danger of an unhappy marriage. There have been divorce cases already, as well as cases of refusal to accept laicisation when the indult arrived! It is difficult for me to intervene, because I have done what depends on me in the presentation of your case. Wishing you God's light and strength,

Yours sincerely,

M. Farrelly

P.S. I apologize for my slowness in replying. I have been to the S.C. Pro Doctrina Fidei quite recently and there is nothing new to report.

Humanae Vitae

Pope Paul VI

In July of 1968 Pope Paul VI issued the encyclical, *Humanae Vitae*, on birth control. His predecessor, John XXIII, had appointed a Commission to make recommendations on the subject after the first appearance of the pill. Paul VI, having forbidden the Fathers of the Vatican Council to debate the subject, expanded the Commission to include

309

theologians and women, as well as other experts in relevant fields. The expanded Commission, though composed of mostly conservative thinkers after the mind-set of the Pope himself, nevertheless recommended that birth control be permitted. That recommendation was leaked to the press before the encyclical appeared and expectations were high that the pope would follow it. So when Humanae Vitae burst on the scene, with its re-affirmation of traditional Church teaching and its condemnation of birth control, the reaction of very many Catholics throughout the world was extremely hostile. For me it was the final crack of the Hierarchical whip that drove me from the Catholic Church. I had read historian John T. Noonan's book: *Contraception: A history of its treatment by the Catholic theologians and canonists,* which convinced me that the ban was yet another rule instituted by a sex-hating Church and that it had no Scriptural or logical justification.

Return to Brazil

Programmer training ended in September, and having passed all the tests – continued employment with IBM depended on passing – I was promoted to Associate Programmer. Niuza and I decided through letters that we would not wait any longer for the dispensation. I decided to go to Brazil towards the end of September to marry, so I booked my passage and went to the Brazilian Consulate in New York to get the required visa. Because of previous experience with Brazilian bureaucracy I specifically asked the Consulate personnel if I would need anything other than the visa to enter and exit the country; they assured him that I would not.

I flew from New York to Rio and then to Sao Paulo, where

310

Niuza met me. She had booked a room for me in a hotel near her relatives' home where she was living. Her parents were there also, preparing for the wedding. They welcomed me and were happy for us both. Which pleasantly surprised me because they were devout Catholics and I had expected them to want a Church wedding. However, since the dispensation had not yet been granted, they were resigned to a civil wedding.

Niuza and I spent the next few days in the city, where she shopped and we did a lot of talking. At night I'd return to my hotel while she went to her relatives' house. About the second evening I begin to feel uneasy about the marriage, though not at all about my relationship with Niuza. Something – I didn't know where it was coming from, but it was very insistent – was warning me against the marriage. I tried to ignore it but it followed me around all next day like a persistent headache. I kept hoping it would go away, but it didn't. That night I challenged it: had my feelings for Niuza changed after a year of separation? I had no doubt that they had not. So what was the problem? I didn't know, only that I continued to be seriously perturbed. The feeling grew stronger that I must not go through with the wedding. I agonized all night without finding a resolution, or understanding the provenance of the problem. But how could I not marry Niuza now, after all we had been through to get to this wonderful point? Still, the voice inside said I must not do it. It was terribly insistent, but quite different from the cold feet that I was later told bridegrooms were said to be prone to on the eve of their weddings.

By the time I met Niuza next day I felt I had no option but to tell her that I could not go through with the wedding. We were both devastated; she still loved me and I loved her and we clung to each other. But she didn't challenge my forced decision, a corollary of which was that I must leave Brazil immediately. We took a taxi to the airline office, a ride I could never forget because of our mutual unhappiness. At the airline office I left her the money I had brought to fly us back to New York and said goodbye.

I ran into a snag at the airline office: the official there said I would not be allowed to leave the country until I produced a document showing that I had paid my Brazilian taxes. I protested that I had been in the country for only four days on a visitor's visa, and that the Brazilian Consulate in New York had assured me I didn't need any other documents to leave the country. Alas, the records showed that I was a permanent resident – which I had been when I lived there. Protests availed nothing against the records of bureaucracy: I must go to the appropriate government office to get the appropriate document in order to leave. It was now four o'clock on Friday afternoon. I raced to the appropriate government office but when I got there it was closing for the weekend. Anyway, an official told me, the earliest I could get such a document would be on Monday. I pleaded emergency so he directed me to another office. I raced there, asked to see the officer in charge, and explained my case. The officer was a kindly man, but he reiterated the difficulty of getting a document at this late hour, and told me to return on Monday. Fortunately, I knew a little about Brazilians. Although, as with most bureaucrats everywhere, they loved to conduct business in an orderly fashion, for them family needs must always top bureaucratic rules. I told the officer that my mother was dying and that I must get to New York as soon as possible. My mother had actually been sick when I left New York, though she wasn't anywhere near death. The officer immediately summoned a subordinate, ordered the document prepared for his signature, and in ten minutes I was on my way back to the airline office.

312

My family, somewhat bemused at my trip to marry a Brazilian, didn't seem perturbed when I returned without a wife. I simply told them, and my IBM colleagues, that it didn't work out, without going into any explanation. Months later I received a letter from Niuza enquiring about my well-being and containing no reproach. I replied, telling her I was still single and that there was no other woman in my life. Shortly after, Father Paddy, one of my former Brazilian confreres, came by for a visit on his way to Ireland. He had spent a year in Florida Paulista before I arrived there and knew Niuza well. He told me that he met her after the non-wedding fiasco and her comment to him was "I hope you're all satisfied now," implying, Father Paddy said, that she held Padre Joao and the confreres responsible for the state of mind that prevented my marrying her.

Marriage

I had not yet heard anything from Rome regarding the dispensation. But having made the decision to marry without it, it was no longer important to me. I considered myself to be no longer a priest, even though Catholic theology said I would always be one – *sacerdos in aeternum* – because of the indelibility of Holy Orders. My commitment to Niuza was broken also, so I was now free to date other women. Which I did, casually, for the next year, without meeting anyone special.

In July of 1969 I went to Ireland, my first visit since leaving for Brazil five years earlier. I felt strange being in my native country but no longer of it, having no home there. I could not visit Aunt Mary since she had declared me to be unwelcome. Neither did I wish to visit other relatives since I didn't know what kind of reception I'd get. At the end of a week I flew to London to visit aunts and uncles and cousins who were not shocked or surprised at my new status. During my stay there, Neil Armstrong and Buzz Aldrin landed on the moon: my relatives and I watched them on television in my aunt's kitchen while looking at the moon from the back door.

Every Friday evening I traveled to New York city and stayed with my mother for the weekend: Poughkeepsie was a rather dull place for single people at that time. Most Saturday nights I went dancing, usually to an Irish ballroom in Queens, but occasionally elsewhere. I met several young women whom I casually dated but none who captured my emotions. Until, one Saturday night in November, 1969, having tired of the Irish ballroom scene, I went to a dance at a yacht club in the Whitestone area. Shortly after arriving I spied a very pretty face peering, for just a moment, from behind a pillar. I asked the owner of the face for a dance. There was instant mutual attraction. We danced together all night. I drove her home to Flushing and made a date for the next Saturday. Her name was Patricia. She worked in Manhattan. We spent subsequent weekends together. Six weeks later we were engaged. Her parents and sisters, devout Catholics all, accepted me, though the sisters didn't tell their children that I was a priest; such was the Catholic mentality at the time. Fortunately for me, Patricia was also a lapsed Catholic. On

Patricia

314

February 14, 1970, Valentine's Day, we married at her sister's home on Long Island. A Lutheran minister, a friend from Poughkeepsie, officiated. Patricia left her job and moved to Poughkeepsie. My marriage to her provided me with not only a physical, but also an emotional release from the burden of celibacy: it replaced the dissatisfaction of being cut off from an intimate relationship with a joy that was diluted only by my fear of losing it. A fear that Patricia's love soon demolished.

Final Break

By now I had been theologically and intellectually detached from the Church for more than a year, but it took my emotions additional time to accept that I no longer belonged. However, they, too, eventually came around, and after the marriage I found myself viscerally indifferent to the beliefs that had guided and controlled me for most of my life. In the heyday of my religious fervor I could never understand how anyone would 'lose the Faith.' Now I myself had sloughed off belief in the Catholic Church without regret. Faith, I determined, was, in computer terms, binary: one believed or one did not. And I no longer believed in the Catholic Church. So I was not excited when, nine months after the wedding, a letter arrived from Father Farrelly, the Secretary General.

Dear Walter,
I went recently to the S.C. for the Doctrine of the Faith to see what had become of your request for laicization, because all the cases presented even a good while after yours had been dealt with. I was informed that the S.C. had written to some of the authorities in Brazil to enquire about the eventuality of your return to that territory. This

letter remained unanswered and so nothing was done to advance your case. I had heard myself that your return to Brazil would not please the ecclesiastical and Religious authorities there, and I must admit that I took a rather passive attitude, while doing all that depends on me officially to get your case through.

From what I have heard from friends of yours, it would appear that you have no intention of returning to Brazil where you were formerly known as a priest. If this is the only obstacle there is no reason for holding up the process.

If you would be so kind as to let me know that you have definitely settled down in the United States I shall set about getting you released from your obligations as soon as the Holy Father returns from his forthcoming journey to the Philippines. Would you also let me know your present diocese, because the rescript of laicization will be executed by the Ordinary of your present residence. As soon as I receive your letter I shall take the necessary action and give you a fairly accurate idea as to when you might expect your Indult.

With best wishes and apologies for this untidy letter, etc.

Though I had no longer any interest in receiving the dispensation, I replied to the letter as a courtesy to Father Farrelly and gave him the information he asked for. Two months later I received a letter from the Brooklyn Chancery.

Dear Mr Keady,
A favorable decision has reached here from Rome today. It would be proper for you to call Father Bevilacqua, our

316

*Vice-Chancellor, so that he can go over the conditions
with you. These dispensations are granted to the Bishop
and he must be sure that the conditions are fulfilled before
he can execute the rescript and grant the dispensation.
Father Bevilacqua can be reached at the above telephone
number. After February first, should it be then that you
call, you can speak with Monsignor King.*

I didn't make the requested call. A little over two months
later I received a letter from the Archdiocesan Court of New
York; Poughkeepsie was in the New York Archdiocese.

*Dear Mr. Keady,
Bishop Mugavero of Brooklyn forwarded to us the
Rescript received in your behalf which grants to you a
dispensation from the obligations attaching to Sacred
Orders and Religious Profession.
In order to discuss the steps necessary to bring this matter
to a conclusion, would you kindly call me on the telephone
in order that we might make an appointment.
With every best wish,
I am sincerely yours in Christ,
Rev. Monsignor Joseph J. Quinn*

Curiosity got the better of me this time, so I rang and spoke
to Monsignor Quinn. "You must come in here to the Chancery in
order to validate the marriage," the Monsignor said, without
preamble or without even asking if I was married.

"Thank you," I replied and hung up. Rude of me, but I was
not about to put Patricia through a meaningless ceremony to
satisfy the Sacred Bureaucracy. So I never formally received the
dispensation.

Becoming an Unbeliever

Rejecting the Church

I left the Church because I no longer believed its claims to infallibility or its doctrines on birth control or enforced clerical celibacy or sex in general. Consequently, I no longer believed that it had a divine mission to represent the will of God on earth. Leaving was difficult: I continued to feel the emotional tug of the Church's comforting rituals: mass, sacraments, even confession for its cleansing affect. I felt alone and lonely and for a time fretful as to whether I had done the right thing. Especially when my believing friends asked me questions like: *But you do believe in God?.... And of course you believe in an afterlife? .... But you're spiritual anyway, aren't you?... You strike me as a very spiritual person....*

I did then what I had always done: read and studied and searched for truth. Which brought an exhilarating sense of freedom. I felt at liberty to appraise all kinds of assertions made by all kinds of authorities. I evaluated them on their merits as I saw them, without having to look over my shoulder, as it were, to see if they had the approval of Mother Church. Or of anyone else.

318

I became a freethinker and in this mode examined the world as I saw it.

The United States was very different from the country in which I had been raised, and was a world removed from the Brazil in which I had worked as a priest. I, who had grown up poor, was overwhelmed by its wealth; I, who had renounced material possessions when I took a vow of poverty, was appalled by its materialism; I, who had just rejected the authority of an arrogant and powerful Church, was disturbed by the arrogance of power that the United States' institutions of government displayed throughout the world. On the other hand, I found American people friendly towards the foreigner in their midst. It probably didn't hurt that I was Irish: President Kennedy had even made my ethnic origin chic. I also found the corporate world, as I experienced it through IBM, to be more caring of its people than either the Catholic Church in general or the Holy Ghost Congregation in particular. And I was impressed by the attitude of Americans towards religion. In Ireland and Brazil those who didn't belong to the Catholic Church were regarded as odd, perhaps even dangerous. In America even Catholics were respectful towards all religions and towards those who espoused no religion.

Natives of Dublin were wont to say, disparagingly, of people who came from rural areas of the country, "you can take the man from the bog but you can't take the bog from the man." I felt somewhat that way now vis a vis the Catholic Church: I no longer belonged to it but a part of it still clung to me. So in my reading and thinking, which were eclectic, I found myself veering towards Catholic doctrine, to validate or refute it. One of the first subjects I delved into was my own new freedom from Catholic orthodox thinking. I was intrigued by the Church's long-held facility in preventing its adherents from independent thinking and

319

thus from challenging its doctrines. In the Book of Genesis God said to Adam: *of every tree of the garden thou mayest freely eat; but of the tree of the knowledge of good and evil, thou shalt not eat.* Likewise, the Catholic Church said to its adherents, every dictum made by man – or woman – you may challenge, but the doctrines declared by Holy Mother Church to be Revealed Truth you shall not challenge. It was a brilliant strategy to hold the faithful in thrall. And it worked for more than thirty years to keep me in subjection to its teaching. When I was studying theology I couldn't challenge any of the wafer-thin arguments used to buttress dubious doctrines because the Church regarded theological study as an exercise of the faithful mind seeking to understand truths it already securely believed.

That strategy had worked successfully on me until the day the twenty-six year old woman came to baptize her tenth child in my church in Florida Paulista. On that day my reason pitted the woman's very real plight against abstract theological doctrine, and screamed that it would be wrong to tell her she couldn't practice birth control. And that scream penetrated my hitherto faith-blocked ears. Though I was not aware of it at that moment, it had punctured the balloon of belief in which the Church had enclosed me and caused the air of my faith to leak away.

I didn't *consciously* reject the Church the day I challenged its teaching on birth control, but *theologically* I did; it just took some time for me to realize the fact. It was that rejection that allowed me to repudiate celibacy when I fell in love a year later, and to abdicate my priesthood another year after that. And it was that rejection that led to my becoming an apostate.

Walter Keady

An Apostate

I *was* now an apostate, a state defined as *total repudiation of the Christian faith[4]*. The Church considers it a very grave sin: you cannot, it says, without malice lose your faith in God and His Holy Church. The malice, according to Catholic teaching, lies in choosing what *you* believe to be true over what the Catholic Church tells you is true. The Church does not allow you to believe what you believe: you must believe what the Church tells you to believe; the Catholic conscience must be informed by Catholic teaching.

I imagined myself back in the seventeenth century, with the Inquisition Tribunal accusing me of repudiating the Faith. The penalty, if I was found guilty, was burning at the stake, a sentence carried out by the civil authority: the Church did not get its hands burned with the grisly details of imposing condign punishment for apostasy. Then I imagined having a modern American attorney defend me at the Tribunal. The dialog between the Inquisitor and the Attorney might go somewhat like this:

Inquisitor: *This man, who is an anointed priest of God, stands accused of repudiating the Catholic faith, which is a grave sin, and is also a criminal offense against the State that is punishable by burning at the stake.*

Attorney: *Would your Eminence be ever so kind as to define what you mean by faith?*

Inquisitor: *Certainly, counselor. Faith is believing that what God has revealed is true not because of the intrinsic truth of the matters grasped by the*

---

[4] *Catechism of the Catholic Church*, 2089

321

natural light of reason but because of the authority of God Himself revealing.

Attorney: Very succinct, I must say. So even if every fiber of my reason screams that something is not true I must believe it because God says so.

Inquisitor: That is correct.

Attorney: And the Catholic Church, and only the Catholic Church, knows infallibly what God says?

Inquisitor: Absolutely.

Attorney: Am I correct in stating that this definition of faith assumes that I believe in God?

Inquisitor: Si, Señor! (Tomás de Torquemada, 'the hammer of heretics' was Spanish). If you don't believe in God you are guilty of an even worse crime, atheism.

Attorney: And I presume that also merits burning at the stake?

Inquisitor: Most certainly.

Attorney: So, I must believe the Catholic Church's authoritative pronouncement that what it teaches has been revealed to it by God.

Inquisitor: That is correct.

Attorney: And I must, if necessary, repudiate the natural light of my reason in order to believe that God exists?

Inquisitor: No, no! You see, reason itself shows us that God exists. Even the pagan Aristotle saw that.

Attorney: Interesting how you invoke the authority of the pagan when it suits your purpose. But never mind. What about the millions of people who don't believe in the God of Christianity? Or the millions

> who don't believe in any God? Are they all being unreasonable?

\Inquisitor: They are either being unreasonable or they are invincibly ignorant of the truth. If they are invincibly ignorant they may in their hearts and desires wish for the truth, which is in the Catholic Church.

Attorney: So you're saying that belief in the Catholic God and His Church and all that the Church teaches is required of every human being?

Inquisitor: Yes. No one can be saved without it. The Fathers of the Church and the Popes have reiterated many times that outside of the Church there is no salvation – extra ecclesiam nulla salus.

This fanciful dialog might seem unreal, but it represents the teaching of the Catholic Church – even in the twentieth century, even after Vatican II – on the necessity of faith in what the Church teaches.[5]

Challenging More Church Doctrines

I realized that repudiating my faith in the Catholic Church didn't mean that I no longer belonged to the Church. Just as, according to Catholic theology, I was a priest forever by the indelible character of the sacrament of Orders, so by the indestructible force of the sacrament of Baptism I remained a member of the Church in spite of my apostasy. I was free of Catholic Church control only because this was the twentieth century and the Church no longer possessed the coercive power

---

[5]Catechism of the Catholic Church, 846ff.

it exercised in the days of the Inquisition. In those times I would have been burned at the stake for my perfidy; now, I was merely looked upon as a refractory Church member.

Challenging Catholic doctrines should logically have led me to join a Protestant sect: the essential difference between a Protestant and a Catholic is that while the latter marches in lock-step to Catholic doctrine the former marches to the beat of his or her own biblical drum. Nevertheless, I did not become a Protestant. Reading and thinking led me to conclude that if the Catholic Church was fallible in purporting to be the voice of God in its interpretation of the Bible and Tradition, then surely Protestants were no less fallible in their individual Biblical interpretations.

Once I felt free to challenge the theological doctrines of the Church, all kinds of fundamental questions arose. The Church declares, in common with Protestants, that the Bible is the Word of God. But how does the Church know that? In the Scholasticate when we studied Scripture I never asked the question that I asked now: how does the Church know that Scripture is the word of God? It knows it was written by men, maybe some of it by women, but how does it know that God spoke through its writers? As I understand the Church's reasoning, it knows that Scripture is the Word of God because the writers of the various books that comprise the Scripture claimed that God spoke through them. So the Church cites the authority of their claims as proof that the sacred books are the word of God because those claims were contained in the Scripture, which is the word of God! Protestants use the same circular argument. Alternatively, they claim that believing in God is a gift of God – the gift of faith; more circular reasoning.

Another basic question that raised its head was: if God

324

exists and wants us all – the whole human race, not just Catholics – to worship and obey Him, why doesn't He make Himself clearly known to all? Why is He so coy, so mysterious, giving His message to only a few people within one tiny ethnic group of nomads and allowing the rest of humankind to go on believing in false gods, or even in no God at all? Why doesn't He make plain to us His existence and wishes? Why play hide-and-seek games, allowing those who seek the truth to be lost in doubt and confusion? I did not think it acceptable to slough off the question with St. Paul's, *who hath known the mind of the Lord?* Or with Christian platitudes like *God's ways are inscrutable*, or *God knows best.* I considered those to be mere pious shibboleths to conceal a lack of information about a dubious deity.

Another question: why doesn't God inform His Church in a clear and consistent way about what He regards as right and wrong, so that the Church doesn't have to confuse its infallibility claims by reversing itself? Or maintain its infallibility claims by refusing to bow to reality – as in the case of contraception? The early Church condemned the rhythm method of contraception as being sinful; today the rhythm method is the only contraceptive method the Church claims to be God's will. The Church once held slavery to be lawful but now acknowledges that it was always wrong.[6] And for centuries it condemned charging interest on loans of money, but now the Vatican loans its own money, for which it receives interest. So, if God speaks to humanity through His Church, He's doing a very poor communications job of giving it accurate and consistent information regarding His Will.

---

[6] In 1993 Pope John Paul II said that slavery was intrinsically evil.

Being & Becoming

Does God Exist?

All of the foregoing raised for me the most fundamental religious question of all: does God really exist? Or is He just a creation of human imagination and desire? Some passages in Scripture say that the author saw God, while others say no man has seen God. Are both correct? To prove from reason that God exists theologians, following St. Thomas Aquinas, trot out versions of the five proofs that Aristotle put forth: First Cause, Prime Mover, etc. For me, while those arguments might bolster a belief already held, they do not prove the existence of God. The whole notion of God, I felt, smacked of a *deus ex machina* to account for those mysteries of life that couldn't otherwise be explained. And there are so many such mysteries in life. Principally free will. And evil.

Regarding free will, I found that alleged faculty to be mysterious enough without positing a God who while controlling every human thought and action yet allows humans to possess freedom of choice! There seemed to me a clear contradiction there. I was aware that the subject had a long history of contentious debate among philosophers and theologians. And that even when they left God out of the discussion they still had problems trying to decide to what extent humans are free in their decisions. In particular, how much of human actions are the result of biologically determined forces from within or environmentally determined pressures from without? Does anyone know the answer to the question: to what degree are people free in their choices of action? In practice, the systems of justice in all human societies act on the principal that people are, in the main, free agents: that they can freely choose, and that they are responsible for the decisions they make. The Church, I felt, had tied itself into verbal knots trying to harmonize the notion of free will with its doctrine of total dependence on God. People must have free will, it taught, otherwise they couldn't be guilty of sin and merit hell, or they couldn't be virtuous and merit heaven. On the other hand, they were, according to Church teaching, totally dependent on God for everything; without Him they could do nothing. Which logically meant that they could not be free. Which led to the conclusion that when they sinned God was the Prime Mover of their sin. So how could a just God – and the Church teaches that God is Just – condemn people to hell for something He Himself did or caused them to do?

Then there was the matter of evil. Catholic theologians exhausted themselves down the centuries in a vain attempt to reconcile the notion of a just God Who cares for all His children with a God who causes all the evils that occur to those children. Even the Biblical parable of Job fails to crack that conundrum. The pious still ask, how can a God Who cares for us permit such evil? Perhaps the most popular explanation of evil in the world is that it is caused by the devil, the enemy of God and of mankind. Ah, the devil! The epitome of evil. The excuse for bad human acts: the devil made me do it. That is the myth of the former angel who out of pride rebelled against God and who, though for his disobedience was sentenced to eternal punishment in hell, is nevertheless permitted by God Himself to continue his rebellion. According to Catholic teaching, God allows the devil to recruit mankind in his battle against the Almighty. So the God who is supposed to love mankind not only saddles us with evil propensities that make it difficult for us to love Him in return, but also lets Satan loose on us to lure us down to hell?

I did not find plausible the Church's stock answers to the question of evil – God knows best, His Will is inscrutable, all will be revealed at the Last Judgment, etc. If the Catholic God really

327

cared for His people why would He let so many bad things happen to them? The story of Job notwithstanding, His behavior belies His definition as a just God. However, I felt, if God were left out of consideration altogether, evil would be reasonably intelligible as due to such things as the apparent randomness of natural phenomena – earthquakes, volcanic eruptions, weather, accidents, etc.– and the variability of human genetic make-up and perspectives – mania, paranoia, greed, hatred, prejudices, etc.

Another question further raised my doubts about the gods of religions: if God is what He is according to religious definition – maker of heaven and earth, supreme lord of the whole universe – why is He constantly in need of praise from His creatures? *...we worship You, we adore You, we praise You for Your glory...* And why is He so easily offended if he designed humans to fail? Even *the just man falls seven times*, according to the Bible. I had spent twenty-five years of my life – from first to last confessions – trying not to offend God, yet I had to confess thousands of offenses against Him, most of them dealing with my failure to resist the onslaughts of those sexual desires that, according to Catholic teaching, He had saddled me with in the first place. Did God *make* me sin – according to Church teaching I could do nothing without Him – so that I would be obliged to adore Him in return for forgiveness? The God that the Church believes in seems to have a terrible inferiority complex, as well as a truly malicious streak. Is it any wonder that His creatures are so mixed up when the Creator Himself is such a Mess?

Would it not be better to believe in no God at all than in such a psychological disaster of a deity?

Immortality of the Soul

Once I doubted God's existence a slew of related questions arose. What of my soul? Did I really possess an immortal soul? St. Thomas Aquinas, the Church's foremost theologian, was much influenced by Aristotle's theory of matter and form – that a substance was generated when matter took on form. So Thomas said that God infuses a soul (form) into each human foetus (matter). That soul must be immortal, Thomas and the Church reasoned, because otherwise heaven and hell, fundamental doctrines of the Church, would have no meaning.[7]

On the question of immortality, I reasoned that if there is no God then there is no heaven or hell and the religious argument for immortality disappears. So when people die do they cease to exist? That's the question that has obsessed mankind for thousands of years. Most people, it would seem, believe in some sort of afterlife. But did belief in immortality come about because people wished it were so? Most don't want to become extinct; they want to go on living. And go on and on. So was this why mankind created gods, and God?

The human race had additional reasons to create a God, and with powers they wished for but didn't possess. They wanted their enemies chastised, but they couldn't always do it themselves. If those enemies were punished during their lifetimes they gave thanks to God for doing it; if not, they looked forward to an afterlife where God would give their enemies a just retribution. As Baldy had taught us long ago about the Final

---

[7]Incidentally, Thomas held that the soul was infused by God about 40 to 80 days after conception; the Church currently teaches that God infuses the soul at the very moment of conception, and that therefore abortion of a one-second-old embryo is murder.

Judgment, *the providence of God which often in this life permits the good to suffer and the wicked to prosper will appear just before all men.*

People have also credited God with being the Creator of all things, including the forces of nature that could harm them. So, when they wanted protection from the blind ferocity of nature they prayed to their created God. And then, because they feared the great power with which they had endowed that created God, they toadied up to Him/Her with thanksgiving and praise and worship for protecting them.

I asked myself if there was any real evidence of an afterlife, such as people craved? I was not aware of any, other than the images supplied by the creative imaginations of theologians and mystics and artists. The dead did not return to tell; the assurances of theologians were based on unverifiable beliefs; the personal visions of mystics were not reliable evidence; accounts of apparitions of the Virgin Mary and other members of the heavenly court were never verifiable; so-called heavenly phenomena – such as miracles, or statues of the blessed that bled or shed tears, or the dancing of the sun – had too often been verified as natural phenomena or hoaxes or the result of individual or mass hysteria. It seemed to me, too, that many believed in an afterlife because it was most comforting: the dear departed loved ones were now in a better place and they would see them again in heaven. And the prospect of heaven for themselves was most alluring. There was also, I thought, the matter of what-if. Many refused not to believe in an afterlife just in case there was one. Belief in an after-life was a can't-afford-to-lose insurance policy: if it existed they were secure; if not, they would never know.

I could find no satisfactory evidence that individual human

330

beings had any existence beyond death. Evolutionary study suggested that even the human species would likely become extinct some time in the future. Nevertheless, immortality remained an attractive prospect for many, which might explain the popularity of vampire and other types of films that portrayed the undead.

What Does Reason Tell Us?

I reasoned that human beings have been endowed with reason – how or by whom or by what, I didn't profess to know. But reason, I determined, was the best tool we have in our search for the truth about our existence. Yet even people of great intelligence and erudition often abdicate their precious reason – as I myself did – in favor of a comforting belief in an all-knowing, all-powerful God, a belief built on the sands of wishful thinking or imagination or whatever. In the various systems of religious belief prevalent throughout the world this thinking, or non-thinking, has been hardened into immutable doctrines by God experts – theologians – who have no greater source of knowing about what lies beyond human existence than have the rest of mankind. So what did reason tell me about where I came from and where I'm going? It told me to look to the evidence unearthed by past and present generations of reason-endowed persons. As regards the human past, a good deal of evidence has been discovered and pieced together by various sciences. I concluded that the theory of human evolution, though still very far from complete, provided the least unsatisfactory explanation of our origins.

The Catholic Church, which for many centuries had insisted that the story of Adam and Eve was to be taken literally, and which for almost a hundred years was reluctant to

331

acknowledge that the theory of evolution might have some merit, now allows that the Book of Genesis need not have quite a literal meaning. Nevertheless, the Church still maintains that all humans are descended from a common ancestral couple and that those common ancestors – whether their names were Adam and Eve or George and Matilda – were endowed, by God's special intervention, with immortal souls. It also maintains that those original ancestors were guilty of committing a major sin – what it calls original sin – that they passed on in some kind of spiritual gene to all their descendants. While the Church nowadays contends that its teachings on the origin of man can be reconciled with the findings of sciences such as paleoanthropology, it qualifies that contention with the entirely arbitrary affirmation that at a certain point in human evolution God intervened directly and placed a human soul in the evolving hominid. And continues to do so with each and every human foetus.

So, do I believe in God? I have found no credible evidence that He/She/It exists. And I have found no credible reason why the existence of a deity has to be posited in order to explain the world and all it contains. I refuse, however, to call myself an atheist, because an atheist is one who denies the existence of God. Such a denial is, to my mind, an act of faith in the non-existence of God and, since a negative cannot be proven, atheism itself is a form of belief. I prefer to call myself an agnostic, one who has no reason to think there is a God but who is willing to acknowledge One should His/Her/Its existence be shown acceptable to my reason.

Believers might ask, and indeed several have asked me, how could I stop believing in God after I once so strongly believed in Him that I became a priest? My answer is that when I believed that the Catholic Church had the answers to life – this life and the next – I followed that belief to its logical conclusion. My belief was that if this life is but a preparation for the next, a next that will be infinitely superior, why would I spend this life doing anything else? When my reason ceased to accept that the Catholic Church had the answers to life I continued to seek the truth about my existence, which brought me to where I am today. Perhaps I am deluded. However, as a seeker of truth I must accept the truth that reason presents to me. And that truth now says that there is no God, no afterlife, only this life here and now.

I have also been asked by curious believers what is it like, having once believed in them, not to believe any longer in God or an afterlife? I answer that initially I felt very lonely: there had been much comfort and security in believing in a Being Who would take care of me and Who promised me eternal happiness. I did not easily abandon that belief. On the other hand, since my search for truth has led me to the conviction that my coming into existence was the result of chance and that when I die I'll cease to exist, I find solace in following that conviction.

This is *my* journey, *my* truth. I do not seek to convince anyone else that I am right, merely to state my convictions.

Also by Walter Keady

Celibates & Other Lovers

Mary McGreevy

The Altruist

The Dowry

The Agitator

Praise for Walter Keady's novels

Keady will leave readers of Irish fiction eager for a sequel
    – Publishers Weekly

Keady is a true storyteller, with an absolute command of the English language
    – St. Petersburg Times

Keady will win the hearts of readers with his charming tale
    – Irish America Magazine

Keady is a refreshing new voice in Irish fiction
    – Library Journal

The great strength of this novel is that it is not afraid to ask big questions
    – The Philadelphia Enquirer

You have to love the title character of Walter Keady's second novel
    – The New York Times

A gem-like celebration of life
    – Dallas Morning News

This novel will connect Irish-Americans with their heritage
    – Booklist

Sweet and funny, with a touch of tartness – an apple pie of a book
    – Orlando Sentinel

Keady ... has cleverly, subtly, captured the warm nostalgic spirit of rural Ireland
    – Boston Sunday Herald

Celibates & Other Lovers

a novel

Walter Keady

Mary McGreevy

Walter Keady

a novel

THE
ALTRUIST

A NOVEL BY WALTER KEADY

the dowry

a novel of Ireland

WALTER KEADY

"Charming Celtic comedy of manners."
—*Kirkus Reviews*

The
AGITATOR

A NOVEL

WALTER KEADY

Author of MARY McGREEVY